ZORA NEALE HURSTON

Zora Neale Hurston

☙

An Annotated Bibliography and Reference Guide

Compiled by
Rose Parkman Davis

Bibliographies and Indexes in Afro-American and African Studies,
Number 34

Greenwood Press
Westport, Connecticut • London

Library of Congress Cataloging-in-Publication Data

Davis, Rose Parkman, 1947–
    Zora Neale Hurston : an annotated bibliography and reference guide
/ compiled by Rose Parkman Davis.
        p.   cm.—(Bibliographies and indexes in Afro-American and
African studies, ISSN 0742–6925 ; no. 34)
    Includes bibliographical references and indexes.
    ISBN 0–313–30387–8 (alk. paper)
    1. Hurston, Zora Neale—Bibliography.   2. Women and literature—
Southern States—Bibliography.   3. Afro-Americans in literature—
Bibliography.   4. Folklore in literature—Bibliography.   I. Title.
II. Series.
Z8428.66.D38   1997
[PS3515.U789]
016.813′52—dc21   97–37459

British Library Cataloguing in Publication Data is available.

Library of Congress Catalog Card Number: 97–37459
ISBN: 0–313–30387–8
ISSN: 0742–6925

First published in 1997

Greenwood Press, 88 Post Road West, Westport, CT 06881
An imprint of Greenwood Publishing Group, Inc.

Printed in the United States of America

The paper used in this book complies with the
Permanent Paper Standard issued by the National
Information Standards Organization (Z39.48–1984).

10 9 8 7 6 5 4 3 2 1

This book is lovingly dedicated to the memory of my mother **Mattie Oatis Parkman** by whose actions and deeds I constantly knew the truth of Eleanor Roosevelt's quotation: "No one can make you feel inferior without your consent."

To Professor Naomi Johnson Townsend, the consummate teacher and scholar, whom I respectfully call advisor, mentor, and role model. To John Usher Monro, colleague, friend, teacher, cheerleader! To L. Zenobia Coleman who taught me to revere books and respect the history reflected in them.

And to my wonderful children, Lumbe Kibebe and Walter Jelani, and my siblings, Robert, Dorothy, Johnie, Columbus, and Joyce.

Contents

Preface

In the last two decades, a revival of interest in Zora Neale Hurston and an unrelenting reexamination of her writings have made Hurston an "industry" in herself. The scholarship generated about her and the re-release of all her primary works mean she is a force to be reckoned with in the academic and publishing worlds.

Several generations of scholars ignored Zora Neale Hurston, and the "revival" and renewed interest in her work as a folklorist, anthro-pologist, dramatist, and writer of fiction have been overwhelming. From Henry Louis Gates, Jr., at Harvard University to students at Coe College writing honors theses, Hurston is garnering a following that seems to have no end in sight. More than one hundred and seventy dissertations and theses have included Hurston. In 1995 alone, sixteen dissertations were completed using Hurston as one of the central literary figures, and several book-length works about Hurston are forthcoming in 1997 and 1998. Her works are included in many new and updated anthologies, and numerous World Wide Web sites are devoted to her writing and works about her life and career.

This project on Zora Neale Hurston began in 1989 to meet the requirements for a graduate course in the School of Library and Information Studies at the University of Alabama. Students had to design a computer database, and I chose Zora Neale Hurston because her works had not been assigned in any of my undergraduate or graduate literature classes in the late 1960s. My interest in Hurston grew as a result of this assignment, and each year I updated my database and read additional works written by this fascinating writer. Early exposure to my mother's feminist views meant I felt an immediate kinship with Zora Neale Hurston.

This volume aims to be a comprehensive, up-to-date reference guide to the scholarship related to one of America's foremost writers. Since so much is written about Zora Neale Hurston, collocating in one source all the diverse arguments, theories, and strategies found in critical, bibliographical, and biographical information and making it easily accessible to researchers and scholars makes good sense. Included are books, essays and book chapters, dissertations and theses, periodical literature, reviews of works by and about Hurston, bibliographies and guides, biographical information, anthologies where Hurston's works are collected, juvenile literature, media, and World Wide Web sites.

Online databases and print indexes were used to seek out every piece of information published about Zora Neale Hurston. OCLC's WorldCat and the online catalogs of several large libraries, such as Harvard University, the Library of Congress, and the University of North Carolina at Chapel Hill, were searched. The main libraries at the University of Alabama at Tuscaloosa, the University of South Carolina, Mississippi State University, and the University of North Carolina at Charlotte were visited.

International Index to Periodicals and *Readers' Guide to Periodical Literature* were used to locate periodical information from the 1920s to the 1970s and to supplement information found in online databases covering the last three decades. *Index to Periodical Articles By and About Blacks* was used to locate information in African American serial literature not indexed by traditional references sources. Exhaustive searches were conducted in: *MLA International Bibliography, America History and Life, Historical Abstracts, Humanities Index, Essay and General Literature Index, Periodical Index*, and *Dissertation Abstracts International*.

Chapter one discusses the book-length works devoted entirely to Hurston or to works where Hurston's name appears in the title. Chapter two looks at the dissertations where Zora Neale Hurston is treated individually, where substantial portions of the theses deal with Hurston, or where at least one chapter is devoted to her work. Also listed are master's theses and undergraduate honors papers. Chapter three provides a comprehensive picture of the myriad essays and book chapters related to Hurston scholarship. Essays that have brief, passing references to Zora Neale Hurston and her works are not included, and if the same essay appears in several sources, each additional source is referenced in a single entry.

Many hours were spent examining the abundance of periodical literature, in print and on microforms, that has been generated about Zora Neale Hurston. She is written about in scholarly publications, foreign journals, and newspapers as well as popular magazines. All periodical literature is listed chronologically so readers may see the escalating interest in Hurston over the years. Selected reviews of Hurston's works written by her contemporaries as well as reviews of recently released publications *by* and *about* Hurston are briefly noted. These are separately analyzed by title of work.

Bibliographies and guides to works about Hurston are annotated as are anthologies where Hurston's works are collected. Biographical information on Hurston is plentiful and diverse, and I have tried to list sources where even brief information is provided, so that students using even the smallest library will be able to locate information on Hurston's life and career. Finally, juvenile literature about Hurston is treated in the last chapter.

The appendices contain information about Hurston's works and life, World Wide Web sites, a guide to special collections where her manuscripts, correspondence, and other materials are housed, and a comprehensive chronology of works written by Hurston, including the latest discovery, "Under the Bridge." The annotated entries are listed in an alpha-numeric sequence, and author subject indexes are provided.

Numerous trips were made to the University of North Carolina at Chapel Hill and to the University of South Carolina. Friends and colleagues in Atlanta and Chicago copied articles, and the Interlibrary Loan department at Winthrop University library was used extensively so this work could be as inclusive as possible. Incorrect citations or missing information forced me to omit several sources, and since this guide is aimed primarily at students and researchers, a decision was made not to include newspaper articles written about Hurston. However, reviews found in newspapers are included. I regret any omissions, but I finally had to set a deadline for receiving materials through interlibrary loan so the book could be finished and indexes could be completed.

I meticulously followed trails and leads. I examined references and bibliographies in each new piece of material to see if citations contained new information. I also did final online searches in key databases so the latest information could be included. It is my hope that researchers, students, and Hurston fans will find this resource beneficial.

Acknowledgments

There are so many wonderful folks to whom I am indebted. To all the strong women who have marched and pranced through my life, who inspired my love of learning and books, and who blazed trails so I could walk this path without stumbling, I say thanks. I give thanks to my Heavenly Father who gave me the courage to run this race and the endurance to cross the finish line. I am grateful for the loving support of my wonderful children, Lumbe Kibebe Davis and Walter Jelani Davis, for their faith in my vision; my sister Joyce Parkman Mallory of Milwaukee, Wisconsin, for her confidence in me; Gail Davis Peyton and Susan Hall, two wonderful friends at Mississippi State University, and special friend Sally Bolding who first told me to publish my work. I also extend sincere thanks to relatives and friends who sent best wishes when they learned Greenwood Press had agreed to publish my book.

I am especially grateful to numerous colleagues for their support of my efforts to get this book to press: Dr. Margaret Steig Dalton, my reference professor at the University of Alabama in whose course I began this bibliography; Robert Gorman and the administration of the Winthrop University Library for approving professional leave to travel and work on the manuscript; the staff of the Interlibrary Loan Department and the Circulation assistants at Dacus Library; and librarians in North and South Carolina and Mississippi who shared resources with me. Finally, I thank Dr. Aldon Morris and his staff at Northwestern University for their invaluable assistance.

A

Books about Zora Neale Hurston

"The sun went on and on to his sky bed at night, pulling the gray and purple hangings of his couch about him and slept, indifferent to human tears."

"Under the Bridge"

A01. Awkward, Michael, ed. New Essays on *Their Eyes Were Watching God*. New York: Cambridge University Press, 1990. For this slim volume, Awkward assembled writers noted for their scholarship on Hurston. Hemenway's "The Personal Dimension in *Their Eyes Were Watching God*," and McKay's "'Crayon Enlargements of Life': Zora Neale Hurston's *Their Eyes Were Watching God* as Autobiography" are two of the new essays included. Awkward writes an excellent introductory essay for the book.

A02. Babcock, C. Merton. *A Word List from Zora Neale Hurston*. Tuscaloosa, AL: University of Alabama Press, 1963. This monograph was published as part of the proceedings of the American Dialect Society's Conference on Dialectology held in 1961 at the University of Alabama. Provides brief background information on Hurston's career. Says her "racy metaphors are a happy marriage of humor and invective." Includes a list of "words, idioms, meanings, functions, and variants" that Hurston used in her published works. These are terms that, at the time, were not included in any standard dictionaries. For example, "doodly-squat" is defined as "the short end of nothing."

A03. Bastin, Bruce. *A Tribute to Zora Neale Hurston*. Sussex, England: Flyright Records, 1974. This is a trifold brochure included as an inset in a sound recording set that was part of "Flyright-Matchbox Library of Congress Series." Bastin wrote the biography and recounts tales of Hurston going to "jook joints" to collect folktales. Some of her "informants" from the 1930s were recorded and documented in the albums this brochure accompanies.

A04.   Bloom, Harold, ed. *Zora Neale Hurston's Their Eyes Were Watching God*. New York: Chelsea House Publishers, 1987. This anthology mainly includes previously published critical essays written by contributors who are noted Hurston scholars. John F. Callahan and Barbara Johnson, Missy Dehn Kubitschek, Robert Stepto, and Houston Baker have articles reprinted. John F. Callahan, Barbara Johnson, and Henry Louis Gates, Jr. provide new essays for this work, and Bloom introduces it. A chronology of Hurston's life and career is provided along with a bibliography of works where Hurston is subject.

A05. Bloom, Harold, ed. *Zora Neale Hurston: Modern Critical Views*. New York: Chelsea House Publishers, 1986. This is another of Chelsea House's books of previously published works that provide "critical views" of Hurston written by several of her contemporaries as well as modern-day scholars who analyze her works. Bloom introduces the book, and selections from Langston Hughes and Alice Walker are among those included.

A06. Brantley, Will. *Feminine Sense in Southern Memoir: Smith, Glasgow, Welty, Hellman, Porter, and Hurston*. Jackson: University Press of Mississippi, 1993: 185-239. One chapter discusses Hurston's autobiography, *Dust Tracks on a Road,* where her "memories of the past tend to become little dramas within themselves." Says the title of autobiography is an "appropriate clue to the book that follows."

A07. Carter-Sigglow, Janet. *Making Her Way With Thunder: A Reappraisal of Zora Neale Hurston's Narrative Art*. New York: Peter Lang, 1994. The preface to this volume indicates that the book grew out of the author's master's thesis in Aachen, Germany. The introduction provides diverse information on Hurston, revisits some old debates, and provides a foundation to understand the analysis of Hurston's works. Each of her primary works are covered in a separate chapter, and each chapter has mini-essays on topics such as "Hoodoo in Eatonville," "Recurring

Themes" and "Stalag Goshen."   Provides a brief yet thoughtful
"reappraisal" of Hurston's works.

A08. Gates, Henry Louis, Jr. and K. A. Appiah, eds. *Zora Neale Hurston:
Critical Perspectives Past and Present*. New York: Amistad, 1993. This
work collocates in one source many of the major reviews of works *by*
Hurston as well as essays written by noted Hurston critics. Twenty reviews
of Hurston's book-length works are included, and they represent a
wonderful sampling of reactions to her works at the time of publication.
Included are reviews by Frank Slaughter, Richard Wright, Alain Locke,
Sterling Brown, and Louis Untermeyer. The second part of this work
presents critical essays that analyze and interpret Hurston's work.

A09. Glassman, Steve and Kathryn Lee Seidel, eds. *Zora in Florida*.
Orlando: University of Central Florida Press, 1991. Fifteen essays explore
Hurston's use of her native land and use of community in her primary
works as well as Hurston's use of the southern oral tradition of storytelling.
A diverse selection of essays is offered, a sampling of which includes:
"Flora and Fauna in Hurston's Florida Novels" by Ann R. Morris and
Margaret M. Dunn; "Voodoo as Symbol in *Jonah's Gourd Vine*" by
Barbara Speisman, and "'De Beast' Within: The Role of Nature in *Jonah's
Gourd Vine*." This book has a selected bibliography of works by Hurston
which includes many of the newspaper articles published during her
lifetime.

A10. Harris, Trudier. *The Power of the Porch: The Storyteller's Craft in
Zora Neale Hurston, Gloria Naylor, and Randall Kenan.* Athens:
University of Georgia Press, 1996. Hurston is one of three storytellers
Harris analyzes as part of a distinguished lecture series at Mercer
University in Georgia. She examines part one of *Mules and Men* for her
essay "Shape-Shifting Through Personalities," discusses in detail Hurston's
self-presentation, and the various personas she assumes as she crafts her
stories. Says her background as a folklorist meant she was committed to
an accurate portrayal of blacks. Argues that Hurston realized she was
going against the grain when she refused to "pretty up" the real world of
rural, lower class blacks, and that she consciously chose to "smooth over
the rough spots."

A11. Grant, Alice Morgan, ed. *All About Zora: Views by Colleagues and
Scholars*. Winter Park, FL: Four-G Publishers, 1991. This work presents
the scholarly proceedings of the Academic Conference of the First Annual
Zora Neale Hurston Festival of the Arts held in Eatonville, Florida, in

1990. Mary Katherine Wainwright, Ann duCille, and Susan Meisenhelder are a few of the participants published.

A12. Hemenway, Robert E. *Zora Neale Hurston: A Literary Biography*. Urbana: University of Illinois Press, 1977. This 371 page work is often called the "definitive study" of Zora Neale Hurston. One of the most quoted-from works about Hurston, it is a well-researched document that opens with Hurston arriving in New York City in 1925 and ends with her death. Hemenway examines her development during the Harlem Renaissance, discusses Hurston's use of folklore and oral storytelling, and provides a picture of her final years in Florida. Photographs appear in the last section of the book, and a comprehensive listing of works by Hurston is appended.

A13. Herbert, Christopher A. *Zora Neale Hurston's Their Eyes Were Watching God*. Piscataway, NJ: Research and Education Association, 1995. This short study guide to the novel is a book in the "MAXnotes Series."

A14. Hill, Lynda Marion. *Social Rituals and the Verbal Art of Zora Neale Hurston*. Washington, DC: Howard University Press, 1996. Hill provides critical analyses and reviews of Hurston's works, looking specifically at the folk expressions and idioms, social change, and language. Also looks critically at some of the materials other scholars have written about Hurston.

A15. Holloway, Karla F. C. *The Character of the Word: The Texts of Zora Neale Hurston*. New York: Greenwood Press, 1987. Another in Greenwood's "Contributions in Afro-American and African Studies" series, Holloway's book provides six chapters that examine the language in Hurston's primary works, discusses Hurston's sophisticated and subtle use of language and the impact of various African philosophies on her novels. Lists Hurston's works, including unpublished materials, and cites a bibliography of secondary sources where Hurston and her works are discussed.

A16. Howard, Lillie P. *Zora Neale Hurston*. Boston: Twayne Publishers, 1980. Howard devotes one chapter to Hurston's "Life and Times," and one to her early works. The remaining chapters are spent on an analysis of Hurston's four major works, and good deal of space is devoted to her non-fiction. Calls Hurston a "black nationalist" in times when such a stance was unpopular. Notes and references included.

A17. Howard, Lillie P., ed. *Alice Walker and Zora Neale Hurston: The Common Bond*. Westport, CT: Greenwood Press, 1993. Book divided into "The Call and the Response," "*Their Eyes Were Watching God* and *The Color Purple*," and "The 'Humming': Expanding the Connections to Other Works by Walker and Hurston." Twelve essays, including Alice Walker's "Zora Neale Hurston: A Cautionary Tale and A Partisan View," are included. Other authors represented are JoAnne Cornwell, Ann Folwell Stanford, and several others not generally associated with Hurston scholarship.

A18. Lowe, John. *Jump at the Sun: Zora Neale Hurston's Cosmic Comedy*. Urbana: University of Illinois Press, 1994. Book resulted from author's interest in American ethnic humor. Lowe's long introduction explores Hurston as a cosmic griot, her "retelling of tales," and provides commentary on African American humor. Says Hurston "conjured" him with her "wit and wisdom" into doing book. Lowe's basic tenant is "Humor was a basic, continuing component in her work; to her, laughter was a way to show one's love for life; an indirect mode useful in saying the unsayable and in negotiating differences." The years of research that went into the making of this book is evident in the scholarly, insightful articles in the three parts designated as "Sunrise," "Sun's Up," and "Sunset." *Jonah's Gourd Vine, Their Eyes Were Watching God*, and *Seraph on the Suwanee* are discussed.

A19. Nathiri. N. Y, ed. *Zora! Zora Neale Hurston, A Woman and Her Community*. Orlando: Sentinel Communications, 1991. This work--in a "scrapbook" format--is compiled and edited by an Eatonville, Florida resident who convenes the Zora Neale Hurston Festival of the Arts and Humanities. Part one is a first-person account of the Nathiri's family tree. A speech given by Alice Walker at the First Annual Zora Neale Hurston Festival: "Anything We Love Can be Saved: The Resurrection of Zora Neale Hurston and Her Work" is included. Photos of people and sights at the Festival, around Eatonville, and of Nathiri's family are included.

A20. Newsom, Adele S. *Zora Neale Hurston: A Reference Guide*. Boston: G.K. Hall, 1987. An annotated bibliography, this reference guide provides a chronology of writings about Zora Neale Hurston from 1931 to 1986. Originally Newsom's dissertation, the work includes early reviews of Hurston's novels, journal articles, dissertations, book chapters and books about Hurston.

A21. Plant, Deborah G. *Every Tub Must Sit on Its Own Bottom: The Philosophy and Politics of Zora Neale Hurston*. Urbana: University of Illinois Press, 1995. A partial listing of the table of contents of this work shows the diversity of articles: "Metaphors of Self, Language, and the Will-to-Power;" "Politics, Parody, Power, and *Moses, Man of the Mountain*;" Politics of Self: Ambivalence, Paradoxes, and Ironies of Race, Color, Sex, Class, and Gender." Plant concludes that Hurston "stands in a long line of female progenitors who were aggressive, forceful, and masculine-identified in one capacity or another."

A22.   Randall, Mary Ella. *Their Eyes Were Watching God: Notes*. Lincoln, NE: Cliff Notes, 1995. Cliff notes on the novel T*heir Eyes Were Watching God*.

A23.   *Sanctified*. Los Angeles: Museum of Contemporary Art. Five hundred of these 12 page books were published on the "occasion of the...theatrical production ...based on the life of Zora Neale Hurston." They were hand-bound on hand-made paper. [catalogers notes]

A24. Sena, Emmanuel. *Novel Guide for Their Eyes Were Watching God by Zora Neale Hurston*. Glenview, IL: Scott Foresman, 1996. This is a study guide for the novel; a bibliography is included..

A25.   Sheffey, Ruthe T., ed. *A Rainbow Round Her Shoulder: Zora Neale Hurston Symposium Papers*. Baltimore: Morgan State University Press, 1982. Sheffey, founder of the Zora Neale Hurston Society housed at Morgan State University in Baltimore, edited the collection of papers presented at the first academic conference held in 1980. Some of the contributors are Robert Hemenway, Addison Gayle, James Miller, and Sheffey.

A26. Several books about Hurston are listed in *Books in Print* as forthcoming publications; however, they are not yet available. Look for these: *Critical Essays on Zora Neale Hurston*. New York: G.K. Hall, 1997. Montgomery, Maxine. *A Zora Neale Hurston Reader*. Sarasota: Pineapple Press, [no date set]. Karanja, Ayana I. *Zora Neale Hurston: Dialogue in Spirit and in Truth*. New York: Peter Lang, 1997.

B

Dissertations, Theses, and Honors Papers about Zora Neale Hurston

"The brother in black puts a laugh in every vacant place in his mind."

Mules and Men

1996

B01. Bauer, Bette B. *Passion and Form: Narrative Strategies and Women's Spiritual Journeys*. Eugene: University of Oregon, 1996. Hurston's *Their Eyes Were Watching God* is used as one example of female authors challenging the "traditional representation of spirituality" in their female characters. Concludes that female sensuality is a "powerful and generative spiritual force." (*DAI* 57-9A: 171)

B02. Dietzel, Susanne B. *Reconfiguring the Garden: Representations of Landscape in Narratives by Southern Women*. Minneapolis: University of Minnesota, 1996. This dissertation explores the representation of southern landscape in selected novels and autobiographies by southern women from different cultural, racial, and class backgrounds. Hurston's *Their Eyes Were Watching God* is one of the cultural texts examined for construction of landscape and garden. (*DAI* 57-9A: 3998)

B03. Epperson-Barak, Julie M. *Liminal Status and Carnival States in the Novels of Hurston, Alvarez, Laurence, and Erdrich*. Lincoln: University of Nebraska, 1996. This study theorizes the "uses of laughter, irony, and the grotesque" in these authors and looks at the concept of carnival "as a tool for feminist writers and readers." (*DAI* 57-03A: 257)

B04.   Glenn, Rochelle Smith. *Reducing the Distance: The Rhetoric of African-American Women's Autobiography*.   Athens: University of Georgia, 1996.   Uses *Dust Tracks on a Road* as one of three autobiographies examined to explore "rhetorical strategies." Contends that metaphor is the "main rhetorical strategy used for persuasion;" the others are irony and direct address. (*DAI* 57-9A: 3938)

B05.   Groover, Kristina Kaye. *The Wilderness Within: American Women Writers and Spiritual Quest*.   Chapel Hill: The University of North Carolina, 1996.   Explores "alternative construction of spirituality" in the works of late nineteenth and twentieth-century American women writers." Believes this spirituality is exemplified through domesticity and storytelling and is rooted in the community, not the individual. (*DAI* 57-10A: 4368)

B06.   Jones, Sharon Lynette. *Rereading the Harlem Renaissance: The "Folk," "Bourgeois," and "Proletarian" Aesthetics in the Fiction of Jessie Fauset, Zora Neale Hurston, and Dorothy West*. Athens: University of Georgia, 1996. Believes Hurston, Fauset and Larsen use folk, bourgeois, and proletarian aesthetics to "create a complex portrait of African American life in their literary work." Examines the writers "appropriation of narrative strategies" to achieve a unique voice in African American literature. (DAI 57-9A: 3940)

B07.   Klawunn, Margaret May. *On the Outskirts of Fiction: American Women Writers and the Politics of Regionalism*. New Brunswick: Rutgers, The State University of New Jersey, 1996. Analyzes regional fiction-- thought to be "ideologically compromised" because of its response to political and geographical activities--in the works of Hurston, Sarah Orne Jewett, and Grace Paley. Believes women regionalists are the major contributors to the genre and examines these works as a subordinate part of realism and as "feminized literature." (*DAI* 57-06A: 2477)

B08.   Lewis, Sharon Anderson. *Spyin' Noble: Money in the Novels by Black American Women*. New Brunswick: Rutgers, The State University of New Jersey, 1996. Examines the works of Hurston, Toni Morrison and Paule Marshall to investigate the "textual fusions of class, race, and gender" and spotlights "a critical but overlooked component of social class positioning, namely money." Uses Houston Baker's interpretation of

Janie's journey in *Their Eyes Were Watching God* being financed by "bourgeois economics" as a springboard to examine "class subjectivity" in novels by three African American female writers. In other words, "Who's funding who?" is the author's question. (*DAI* 57-06A: 2478)

B09.   Lewis, Barbara Williams. *Prodigal Daughters: Female Heroes, Fugitivity and "Wild" Women in the Works of Toni Morrison*. Los Angeles: University of Southern California, 1996. Hurston's fictionalized heroine Janie Crawford is used to show a connection to real heroines such as Sojourner Truth. (*DAI* 57-9A: 3940)

B10.   Mechling, Kelly Ann. *Creative Dimensions in Autobiographies of Selected Twentieth Century American Women Writers*. Indiana, PA: Indiana University of Pennsylvania, 1996.   This study examines autobiographies of a cross-section of twentieth-century American women writers, including Hurston. Analyzes their autobiographies within the framework of "memory, creative origins, and textual construction." (*DAI* 57-7A: 3023)

B11.   McGowan, Todd Robert. *The Empty Subject: The New Canon and the Politics of Existence*. Columbus: Ohio State University, 1996. Dissertation begins with historical coincidence and examines "recent changes in the canon of American literature and the emergence of global capitalism." Looks at the interpretation of recently "recovered" works, one of which is *Their Eyes Were Watching God*. Feels it an "appropriate gesture" to include Hurston. (*DAI* 57-02A: 683)

B12.   Rogers, Kenneth Scott. *The Literary Study of Non-Fiction: An Analysis of Selected Works by George Orwell, Richard Wright, Zora Neale Hurston, and Virginia Woolf*. Chicago: Loyola University of Chicago, 1996.   Dissertation looks at the causes for the general disinterest in non-fiction, provides a "model of analyzing non-fiction works as primary works," and applies this model to the works of the three authors. Hurston's *Mules and Men* is one work analyzed. (*DAI* 57-03A: 1153)

B13.   West, Roger Wade. *"God's Eunuch Race": The Mule in Southern Literature and Folk Culture*. Hattiesburg: University of Southern Mississippi, 1996. Examines the role of the mule as a symbol of the southern African American and white underclass. Believes Hurston compares the lives of her "female characters with the mule's because of the pervading sexism and racism." (*DAI* 57-7A: 3025)

1995

B14. Barks, Cathy W. *The Second Act: American Autobiography and the Moderns*. College Park: University of Maryland, 1995. This dissertation argues that as "many of the modernist writers moved beyond their youth and early work, they took up autobiography in a pragmatic spirit, using the form to reinvent themselves according to their mature needs." Chapter three, "Autobiography and the Harlem Renaissance," argues that Hurston used the journey narrative to demonstrate competence and resourcefulness in overcoming obstacles. (*DAI* 56-8A: 3122)

B15. Berni, Christine. *Writing the Body Across the Disciplines: Social Science and Literature, 1880-1940*. Rochester: University of Rochester, 1995. Critically re-examines Hurston as one of the authors who used the "newly enfranchised disciples of psychology and anthropology" in their literary representations of the "body as a vehicle of gendered, sexual, and racial identity." (*DAI* 56-03A: 921)

B16. Carlson, Elizabeth Mary. *"In Dixie Land Where I Was Born": The Southern Autobiographer as Historian, 1932-1945*. Bloomington: Indiana University, 1995. Dissertation investigates the "role of southern autobiographical writings in representing regional history and constructing cultural identity." Hurston one of the authors used to learn how several southern writers "represent regional history" and "construct notions of cultural identity." (*DAI* 56-06A: 2235)

B17. Desy, Jeanne N. *The Effect of Metaphor on Narrative Progress*. Columbus: Ohio State University, 1995. Analyzes metaphor as it relates to a "pattern of desires and satisfaction" in the works of Hurston, Hemenway, and Fitzgerald. Believes that in *Their Eyes Were Watching God*, Hurston uses metaphors--pear tree, death, and the horizon--to "influence the progression" and get readers to understand the characters. *(DAI* 56-06A: 2236)

B18. Fernandez, Ramona. *Imagining Literacy*. Santa Cruz: University of California, 1995. This work discusses "literacy as an epistemological question rooted in imaginative constructs." Hurston examined in the chapter "Reading Trickster Writing." Believes the texts of the authors examined--Kingston, Anzaldau, Silko and Hurston--prove that cultural literacy is the "concatenation of multiple knowledge, requiring a collection of skills." (*DAI* 57-03A: 1136)

B19.   Grant, Nathan L., Jr.   *Jean Toomer and Zora Neale Hurston: Modernism and the Recovery of Black Male Identity*. New York: New York University, 1995. Study posits that Hurston and Toomer are two Harlem Renaissance writers whose works use their southern roots, and they examine "notions about Black maleness whose expression had lain buried...and had always sought expression in the African-American community." Also discusses characterizations of black men in literature. (*DAI* 56-5A: 1778)

B20.   Kuenz, Jane Ellen. *Producing the New Negro: The Work of Art in the Harlem Renaissance*. Durham, NC: Duke University, 1995. Examines the "cultural production of the 'New Negro' in the Harlem Renaissance debates about the purposes and form of African American self-representation." Chapter three looks at the use of "the folk" and Hurston's reception as a guide for tracing the evolution of "the Negro-Art hokum." (*DAI* 56-5A: 1779)

B21.   Lewis, Krishnakali Ray. *Ambivalence and Pastoral Strategy: Colonization in the Caribbean*.   University of Pennsylvania, 1995. Examines narratives from the "New World tradition, specifically the Caribbean and African American cultures." Hurston's *Their Eyes Were Watching God* is one of the works examined.   (*DAI* 56-8A: 3114)

B22.   Liang, Iping Joy. *The Lure of the Land: Ethnicity and Gender in Imagining America*. Amherst: University of Massachusetts. Pairs Hurston and Claude McKay in her study of the manner in which different ethnic group writers deal with the "lure of the land." Investigates the ethnic woman's need to "carve out the 'land before her' in both racial and gender terms." (*DAI* 56-11A: 4402)

B23.   Lumumba, Beverly Yvonne. *Words Without Masters: Harriet Jacobs' and Zora Neale Hurston's Listernerly Text*. Boulder: University of Colorado, 1995. Study uses Jacobs' *Incidents in the Life of a Slave Girl* and Hurston's *Their Eyes Were Watching God* to explore the "storytelling experience of the African American oral tradition and black feminist theory." Chapter three, "The Woman-Listerner Text as Communal Self" examines the "listernerly text's perspective" in Hurston's work. (*DAI* 57-1A: 21 7)

B24.   Nichols, David Green. *Conjuring the Folk: Modernity and Narrative in America 1915-1945*. Chicago: University of Chicago, 1995. Chapter three, "*Mules and Men* and Migrant Labor" considers "how the narrative frame in Zora Neale Hurston's ethnography displays folklore operating as a language of dissent in a lumber camp." (*DAI* 56-8A: 3128)

B25.   Obropta, Mary M.   *Hunters and Gatherers: American Women Working in the Documentary Arts, 1928-1939.*   Buffalo: State University of New York, 1995.   Focuses upon a "generation of American women working in the documentary arts;" these professional women were folklorists and anthropologists, one of whom was Hurston. Studies these women as part of a larger movement of professional, liberated women whose achievements as "hunters and gatherers" marked a new era in American history. (*DAI* 56:10A: 3962)

B26.   Patterson, Tiffany Ruby Ladelle.   *"You Got Tuh Go There Tuh Know": Social History as Knowable Through the Writings of Zora Neale Hurston, 1890-1945.*   Minneapolis: University of Minnesota, 1995. Examines the life and career of Hurston as "a means of reconstructing the consciousness of her time." Believes Hurston's willingness to examine social class and gender identity as well as segregation that other intellectuals at the time ignored, set her apart. (*DAI* 57-1A: 419)

B27.   Pavloska, Susanna.   *Primitivism in the Modern Era: A Study of Stein, Hemingway and Hurston.*   Princeton: Princeton University, 1995. Hurston's *Mules and Men* is one work examined. Says in it she "achieves an intersubjective ethnographical style that answers current postmodern concerns." Feels Hurston's model of "pure" African American culture are "complicated by the assimilationist underpinings of her pluralist stance." Believes primitivism provided "a system of eloquent symbols." (*DAI* 56-4A: 1358)

B28.   Vega, Maria Moreno.   *Yoruba Philosophy: Multiple Levels of Transformation and Understanding.*   Philadelphia: Temple University, 1995. This study provides "an historic and contemporary analysis of the continuity of Yoruba thought and contemporary analysis in the African Diaspora." Says Hurston one of the African-American professionals, who, through her anthropological research, promulgated the Yoruba tradition. (*DAI* 56-6A: 2285)

1994

B29.   Caron, Timothy Paul.   *"Rag-Tag and Bob-Ends of Old Stories": Biblical Intertextuality in Faulkner, Hurston, Wright, and O'Connor.* Baton Rouge: Louisiana State University, 1994. Examines the literature of southerners whose works rely on and borrow from religious tradition. Believes each recognizes the "authority" given to the Bible. Feels that with *Moses, Man of the Mountain*, Hurston contributes to the "South's intra-cultural conversation on race." (*DAI* 55-9A: 2828)

B30.   Chelte, Judith Segzdowicz. *Philomela's Tapestry: Empowering Voice Through Text, Texture, and Silence.* Amherst: University of Massachusetts, 1994.   Uses the Philomela legend to examine how "verbalizing silence creates a powerful textual and textural eloquence." Uses *Their Eyes Were Watching God* as on of seven texts analyzed to see how Hurston "explicitly or implicitly" uses the legend. (*DAI* 55-11A: 3510)

B31.   Holmes, Gloria Graves. *Zora Neale Hurston's Divided Vision: The Influence of Afro-Christianity and the Blues.* Stony Brook: State University of New York, 1994.   This study attempts to show how "Christianity, and the experience of American slavery combined to inform the fiction of Zora Neale Hurston." Says an examination of Hurston's fiction allows a "focus on the black church and black religious rituals and practices as creative sources." (*DAI* 55-9A: 2831)

B32.   Karell, Linda Kay. *Literary Borderlands and Unsettling Stories: Storytelling and Authority in Willa Cather, Mary Austin, Mourning Dove, and Zora Neale Hurston.* Rochester: University of Rochester, 1994. Hurston one of several authors examined in order to "explore how stories and storytelling, when used by marginalized women writers, engage questions of cultural and racial identity, literary authority, and transcendence." (*DAI* 55-5A: 1262)

B33.   Kawash, Samira. *Racial Properties, Racial Improprieties: Structures of Race in African American Narrative.* Durham, NC: Duke University, 1994.   Examines how racial identity is presented in African American literature.   The final chapter argues that in *Dust Tracks on a Road* and *Their Eyes Were Watching God*, Hurston presents "a sophisticated reflection on the violence of a racializing discourse of difference." (*DAI* 55-8A: 2391)

B34.   Kodat, Catherine Gunther. *Southern Modernists in Black an White: Jean Toomer, Allen Tate, William Faulkner, and Zora Neale Hurston.* Boston: Boston University, 1994. Examines Hurston's *Their Eyes Were Watching God* to understand two common concerns of modernism--"the role of history in the formation of the subject and the constraints of textuality upon the representation of consciousness." (*DAI* 54-10A: 3749)

B35. McFarlin, Patricia Ann. *Embodying and Disembodying Feminine Selves: Zora Neale Hurston's "Their Eyes Were Watching God," Djuna Barnes's "Nightwood," and Gertrude Stein's "Ida, A Novel."* Houston: University of Houston, 1994. "Traces a fiction which creates self-hood against the grain of the social norm." Says Hurston "splits her protagonist between the socially created self and the essentialist, nature-created self" and that she then "refashions a dialogic-self ready to shape its community." (*DAI* 56-2A: 553)

B36. McLaughlin, Patrick G., III. *Narrative Structure and Narrative Sense: Women's Writing and Identity in the Works of Zora Neale Hurston, Margaret Drabble, and Isabel Allende.* Indiana, PA: Indiana University of Pennsylvania. Looks at three twentieth-century women authors and explores the "relationship between cultural and personal identity as exemplified in the meshing and juxtaposing of the two within their writing." (*DAI* 55-7A: 1942)

B37. Monda. Kimberly Ann. *Resisting Self-Sacrifice: Subjectivity and Sexuality in Six American Women's Novels from Chopin to Hurston.* Los Angeles: University of California, 1994. Looks at female self-sacrifice in novels by six early twentieth-century female writers. *Their Eyes Were Watching God* is the Hurston novel analyzed. (*DAI* 55-11A: 3513)

B38. Musser, Judith A. *Engendering the Harlem Renaissance: The Short Stories of Marita Bonner, Zora Neale Hurston, and Other African American Women, 1921-1950.* West Lafayette, IN: Purdue University, 1994. "This study surveys 135 stories published by women in two of the Harlem Renaissance's leading African American journals-- *Opportunity* and *The Crisis*." Says these women created stories which reflected their own "gendered viewpoint," and that Hurston's stories deal with the hidden power of African Americans. (*DAI* 55-12A: 3844)

B39. Rummage, Ronald Glynne. *The Raceless Novels of the 1930s: African American Fiction by Arna Bontemps, George Henderson, Countee Cullen, Jessie Fauset, and Zora Neale Hurston.* Murfreesboro: Middle Tennessee State University, 1994. Examines the works of five African American novelists whose fiction "de-emphasized racial problems" and provided a "dispassionate rendering of black life." Hurston's writings are covered in chapter four. (*DAI* 56-3A: 934)

B40. Stein, Nancy Rachel. *Shifting the Ground: Four American Women Writers' Revisions of Nature, Gender and Race.* New Brunswick: Rutgers,

The State University of New Jersey, 1994.   Studies the relationship between "cultural conceptions of nature and gendered, racial and national identities." Argues that Hurston is one writer who incorporates "alternative conceptions of nature" using Voodoo and other African American traditions. (*DAI* 55-7A: 1972)

B41. Wright, Charlotte Megan. *Plain and Ugly Janes: The Rise of the Ugly Woman in Contemporary American Fiction*. Denton: University of North Texas, 1994. Discusses evolution of "plain Jane" and homely characters into powerful figures in the literature of twentieth-century authors, including Hurston.   These new characters question "the overwhelming value placed on beauty." (*DAI* 55-9A: 2837)

1993

B42. Batker, Carol J. *Ethnic Women's Literature and Politics: The Cultural Construction of Gender in Early Twentieth-Century America*. Amherst: University of Massachusetts, 1993. This study demonstrates the heterogeneity of gender politics early in this century by detailing how ethnic women's fiction contests the political discourses of ethnic women." Argues that *Their Eyes Were Watching God* "employs the language of the black women's club movement...to refute racist and classist sexual ideologies." *(DAI* 54-2A: 518)

B43. Cataliotti, Robert Henry. *The Words to the Song: Representing Music in African American Fiction*. Stony Brook: State University of New York, 1993. Traces how African American music is represented in works by African American authors. Hurston is one of several from the Harlem Renaissance whose works are analyzed. (*DAI* 54-10A: 3746)

B44. Donlon, Jocelyn Hazelwood. *Orality and the South: The Personal Narrative in Black and White Southern Fiction*.   Urbana-Champaign: University of Illinois, 1993. The dissertation looks at intraracial and cross-racial storytelling, and examines oral and literacy traditions in southern, rural locales. Hurston is discussed in chapters one and two. (*DAI* 54-5A: 1802)

B45. Drolet, Anne McCart. *Telling Her Stories to Change the (Con)Text of Identity: Four Novels by Contemporary American Women Authors of Color*. Binghamton: State University of New York, 1993. Feels that Hurston, along with Tan, Silko, and Cisneros, gives "radical new perspectives to what constitutes 'novel,' 'American', 'self,' 'community,' and 'identity.'" All use "folklore and cultural narratives to undermine expectations of women as passive and male-defined." Hurston discussed in chapter one which asserts *Their Eyes Were Watching God* "incorporates the subversive messages of the tall tale into the traditional quest romance." (*DAI* 54-8A: 3027)

B46. Hawkins, Alfonso Wilson, Jr. *The Musical Tradition as an Affirmation of Cultural Identity in African American Autobiography.* Columbus: Ohio State University, 1993. Explores the musical reading of African American autobiographical writing and attempts to show how Hurston, among others, "constructed personas of the black folk character whose life and vision echoed the black musical tradition." (*DAI* 54-2A: 519)

B47. Hill, Lynda Marion. *Social Rituals and the Verbal Art of Zora Neale Hurston.* New York City: New York University, 1993. This dissertation examines Hurston's work from the 1920s and 1930s for "ways performance can be a common reference point for interdisciplinary research." Asserts that her ethnographic texts use more than one genre and her literary techniques "expose central conflicts inherent in the paradigms used to represent cultural knowledge." (*DAI* 54-7A: 2687)

B48. Holmes, Carolyn Louise. *New Visions of a Liberated Future: Afrocentric Paradigms, Literature, and a Curriculum for Survival and Beyond.* Philadelphia: Temple University, 1993. Hurston one of several African American writers whose works were analyzed using Afrocentric paradigms as guidelines. "Each author was 'located' to determine his or her historical, cultural, and geographical centricism." Dissertation designed as a model for changing the bleak picture related to the educational status of African American youth. (*DAI* 54-7A: 2445)

B49. Maxwell, William Joseph. *Dialectical Engagements: The 'New Negro' and the 'Old Left,' 1918-1940.* Durham, NC: Duke University, 1993. Dissertation examines "the relations among black writers, white writers, and Marxism on the 'Old,' pro-Soviet left" in view of several recent developments and schools of thought. Hurston included in chapter four, which begins by "re-rooting the Wright-Hurston dispute within the larger Depression-era debates." Believes that Hurston, unlike Wright who embraced communism, was "enabled" by her "anthropologized memories" of her hometown of Eatonville. (*DAI* 54-3A: 567)

B50. McHenry, Elizabeth Ann. *Setting Terms of Inclusion: Storytelling as a Narrative Technique and Theme in the Fiction of Zora Neale Hurston, Eudora Welty, Leslie Marmon Silko and Maxine Hong Kingston.* Palo Alto: Stanford University, 1993. This study addresses "the strategy of storytelling as a narrative technique and theme." Hurston one of the authors whose linguistic structures draw upon her regional and cultural backgrounds. (*DAI* 54-5A: 1805)

B51. Mermann-Jozwiak, Elisabeth Maria. *A New Cultural Politics: Women Writers and Postmodernism.* Madison: University of Wisconsin, 1993. This dissertation examines "intersections among Postmodernism, feminism, and multiculturalism to reclaim women's experimental works as part of the postmodern tradition in the contemporary novel." Concludes that Hurston was one of several early women writers whose works foreshadow postmodern concerns. (*DAI* 54-6A: 2152)

B52. Mishkin, Tracy Ann. *Black/Irish: Comparing the Harlem and Irish Renaissances.* Ann Arbor: University of Michigan, 1993. This project explores the parallels between the two renaissances. It provides historical grounding and investigates comparisons made in the early twentieth-century. Hurston one of the Harlem Renaissance writers included in this comparative analysis. Looks at such issues as language, identity, and representation and at women writers whose works were often "marginalized." (*DAI* 54-3A: 925)

B53. Orlow-Klein, Ingrid Maria. "Real Voices Speak Multitudes: The Rhetoric of Analogy in *Kindheitsmuster, Mules and Men,* and *Goedel, Escher, Bach.*" Providence: Brown University, 1993. Examines "self-referential texts" by Hurston, Douglas Hofstadte, Christa Wolf, and Jorge Luis Borges to see how autobiography "has generated forms that counter theoretical definitions developed in the past 150 years." Uses Hurston's *Mules and Men* as one text to "outline a model of persuasive texts that could be termed 'analogical narrative.'" (*DAI* 54-10: 3739)

B54. Rodriguez, Barbara Ruth. *Generic Revisions: Form, Personhood, and Self-Representation in Autobiography by American Women of Color.* Cambridge: Harvard University, 1993. Study is a response to the "prescriptive and male-centered theories of the genre of autobiography." The texts of Hurston, Harriet Jacobs, Mary Rowlandson, Kingston, Hisaye Yamamoto, Silko, Adrienne Kennedy, and Pineda are examined in author's analysis of the ways they "illuminate the issues of subject construction" in the autobiographical genre. (*DAI* 54-11A: 4096)

B55.   Rony, Fatimah Tobing. *On Ethnographic Cinema: Race, Science and Spectacle, 1895-1933*.   New Haven: Yale University, 1993. Dissertation focuses on "ethnographic cinema before World War II." Rony's examination of "alternative forms of spectacle and ethnography" in cultural productions includes artists such as Hurston, Josephine Baker, and Katherine Dunham. (*DAI* 55-8A: 2188)

B56.   Shankar, Subramanian. *From the Hearts of Darkness to the Temples of Doom: The Discursive Economy of the Travel Narrative in the Colonial Context*. Austin: University of Texas, 1993. This study examines the colonial travel narrative as a genre. Looks at Hurston and several other authors in a side-by-side reading of the texts as both literature/culture and history/politics. (*DAI* 54-8A: 3021)

B57.   Wright, Pamela Stennes. *"Hitting a Straight Lick With a Crooked Stick"; Strategies of Negotiation in Women's Autobiographies From the United States 1940s: Zora Neale Hurston, Mine Okubo, and Amelia Grothe*. San Diego: University of California, 1993. The dissertation examines the "relationship between women's writing practices and strategies of cultural domination." Hurston's *Dust Tracks on a Road* examined "within a tradition in Afro-American modernism which 'gives the trick' to white expectations." (*DAI* 54-2A: 525)

1992

B58.   Basu, Biman. *Hybridity and the Dialogic in Black Women's Fiction*. Minneapolis: University of Minnesota, 1992. Considers the "politics of theory in general, and post-colonial and Afro-American literary theories in particular." The hybridity and dialogic metaphors are used as a framework to analyze Hurston's *Their Eyes Were Watching God* and works by Paule Marshall and Toni Morrison. Says a close readinig of the texts shows "deeply embedded hybridity in black women's fiction." (*DAI* 53-7A:2367)

B59.   Birns, Nicholas. *Spirits Lingering: Christianity and Modernity in Twentieth Century American Literature* (Melville, Stevens, Cather, Hurston, and Lowell). New York: New York University, 1992. Using the techniques of rhetorical and historical criticism, this dissertation discusses Christianity and modernity. Hurston included in the fifth chapter which examines her novels which "display the interaction between Christianity and modernity." (*DAI* 53-3A: 809)

B60.   Holland, Sharon Patricia. *Qualifying Margins: The Discourse of Death in Native and African American Women's Fiction*.   Ann Arbor: University of Michigan, 1992.   Looks at the "margin/center debate in literary criticism," and uses Hurston's *Their Eyes Were Watching God* to examine the "discourse between the living and the dead."   (*DAI* 53-12A:4320)

B61.   Johnson, Maria Virginia. *Voices of Struggle: An Exploration of the Relationship Between African American Women's Music and Literature*. Berkeley: University of California, 1992.   This dissertation explores the relationship of the union between music and literature and the unique influences on the creative process.   Writers Hurston and Walker and musicians Bernice Reagon Johnson and Bessie Smith are the specific artists examined to explore the connection between these artists and their creative processes and to "describe the basic aesthetic principles which characterize traditional African American approaches to performative processes." (*DAI* 54-9A: 3257)

B62.   Johnson, Yvonne. *The Voices of African-American Women: The Use of Narrative and Authorial Voice in the Works of Harriet Jacobs, Zora Neale Hurston, and Alice Walker*.   Dallas: University of Texas, 1992. Hurston's *Their Eyes Were Watching God* is one work used to examine authorial voice in narratives by African American women writers. (*DAI* 53-3A:810)

B63.   Mendelsohn, James Robert. *The Brute Fact: The Cultural Authority of Science in Twentieth-Century American Literature*.   St. Louis: Washington University, 1992.   This study looks at the "changing manner in which sciences are represented in the works of Williams James, Gertrude Stein, Zora Neale Hurston, Don DeLillo and others."   Believes the works of these authors show the imaginations of science "that map central issues within the culture" of twentieth-century America. (*DAI* 52-7A:2372)

B64.   Monroe, Barbara Jean. *Mother Wit: American Women's Literary Humor*.   Austin: University of Texas, 1992.   This dissertation uses the "differences in race, ethnicity, marital status, regionalism, age, sexual preference, and class" to look at the diversity within women's literature. Hurston, Anita Loos, June Arnold, and Mary McCarty are the authors whose works are examined. (*DAI* 53-4A: 1160)

B65.   Nelson, Linda Williamson. *Cultural Context and Cultural Code in the Oral Life Narratives of African-American Women: An Ethnography of*

Speaking. New Brunswick: Rutgers, The State University of New Jersey, 1992. The study looks at the "influence of cultural context on the linguistic form and thematic content of life narrative discourse." Analyzes vernacular use and the "speakers' personal agency" in Hurston's *Their Eyes Were Watching God*. (*DAI* 53-2A:544)

B66. Trefzer, Annette. *The Politics of In-Difference: Zora Neale Hurston and William Faulkner*. New Orleans: Tulane University, 1992. Looks at *Seraph on the Suwanee* and *Wild Palms* to argue that these works are not "aesthetically inferior" to the works considered masterpieces by the authors. Believes the novels have value because they "contest both traditional and revisionist canonizing efforts." (*DAI* 53-6A: 1918)

B67. Walther, Malin Lavon. *Embodying Beauty: Twentieth-Century American Women Writers' Aesthetics*. Madison: University of Wisconsin, 1992. Hurston is one author used to explore the "representation of female beauty" in the works of three generations of women writers. Hurston discussed in "relation to changing cultural standards of female beauty and the figure of the mulatta." (*DAI* 53-10A:3532)

1991

B68. Anokye, Akua Duku. *Linguistic Form and Social Function: A Discourse Analysis of Rhetorical and Narrative Structure in Oral and Written African-American Folk Narrative Texts*. New York: City University of New York, 1991. Study uses field notes and a previously unknown manuscript by Hurston to analyze "some African American folk narratives from the John and Master genre." Live recordings of folktales from the WPA era are also used for a performance-based analysis to show that the "prosodic structure...underlies comprehension in the oral texts." (*DAI* 52-5A: 1729)

B69. Bordelon, Pamela G. *The Federal Writers' Project's Mirror to America: The Florida Reflection*. Baton Rouge: Louisiana State University, 1991. This dissertation looks at the Florida project of the Works Progress Administration. Florida was one of three states which had an African American unit. Hurston was the only trained African American folklorist in the South, and this study looks at her contributions to the project. (*DAI* 52-9A: 3400)

B70. Brantley, William Oliver. *Women of Letters, the Southern Renaissance and a Literature of Self-Determination*. Madison: University of Wisconsin, 1991. This study provides an "intertextual examination" of women from the Southern Renaissance. Chapter five "considers the nexus of gender, region, nation, and race" in *Dust Tracks on a Road*. (*DAI* 52-10A: 3599)

B71. Cassidy, Thomas John. *Desire and Representation in Twentieth-Century American Realism* (Hurston, Dreiser, Cather, Morrison). Binghamton: State University of New York, 1991. This study examines relationships based on desire and critiques several novels to explore " male centered forms of marriage and self/other relationships." *Their Eyes Were Watching God* one novel used to study the representation of desire and what is real. (*DAI* 52-3A:914)

B72. Connor, Kimberly Rae. *Conversions and Visions in the Writings of Afro-American Women*. Charlottesville: University of Virginia. Rebecca Jackson, Harriet Jacobs, Toni Morrison, Alice Walker, Paule Marshall, and Hurston are authors whose works are examined for a "recurring pattern concerned with identify formation." Believes Hurston "occupies a pivotal position in the development of Afro-American women's writings." (*DAI* 53-2A: 497)

B73. Davies, Kathleen. *The Goddess in the Landscape: A Tradition of Twentieth Century American Women's Pastoral*. Bloomington: Indiana University, 1991. Looks at how women novelist "claim literary authority for women by appropriating the pastoral mode." Hurston appears in chapter four where an examination of *Their Eyes Were Watching God* shows she exploited the "discourse of the romance plot to simultaneously protect herself, the heroine, and black men." (*DAI* 53-1A: 149)

B74. duCille, F. Ann. *Coupling and Convention: Marriage, Sex, and Subjectivity in Novels by and About African American Women, 1853-1948*. Providence: Brown University, 1991. This work explores the relationship between "literary convention and racial and sexual ideology." Looks at early representations of marriage as the "bourgeois ideal" in the works of such nineteenth century writers as Harriet Wilson, Frances Harper, and Pauline Hopkins. Then examines early twentieth century writers--Fauset, Larsen and Hurston--who show that the "legal right to desire is not the same thing as sexual or reproductive freedom." (*DAI* 52-11A: 3977)

B75. Gillespie, Carmen Renee. *Visions of the Goddess: Self-Affirmation and Contemporary African-American Women Writers: A Womanist Reading*. Atlanta: Emory University, 1991. Study examines the protagonists in the novels of Hurston, Alice Walker, Morrison, Shange, Bambara, and Naylor who create "self-affirming" protagonists who discover their "inherent divinity." Texts examined chronologically to emphasize the "progressive emergence of the goddess." Womanism as a critical paradigm is also discussed in this dissertation. (*DAI* 52-12A: 4328

B76. Kaplan, Carla. *Opposing Stories: Fictions of Resistance and the Case of Zora Neale Hurston.* Evanston, IL: Northwestern University, 1991. Part one of this study focuses on critical debates about women's and African-American literary theories. The second section concentrates on Hurston: recuperating Hurston as a "model of resistance," looking at the changing reception to her work, examining her status as a "double-outsider" during the Harlem Renaissance, and using *Their Eyes Were Watching God* to focus on her "revision of the romance." (*DAI* 51-12A: 4121)

B77. Lee, Carol Diane. *Signifying as a Scaffold for Literary Interpretation: The Pedagogical Implications of an African American Discourse Genre.* Chicago: University of Chicago, 1991. This study investigates "signifying" as a scaffold for teaching literary interpretation skills to high school students. High school students in control and experimental classes analyzed samples of "signifying dialogues" and applied those strategies to "complex inferential questions" based on *Their Eyes Were Watching God* and *The Color Purple*.

B78. Levecq, Christine. *"Hitting a Straight Lick With a Crooked Stick": Humor and the Subversive in Three Novels by Zora Neale Hurston.* Urbana-Champaign: University of Illinois, 1991. This study examines *Jonah's Gourd Vine, Their Eyes Were Watching God*, and *Moses, Man of the Mountain* for Hurston's recurrent use of humor. Believes Hurston "appears as a subversive presence whose manipulation of humor underscores a complex political vision." (*DAI* 51-11A: 3939)

B79. Mayne, Heather Joy. *Biblical Paradigms in Four Twentieth-Century African-American Novels.* Palo Alto: Stanford University, 1991. This study examines the use of four Biblical paradigms. The "paradigm of the journey" is examined in *Their Eyes Were Watching God*. Discussed with Baldwin's *Go Tell it on the Mountain* is the "paradigm of the apocalypse;" Morrison's *Song of Solomon* is used to discuss the "paradigm of the canticle," and Walker's *The Color Purple* is used for the "paradigm of the epistle." Believes these paradigms function as "powerful systems of meanings which affirm identity and provide empowerment." (*DAI* 52-9A: 3284)

B80. Parke-Sutherland, Christine Marie. *Imagining Relation: Otherness in American Women's Experimental Fiction*. Ann Arbor: University of Michigan, 1991. This study describes the experimental point of view strategies found in novels written by Hurston, Olsen Tillie, and Stein. Argues that point of view is the "knowledge and power relationships constructed between the verbal-ideological works of authors, narrators, characters, and readers." Says Janie in *Their Eyes Were Watching God* had a "fully articulated and functional chorus of voices" that came together to tell her story. (*DAI* 52-10A: 3599)

B81. Perreault, Donna Marie. *Questions of Authorship in Twentieth-Century Literary Autobiography*.   Baton Rouge: Louisiana State University, 1991. Hurston one of the writers in this study which examines "narrative autobiographies by some of this century's most prominent and rebellious professional writers." Perreault examines how these narratives "put into question both processes of authorization and the cultural contexts in which they occur." (*DAI* 53-2A: 499)

B82. Peterson, Elizabeth. *A Phenomenological Investigation of Self-Will and Its Relationship to Success in African-American Women*. DeKalb: Northern Illinois University, 1991. This study collected life stories from black women aged 29 to 95 who "exhibited qualities of determination and courage" and compared the themes to those found in the writings of Alice Walker, Morrison, Angelou and Hurston. The themes from the interviews and the literature were analyzed using phenomenological methods. (DAI 51-4A: 1179)

B83. Raynaud, Claudine. *Rites of Coherence: Autobiographical Writings by Hurston, Brooks, Angelou and Lorde*. Ann Arbor: University of Michigan, 1991.   This dissertation looks at the constraints and contradictions found in autobiographical narratives written by contemporary African American female writers. Zora Neale Hurston's *Dust Tracks on a Road* is "analyzed as the tensional exploration of the self in folklore which eludes the demands of self-discovery and begrudgingly comes to terms with the politics of publishing." (*DAI* 53-3A:812.)

B84. Ward, Cynthia Ann. *Writing from the Margin, Speaking the Centers: An Oral Anti-Aesthetic*. Palo Alto: Stanford University, 1991. Examines the "marginal" writers, the "other," in an attempt to "locate a non-representable, non-authorizing 'speech' by redefining 'oral.'" Hurston, Emecheta, Flann O'Brien, and Carolyn Chute discussed in part two as "marginal" writers. Believes these works "point outside of textuality itself, to what literally cannot be communicated." (*DAI* 52-9A: 3269)

1990

B85.   Berg, Rebecca Louise. *How to Tell Lies: Epistemology and Gender Politics in Modernist Narratives*. Ithaca, NY: Cornell University, 1990. The works of four modernists--Hurston, Stein, Nietzsche, and Wilde--who "construct" or manufacture "truths" are examined in ths study. *Their Eyes Were Watching God* is analyzed as an example of a work where lies are told and then made to come true. Believes the writer's success depends upon gender politics. (*DAI* 51-11A: 3738)

B86.   Gambrell, Alice Kathleen Hagood. *The Disquieting Muse: New World Artists and Modernist Fictions of Alterity.* Charlottesville: University of Virginia, 1990. An analysis of the "dynamics of male/female intellectual collaboration in the contest of Modernism" is discussed in this work. Gambrell examines and reappraises four well-known cases--Hurston and Franz Boas being one, to learn what it means to study within a school, discipline or movement and be considered "Other." Examines "professional couplings" and in Hurston's case, her role as ethnographer/informant. (*DAI* 51-11A:3738)

B87.   Johnson, Gloria Carniece. *The Folk Tradition in the Fiction of Black Women Writers*. Knoxville: University of Tennessee, 1990. Study looks at the works of Hurston, Morrison, and Marshall, African American women writers who incorporate folk materials into their fiction. In chapter two Hurston is examined as a forerunner in the use of "folk expression, folktales, folkloric setting, and creation of the folk hero and heroine." (*DAI* 52-3A: 917)

B88.   Kuhel, Patty Joan Farris. *Remembering the Goddess Within: The Functioning of Fairy Tale and Mythic Motifs in the Novels of Hurston, Walker, Morrison, and Shange*. Tulsa, OK: University of Tulsa, 1991. Examines the works of Hurston, Alice Walker, Morrison, and Shange which "overturn the myths about beauty and worth...and celebrate women." Believes their characters grow into strong, self-confident women despite their communities' ideals and views. (*DAI* 52-2A: 539)

B89.   McAninch-Runzi, Wolfgang Manfred.   *African-American Women Writers and Liberation Theologies: Religion, God, and Spirituality in the Works of Zora Neale Hurston and Alice Walker*.   Eugene: University of Oregon, 1990.   This study looks at *Their Eyes Were Watching God* and *The Color Purple* as challenges to traditional, conventional, white male theology.   Feels Janie, and especially Celie, recognize theology's "dehumanization of the 'other'" and their religious disenfranchisement, but their own theologies allow them to "alter the social and economic structures of their environment." (*DAI* 51-8A: 2746)

B90.   Ryan, Judylyn Susan.   *Water from an Ancient Well: The Recuperation of Double-Consciousness in African-American Narrative*.   Madison: University of Wisconsin, 1990.   Using DuBois's definition of double-consciousness, this study examines the "African American narrative tradition in terms of this conflict of identity."   An individual chapter is devoted to Hurston's narratives.   (*DAI* 51-10A: 3405)

B91.   Schuyler, Sarah Elizabeth.   *Running Hot and Cold: A Cultural History of Late-Modern Bodies*.   Seattle: University of Washington, 1990.   Hurston examined in part two of this study which investigates "twentieth-century theoretical and cultural-studies work drawn from ...ethnographic contexts," one of which is the "new social scientific thinking" of the early twentieth century.   Hurston discussed in Part II which provides an historical view of interest in the body. (*DAI* 51-9A: 3070)

1989

B92.   Adams, Ann Josephine.   *Sisters of the Light: The Importance of Spirituality in the Afra-American Novel*.   Bloomington: Indiana University, 1989.   Adams examines Afrocentric values in the literature of African American women.   The novels of Hurston are explored in Adams' interdisciplinary approach to her analysis. (*DAI* 50-12A: 3948)

B93.   Adams, Brenda Byrne.   *Patterns of Healing and Wholeness in Characterizations of Women by Selected Black Women Writers*.   Muncie, IN: Ball State University, 1989.   Hurston, Bambara, Marshall, Naylor, and Alice Walker are the African American female writers whose fiction is examined for "written characterizations of winning women."   Their characters deal with "traumatic personal histories in a growth-enhancing manner." (*DAI* 50-11A: 3584)

B94. Hewitt, Mary Jane C. *A Comparative Study of the Careers of Zora Neale Hurston and Louise Bennett as Cultural Conservators*. Mona, Jamaica: University of the West Indies, 1989. (Dissertation from a foreign university; no other information available.)

B95. St. Clair, Janet Alcina. *The Struggle Through Despair: Heroic Affirmation in Modern American Fiction*. Atlanta: Emory University, 1989. Examines the fiction of Hurston, Faulkner, Nathanael West, Bellow, Silko, Katherine Ann Porter, and Cecile Pineda to look at "protagonists...who struggle toward an affirmation of both personal integrity and communal cohesiveness." Believes Hurston's character Arvay Meserve rejects oppression and the "mental submission to oppression that constricts her spirit and blights her efforts at involvement." (*DAI* 50-10A: 3228)

B96. Wainwright, Mary Katherine. *"Through Different Eyes": The Aesthetics of Community in the Texts of Zora Neale Hurston, Toni Morrison, and Alice Walker*. West Lafayette, IN: Purdue University, 1989. Study uses key elements of literary convention to look at selected texts by these three writers. Identifies an "Aesthetics of Community" that connects these three, and identifies a "politics of gender which counters the traditional emphasis on the theme of racial conflict as the major motif in African American literature." (*DAI* 50-9A: 2901)

1988

B97. Dawson, Emma J. Waters. *Images of the Afro-American Female Character in Jean Toomer's* Cane, *Zora Neale Hurston's* Their Eyes Were Watching God, *and Alice Walker's* The Color Purple. Tampa: University of South Florida, 1988. This study focuses on the depiction of African American women characters to examine the "evolving image" of African American women in the selected novels. Examination shows women in *Cane* lacked substance and were invisible; Hurston expands female characterization to a more complex, realistic woman looking for a meaningful relationship and an identity of her own. Says *The Color Purple* is an example of how a woman sustains herself after she is "self-defined and fulfilled." (*DAI* 48-10A: 2627)

B98. Fisher-Peters, Pearlie Mae. *"Don' Say No Mo' Wid Yo' Mouf Dan Yo' Back Kin Stan": The Assertive Woman in Zora Neale Hurston's Fiction, Folklore and Drama*. Buffalo: State University of New York, 1988. This dissertation provides a "critical study of Hurston as an assertive woman and includes an analysis of a "mighty fighter in her art." Says talking and fight were Hurston survival strategies in her quest for "assertive individualism." (*DAI* 50-1A: 139)

B99. Hardin, Shirley Hodge. *Reconciled and Unreconciled Strivings: A Thematic and Structural Study of the Autobiographies of Four Black Women*. Tallahassee: Florida State University, 1988. This study looks at the contribution of African American women to the autobiographical genre. Hurston's *Dust Tracks on a Road* analyzed in a separate chapter. Argues that the autobiographies of Hurston, Angelou, Gwendolyn Brooks, and Lorraine Hansberry give voice to women and "reveal what it means to be human in a society that denies humanity, growth, and fulfillment." (*DAI* 49-6: 1456)

B100. McCaskill, Barbara Ann. *To Rise Above Race: Black Woman Writers and Their Readers, 1859-1939*. Atlanta: Emory University, 1988. An examination of how "black American women writers have shaped their works as challenges to their readers' and reviewers' expectations of black women" is presented in this study. Hurston is one of three Harlem Renaissance female writers whose novels use a theme and structure to develop works that are set apart from "mainstream American literature." (*DAI* 50-1A: 140)

B101. Mugambi, Helen Nabasuta. *The Wounded Psyche and Beyond: Conformity and Marginality in Selected African and Afro-American Novels.* Bloomington: Indiana University, 1988. This study examines the "predicaments of female characters" in novels of Hurston and other African and African American women writers. *Their Eyes Were Watching* is one novel in a sequence "designed to illustrate the protagonists' progressive movement away from conformity to marginality." (*DAI* 50-4A: 944)

B102. Speisman, Barbara Waddell. *"Zora," "Color Struck and Weary Blues" and "Tea With Zora and Marjorie."* Tallahassee: Florida State University, 1988. Three original plays about the life and career of Zora Neale Hurston are presented in this dissertation. Hurston's works, her letters, and conversations with people who knew her are used to create the plays. Also used is her correspondence with Marjorie Rawlings, Carl Van Vechten, and Langston Hughes. (*DAI* 49-6A: 1458)

1987

B103. Dorsey, Peter Andrew. *The Rhetoric of Conversion in Early Twentieth-Century American Autobiography*. Philadelphia: University of

Pennsylvania, 1987. This study uses the autobiographies of Henry James, Edith Wharton, Ellen Glasgow, Richard Wright, and Hurston to examine *conversion* in the works of "conservatives, radicals, traditionalists, and innovators." Believes these writers "increasingly used conversion as an index of estrangement...from mainstream America." (*DAI* 49-2A: 253)

B104. Meeks, Catherine. *The Mule of the World: An Exploration of Sexist Oppression With Zora Neale Hurston and Alice Walker*. Atlanta: Emory University, 1987. Uses Jungian psychology and Greek mythology to examine "sexist oppression, the development of feminist consciousness in the black woman, and patterns of continuity in the expression of that consciousness." Chapter three provides background information on Hurston, and *Their Eyes Were Watching God* is analyzed for patterns of feminist behavior. (*DAI* 48-4A: 1036)

B105. Newsom, Adele Sheron. *An Annotated Bibliography of Critical Response to Zora Neale Hurston*. East Lansing: Michigan State University, 1987. This selective, annotated bibliography traces responses to Hurston's writings and documents her journey from Eatonville and back again. (*DAI* 47-9A: 3429)

B106. Simmons, Brenda Robinson. *Humanistic Influences in Two Novels and One Book of Folklore by Zora Neale Hurston*. Indiana, PA: Indiana University of Pennsylvania, 1987. Discusses a "humanistic perspective useful in reading selected fiction and folklore by Zora Neale Hurston." The three humanistic characteristics used are: verbal acumen, consuming curiosity, and singular initiative. Uses these three to examine *Jonah's Gourd Vine, Their Eyes Were Watching God*, and *Mules and Men*. (*DAI* 48-5A: 1205)

B107. Witherspoon-Walthall, Mattie L. *The Evolution of the Black Heroine in the Novels of Jessie Fauset, Nella Larsen, Zora Neale Hurston, Toni Morrison, and Alice Walker: A Curriculum*. Jamaica, NY: St. John's University, 1987. This study explores the "plight of the black heroine" in the fiction of five black American women. Hurston discussed in chapter two as one of three Harlem Renaissance writers whose characters are assessed in terms of how stereotypical images have "affected the black heroines in their search for self-awareness." (*DAI* 48-7A: 1772)

1986

B108. Awkward, Michael. *Circle of Sisters*. Philadelphia: University of Pennsylvania, 1986. The "intertextual connections" between Hurston's *Their Eyes Were Watching God* and selected texts of Morrison, Naylor and Alice Walker is studied in this dissertation. Discusses Hurston's female protagonist and her quest for "self-integration and a supportive community." Argues that Hurston and her descendants provide a "'circle of texts' that represents a cooperative system of tropological refiguration." (*DAI* 47-10A: 3756)

B109. Cherry, Amy Lynn. *Crowded Lives: A Bakhtinian Analysis of the Novels of Hurston, Arnow, Morrison, and Kingston*.   Ann Arbor: University of Michigan, 1986. Four novels from three sub-cultures are analyzed individually, and then a conversation is set up between them. Hurston's *Their Eyes Were Watching God* is one of the novels used for this project. (*DAI* 47-10A: 3791)

B110. Cooper, Jan Allyson. *Rhetoric, Lies, and Myth: Language and the Shape of Community in Six Southern Novels*. Iowa City: University of Iowa, 1986. Cooper looks at three "racially-mixed pairs" of novels written by southern writers. Hurston's *Their Eyes Were Watching God* is paired with Welty's *Delta Wedding* to "demonstrate the special ways southerners use language to create and sustain an identifiably southern sense of communal harmony." (*DAI* 47-12A: 4389)

B111. Fryar, Lillie B. *The Aesthetics of Language: Harper, Hurston and Morrison*. Buffalo: State University of New York, 1986. The language and literary styles of Frances Harper, Hurston, and Morrison is investigated in this dissertation. Believes Harper's literary voice is reflected in the "sorrow song;" Hurston's championing of African American folk culture is reflected in the "blues aesthetics," and Morrison's social commentary is reflective of "rhythm and blues."

B112. Holland, Endesha Ida Mae. *The Autobiography of a Parader Without a Permit*. Minneapolis: University of Minnesota, 1986. A Mississippi native documents her experiences growing up in Mississippi and explores the autobiographies of Hurston, Ida B. Wells, Mary Church Terrell, Septima Clark, and others who grew up as activists in the South. Holland's autobiography is presented in the form of a drama. (*DAI* 47-6A: 2206)

B113. Saunders, James Robert. *Great "Truth" in "Fiction": A Study of Four Black Writers* (Hurston, Wright, Hughes, James Weldon Johnson). Ann Arbor: University of Michigan, 1986. The study investigates the accuracy of self-representations in the works of these four authors. It examines their creation of characters and circumstances in an attempt to learn who these writers really were. Feels more is probably revealed about them in their fiction than in their autobiographies. (*DAI* 47-6A: 2161)

B114. Tooms, Charles Phillip. *For My People: The Development of Self in Afro-American Fiction--The Example of Alice Walker*. West Lafayette: Purdue University, 1986. Hurston is examined in chapter three where her fiction is investigated for its presentation of self. Says one of Hurston's concerns is the "relationship between the individual's development of a healthy self and the black community." (*DAI* 48-1A: 128)

1985

B115. Byers, Marianne Hollis. *Zora Neale Hurston: A Perspective of Black Men in the Fiction and Non-Fiction*. Bowling Green, KY: Bowling Green State University, 1986. Study examines the roles of African American men in Hurston's fiction and concludes that she draws "full portraits of black male characters" in her works. Select fiction, non-fiction, and other manuscripts are used to "show the impact of the black male's relationship with his family, his woman, with his community." (*DAI* 47-2A: 528)

1984

B116. Alexander, Estella Conwill. *Tell Them So You'll Know*. Iowa City: University of Iowa, 1984. Studies the autobiographies of Hurston, Angelou, Giovanni, and Brooks and explores how they use "their metaphors for themselves" to examine the worlds they created in their writing. Says Hurston uses them to frame and "order" her own past selves. (*DAI* 45-7A: 2153)

B117. Branzburg, Judith Vivian. *Women Novelists of the Harlem Renaissance: A Study in Marginality*. Amherst: University of Massachusetts, 1984. Explores the relationship between the "marginality" phenomena and the mind and body. Says the fiction of Hurston, Larsen, and Fauset reveals "an acceptance of some kind of encounter between the mind and body." (*DAI* 44-10A: 3063)

1983

B118.   Alladi, Uma Kuppuswama. *Woman and Her Family: Indian and Afro-American: A Literary Perspective*. Buffalo: State University, 1983. The study focuses on "the position of women in the family." Examines the roles of women in two dissimilar cultures. Begins with a socio-historic survey, then looks at the works of Hurston, other African American and Indian women writers to examine the survival skills of women. (*DAI* 44-10A: 3056)

B119.   Cannon, Katie G. *Resources for a Constructive Ethnic for Black Women With Special Attention to the Life and Work of Zora Neale Hurston*. New York: Union Theological Seminary, 1983. From an historical perspective, examines the unique "moral characteristics" of the African American women's community. Hurston's life and writings specifically addressed in chapters four and five as she examines "moral wisdom in the Black community." (*DAI* 45-3A: 865)

B120.   Holt, Elvin. *Zora Neale Hurston and the Politics of Race: A Study of Selected Modernist Fictions of Alternity*. Lexington: University of Kentucky, 1983. Study argues that Hurston's non-fiction prose provides comprehensive documentation of her views on the politics of race. Believes she provides a "romantic image of the South," and stresses the positive in her writing. Feels her views allowed her to "rise above self-pity and to view racism as a test of her ingenuity and strength." (*DAI* 44-10A: 3065)

B121.   Schmidt, Rita Terezinha. *With My Sword in My Hand: The Politics of Race and Sex in the Fiction of Zora Neale Hurston*. Pittsburgh University of Pittsburgh, 1983. Study concludes that an examination of Hurston's fiction shows "political coherence between her fiction's racial expression and its thematic concern with female oppression." Explores the male-female power relationships, which author feels is the "core of her narratives." (*DAI* 45-2A: 522)

1982

B122.   Crouther, Lou Ann. *Returning Home: Heroines as Rebuilders and Victims in American Fiction by Women*. Bloomington: Indiana University, 1982. Studies the fiction of Hurston, Cather, Glasgow, and Larsen to examine the various responses of the women characters to their communities. *Their Eyes Were Watching God* and *Seraph on the Suwanee* are two Hurston works whose female protagonists are analyzed. (*DAI* 43-11A: 3593)

1981

B123.   Babb, Valerie Melissa. *The Evolution of American Literary Language.* Buffalo: State University of New York, 1981. Hurston is one of the authors used to examine the development of American literary language.   Believes that with Hurston, the reader is provided with a language that uses "many techniques--compounding, dialect, vernacular, and borrowing." (*DAI* 41-6A: 2672)

B124.   Lewis, Vashti Crutcher. *The Mulatto Woman as Major Female Character in Novels by Black Women, 1892-1937.* Iowa City: University of Iowa, 1981. Uses thirteen novels written between 1892 and 1937 to explore the characterization of mulatto women. *Their Eyes Were Watching God* is analyzed, and Lewis feels Hurston foreshadows modern women novelists whose female heroines are not traditional feminine beauties. (*DAI* 42-11A: 4827)

B125. McDonald, Susan Sias Waugh.   *Writing and Identity: Autobiographies of American Women Novelists, 1930-1955.* St. Louis: St. Louis University, 1981. Hurston included in this study which analyzes twelve autobiographies of American women novelists.   All works examined were written before the "current wave of feminism which began in the early 1960s," and all look at women's "expanding awareness" of who they are. (*DAI* 42-10A: 4500)

B126.   O'Banner, Bessie Marie. *A Study of Black Heroines in Four Selected Novels (1929-1950) by Four Black American Women Novelists: Zora Neale Hurston, Nella Larsen, Paule Marshall, Ann Lane Petry.* Carbondale: Southern Illinois University, 1981. Looks at the fiction of these authors to explore the survival of black women in a bi-cultural society. Also studies how they strive for self-fulfillment and self-identity. (*DAI* 43-2A: 447)

B127. Varga-Coley, Barbara Jean. *The Novels of Black American Women.* Stony Brook: State University of New York, 1981. The African American experience in America is defined using the novels of writers who represent life using the African American experience. Hurston one of thirteen women whose work is analyzed. (*DAI* 42-2A: 707)

1980

B128.   Grimes, Joanna Lucille. *The Function of the Oral Tradition in Selected Afro-American Fiction*. Evanston: Northwestern University, 1980. Hurston, Morrison, Leon Forrest, and Albert Murray are writers whose novels are used to examine the use of folklore. Chapter one focuses on Hurston's use of the rural South, folk settings, and oral traditions in *Their Eyes Were Watching God*. Two of her short stories are also analyzed. (*DAI* 41-6A: 2604)

B129.   Ingram, Elwanda Eloris. *Black Women: Literary Self-Portraits*. Eugene: University of Oregon, 1980. The selected poetry and fiction of Hurston and several other African American women writers who created real, multi-dimensional characters are analyzed.   Categorizes these characters as "Suspended," "Color-Conscious," "Assimilated," and "Emergent-Assertive." Hurston's characters fit the latter category. (*DAI* 41-8A: 3573)

B130.   McDowell, Deborah Edith. *Women on Women: The Black Woman Writer of the Harlem Renaissance*. West Lafayette: Purdue University, 1980.   Examines the works of Fauset, Larsen and Hurston who were "pioneers in the development of a black female literary tradition." Feels Hurston's women "embrace more universal and humanistic concerns." (*DAI* 42-1A: 215)

1978

B131.   Holloway, Karla Francesca Clapp.   *A Critical Investigation of Literary and Linguistic Structures in the Fiction of Zora Neale Hurston*. East Lansing: Michigan State University, 1978. Believes that the critical reader who can make linguistic and literary judgments will find that Hurston's "structures of the dialect...provide additional insight into the significance of the text."   Believes critical inquiry and investigation requires a knowledge of a "linguistic system." (*DAI* 39-10A: 6131)

B132.   Jenkins, Joyce Odessa.   *To Make a Woman Black: A Critical Analysis of the Women Characters in the Fiction and Folklore of Zora Neale Hurston*. Irvine: University of California, 1978. Examines Hurston's creative union of folklore and literature, and explores characterization in her works. (*DAI* 39-7A: 4257)

B133.   Johnson, Gloria J. *Hurston's Folk: The Critical Significance of Afro-American Folk Tradition in Three Novels and the Autobiography.* Irvine: University of California, 1978. This study posits that all but a few of Hurston's characters are "folk." Says Hurston counted on her readers to participate and "flesh out" her characters. Also argues for folklore as a valid criterion for evaluating literature and explores the "relationship between her folk characters and their folkloric prototypes." (*DAI* 38-9A: 5480)

1976

B134.   Wall, Cheryl A. *Three Novelists: Jessie Fauset, Nella Larsen, and Zora Neale Hurston.* Cambridge: Harvard University, 1976. No abstract available from *Dissertation Abstracts*--online or in print.

1975

B135.   Davidson, Colleen Tighe. *Beyond the Sentimental Heroine: The Feminist Character in American Novels, 1899-1937.*   Minneapolis: University of Minnesota, 1975. Examines *Their Eyes Were Watching God* and novels by Thomas Bell and Edith Wharton and concludes that their female characters achieve a "balance between their senses of personal and social identity." These authors are all advocates of feminism. (*DAI* 37: 306)

B136.   Howard, Lillie Pearl. *Zora Neale Hurston: A Non-Revolutionary Black Artist.* Albuquerque: University of New Mexico, 1975. This study is a "critical and extensive" examination of five of Hurston's short stories, four novels, two books of folklore, and her autobiography. Believes she is a writer "deserving of sustained attention" because her themes are "universal." (*DAI* 36-10A: 6673)

B137.   Royster, Beatrice Horn. *The Ironic Vision of Four Black Women Novelists: A Study of the Novels of Jessie Fauset, Nella Larsen, Zora Neale Hurston, and Ann Petry.* Atlanta: Emory University, 1975. Study asserts that each writer reflects a "common sense of irony in their perception of the universe." Separately analyzes novels of each author and argues that Hurston dramatically rejects the "genteel tradition" found in earlier novels. Says Hurston uses the folk tradition, but also has an idealistic and comic vision of the universe. (*DAI* 36-12A: 8051)

MASTER'S THESES

B138. Alexander, Rosalind. *Voodoo Essentials in Zora Neale Hurston's Published Fiction*. Washington, DC: Howard University, 1986.

B139.   Appleton, Karen Alecia. *Leadership and Freedom: Zora Neale Hurston's Moses, Man of the Mountain*. East Lansing: Michigan State University, 1992.

B140.   Bit, Sandra Lisa. *Making the Ancient Image New: Identity and Family Origins in Three Novels by Toni Morrison*. (Hurston analyzed in conclusion.) Halifax, Nova Scotia: Dalhousie University, 1990.

B141. Blanchard, Thomas Knudson. *A Radical Feminist Materialistic Reading of Zora Neale Hurston's Fiction*.   Recinto de Rio Piedras: Universidad de Puerto Rico, 1993.

B142. Boyles, Janice Wilson. *The Quests of Zora Neale Hurston and the Protagonists in Her Novels Their Eyes Were Watching God and Jonah's Gourd Vine*. Clemson: Clemson University Press, 1992.

B143. Davis, Mella Jean. *Zora Neale Hurston: The Voice of the Goddess*. Bowling Green: Western Kentucky University, 1991.

B144.   Foster, Delores. *Love, Hate, and Protest in the Novels of Zora Neale Hurston*. Jackson: Jackson State University, 1981.

B145.   Frias, Maria. *Zora Neale Hurston: Marriage Does Not Make Love*. Chapel Hill: University of North Carolina, 1992.

B146. Halpin, Gerald. *Blues Voices and Echoes: Zora Neale Hurston's Their Eyes Were Watching God*. Tempe: Arizona State University, 1993.

B147. Hannah, Kathleen Powell. *"He Was a Glance From God:" Mythic Analogues for Tea Cake Woods in Zora Neale Hurston's Their Eyes Were Watching God*. Bowling Green: Western Kentucky University, 1992.

B148. Hooks, Rita Daly. *Conjured Into Being: Zora Neale Hurston's Their Eyes Were Watching God*. Tampa: University of South Florida, 1990.

B149. Imperato, Lynn Rossetti. *Community, Canon, and the Classroom in Three Works by African American Women Writers: Incidents in the Life of a Slave Girl, Their Eyes Were Watching God, and Sula: A Thesis.* Upper Montclair, NJ: Montclair State University, 1995.

B150. Inman, James A. *Journeys of the Self: Connecting the Experiences of Henry James's Isabel Archer, James Joyce's Stephen Dedalus, and Zora Neale Hurston's Janie Mae Crawford.* Valdosta, GA: Valdosta State University, 1995.

B151. Jenkins, Pamela J. *The Wandering Soul: The Search for Identity in Chopin's The Awakening, Hurston's Their Eyes Were Watching God, and Walker's The Color Purple.* Greenville, NC: East Carolina University, 1995.

B152. Lain, Rodney O'Neale. *Signifyin(g) as a Rhetorical Device in the Selected Writers of the Harlem Renaissance* (Hurston, Hughes, and Wright). Natchitoches: Northwestern State University of Louisiana, 1994.

B153. Lopez, Judith Anne. *Narrative and Thematic Tension in the work of Zora Neale Hurston.* San Jose: San Jose State University, 1991.

B154. Lovegrove, Marie Valerie. *The Carnivalesque Blues of Zora Neale Hurston.* Guelph, Ontario: University of Guelph, 1994.

B155. Manetti, Marina Margherita. *The Issue of the Self Traced Through African American History, Twentieth-Century African American Novels, and an Aesthetic Theory. (Hurston, Ellison, and Morrison)* East Lansing: Michigan State University, 1993.

B156. MacGillis, Julie. *The Use of Rural Southern Landscapes to Rewrite History in the Fiction of Jean Toomer, Richard Wright, Zora Neale Hurston, and Ernest J. Gaines.* Tallahassee: Florida State University, 1995.

B157. Meehan, Kevin. *Decolonizing Ethnography: Zora Neale Hurston and the Caribbean.* College Park: University of Maryland, 1991.

B158. Mock, Jennifer A. *Southern Women Writers: Exploring Self-hood (Hurston, Glasgow, Porter, Alice Walker).* Winter Park, FL: Rollins College, 1995.

B159.   Moen, Joelle C. *Breaking Boundaries, Inciting Revolutions: Negotiating the Re-Doubled Conscious and the American Grotesque in Zora Neale Hurston's Their Eyes Were Watching God.*   Pullman: Washington State University, 1995.

B160.   Morgan, Cathy L. *Fiction as Autobiography, Autobiography as Fiction: Zora Neale Hurston's Their Eyes Were Watching God and Dust Tracks on a Road.* Farmville, VA: Longwood College, 1991.

B161. Noll, Elizabeth O'Donnell.   *Three From the Margins of Anthropology: Hurston, Bohannan and Powdermaker.* Tuscon: University of Arizona, 1994.

B162.   Raphael, Heike Juliane. *The Concept of the "Critical Utopia" in the Works of Zora Neale Hurston, Alice Walker, and Toni Morrison.* Louisville: University of Louisville, 1989.

B163. Rasmussen, Patricia Ann. *Zora Neale Hurston: Freedom From the Inside Out.* Corvalis: Oregon State University, 1994.

B164.   Redding, Andrey J. *Symposium on Women.* Winter Park, FL: Rollins College, 1992.

B165. Redling, Erik Karl. *Early Twentieth Century Scientific Theories of Race and Their Impact on Zora Neale Hurston and William Faulkner.* Raleigh: North Carolina State University, 1994.

B166. Scott, Kathleen J. *The Ethnographic Works of Zora Neale Hurston.* Northridge: California State University, 1994.

B167. Sheldon, Ricky Weaver. *Southern Women's Literature: Reaching Back Through Myth to Recover Woman's Artistic Selfhood.* Shippensburg: Shippensburg University of Pennsylvania, 1995.

B168.   Smith, Christopher Stewart. *Implications of Race Identity in the Black Autobiographical Tradition.* Auburn, AL: Auburn University, 1996.

B169.   Uber, Nancy E. *Double-Figuring, Double-Reading: The Problematics of Texts Grounded in Multiple Cosmologies.* Sonoma: Sonoma State University, 1992.

B170. Whelcher, Karen L. *Hurston's Black Feminist Vision and Voice.* Radford, VA: Radford University, 1992.

B171. Zambo, Tammy J. *Adoptations, the Self-Writings of Three African American Women.* University of North Dakota. 1993.

HONORS PAPERS

B172. Basalla, Susan Elizabeth. *The Field of Imagination: Art and Anthropology in Zora Neale Hurston's Mules and Me*n. Lewisburg, PA: Bucknell University, 1992.

B173. Brown, Elizabeth Ann Barnes. *Family Relationships in the Novels of Black Women Authors.* Abilene, TX: Abilene Christian University, 1994.

B174. Flores, Joy. *Zora Neale Hurston: The Mingling of Fact, Fiction and Conviction.* San Luis Obispo: California Polytechnic State University, 1996.

B175. Myers, Teresa. *Past and Present in Negro Humor: Langston Hughes and Zora Neale Hurston.* Clinton: Mississippi College, 1974.

B176. Roark, Kira. *Zora Neale Hurston's Their Eyes Were Watching God and Leslie Marmon Silko's Ceremony.* Denver: Metropolitan State College of Denver, 1994.

B177. Smith, Naomi Catherine. *Zora Neale Hurston's Their Eyes Were Watching God: An Analysis of Janie Mae Crawford's Growth and Development in Relation to Her Three Marriages.* Cedar Rapids, Iowa: Coe College, 1993.

C

Essays and Book Chapters about Zora Neale Hurston

"What seems to be a returning pilgrim is another person born in the strange country with the same-looking ears and hands."

Dust Tracks on a Road

C01. Angelou, Maya. Foreword to *Dust Tracks on a Road*. New York: Harper Perennial, 1991: vii-xii. Notes that Hurston's autobiography, though written when she was fifty years old, deals primarily with the very early part of her life. Angelou also comments that Hurston "does not mention one unpleasant racial incident," and feels the book is written with "royal humor and an imperious creativity."

C02. Awkward, Michael. "Mah Tongue Is in Mah Friend's Mouf." In *Inspiriting Influences: Tradition, Revision, and Afro-American Women's Novels*. New York: Columbia University Press, 1989: 15-56. The book discusses four black women novelists, with Hurston examined in chapter one. Essay provides an "intertextual reading" of *Their Eyes Were Watching God* and concludes that Janie resolves a "double consciousness into a unified, black sensibility."

C03. Awkward, Michael. "'The inaudible voice of it all': Silence, Voice, and Action in *Their Eyes Were Watching God*." In *Black Feminist Criticism and Critical Theory*. Eds. Joe Weixlmann and Houston A. Baker, Jr. Greenwood, FL: Penkevill Publishing Company, 1988. This is a reprint of an article first published in *Studies in Black American Literature*.

Argues that Hurston deliberately uses the African American pattern of "call and response" to tell Janie's story, rather than have Janie narrate her own story. Article cites the work of other Hurston scholars.

C04. Baker, Houston. "Figurations for a New American Literary History: Archaeology, Ideology, and Afro-American Discourse." *Blues, Ideology, and Afro-American Literature: A Vernacular Theory*. Chicago: University of Chicago Press, 1984: 56-60. Links *Their Eyes Were Watching God* to slave narratives. Says Janie as "singer" represents the experiences of African American women who are used and treated as mules. Discusses the economic problems associated with telling one's history or selling ones blues and cites examples from the novel.

C05. Baker, Houston. *Working the Spirit: The Poetics of Afro-American Women's Writing*. Chicago: University of Chicago Press, 1991: 66-69; 77-79, 82-99. Various sections of Baker's essay, "Workings of the Spirit: Conjure and the Space of Black Women's Creativity," are devoted to Hurston's use of "spiritual agents" and a discussion of their use in *Mules and Men*. Believes Hurston's creative use of conjuring influenced Walker and other black women writers.

C06. Bambara, Toni Cade. Foreword to *The Sanctified Church*. Zora Neale Hurston. Berkeley: Turtle Island Foundation, 1981: 7-11. Clearly a Hurston fan, Bambara feels more African Americans should "discover Zora." Said Hurston knew what her mission in life was and pursued it.

C07. Barksdale, Richard, and Keneth Kinnamon. In *Black Writers of America*. New York: Macmillan, 1972: 611-618. This entry provides a reprint of "The Gilded Six-Bits," a Hurston short story, critical comments on several works, and biographical information.

C08. Barthold, Bonnie J. *Black Time: Fiction of Africa, the Caribbean, and the United States*. New Haven: Yale University Press, 1981: 131-134. Janie from *Their Eyes Were Watching God* discussed in a chapter entitled "Women: Chaos and Redemption." Discusses Janie's marriages as rebellion and "flight from a spiritually destructive respectability" and analyzes her redemption and rebirth.

C09. Bass, George Houston. "Another Bone of Contention: Reclaiming Our Gift of Laughter." Introduction to *Mule Bone: A Comedy of Negro Life*. New York: Harper Collins, 1991: 1-4. Discusses Hurston's and Hughes' understanding of and appreciation for the black oral tradition and the blacks' use of humor as a "coping mechanism for personal and group survival. Explores their deliberate use of comic characters, telling tall tales, signifying, and other devices used to establish a sense of self.

C10.   Bell, Bernard W. *The Afro-American Novel and Its Tradition.* Amherst: University of Massachusetts Press, 1987: 119-128. Hurston appears in the chapter, "The Harlem Renaissance and the Search for New Modes of Narrative." Says *Their Eyes Were Watching God* is a love story written by a visionary feminist. Also feels Hurston was "destined to achieve distinction for her imaginative use of ethnic folklore." Believes one main problem with the novel is Hurston's awkward handling of point of view.

C11.   Bell, Bernard W.   "Zora Neale Hurston."   In *The Reader's Companion to American History.* Eds. Eric Foner and John A. Garraty. Boston: Houghton-Mifflin, 1991: 528-529.   Notes that Hurston was "outspoken, spirited, and gifted," and her upbringing in an all-black town was "the major shaping influence of her affirmative vision of African-American rural folk culture." Bell summarizes author's life and major works, states that *Dust Tracks on a Road* is her "most commercially successful" work, and *Their Eyes Were Watching God* is her "most critically acclaimed" one.

C12.   Bell, Bernard W.   "Zora Neale Hurston."   In *The Reader's Companion to American History.* Eds. Eric Foner and John A. Garraty.Boston: Houghton-Mifflin, 1991: 528- 529. Brief entry provides biographical information on Hurston and lists and summaries each of her primary works. Says *Their Eyes Were Watching God* has a "mixture of formal rhetoric and black idiom."

C13.   Berzon, Judith R.   "Mulatto Fiction: Myths, Stereotypes, and Reality." In *Neither White Nor Black: The Mulatto Character in American Fiction.* New York: New York University Press, 1978: 75-76. Says that writers of mulatto fiction do not generally endow their female characters with much "breadth or depth, or very many options," but that Hurston's Janie was an exception.

C14.   Bethel, Loraine.   "'This Infinity of Conscious Pain': Zora Neale Hurston and the Black Female Tradition."   In *But Some of Us are Brave.* Ed. Gloria T. Hull, Patricia Bell Scott, and Barbara Smith. Old Westbury: Feminist Press, 1982: 176-188. Says Hurston faced life and literature as a strong and courageous black female and portrayed women characters as worthy. Believes her use of storytelling confronted the stereotypes established and perpetuated by white males.

C15. Bloom, Harold, ed. *Black American Prose Writers of the Harlem Renaissance*. New York: Chelsea House, 1994: 78-93. Critical extracts/reprints of writings by H.I. Brock, Sterling Brown, Richard Wright, Worth Tuttle Hedden, Robert Bone, Henry Louis Gates, Jr., John Lowe, Karla Holloway, S. Jay Walker, Nellie McKay, Jennifer Jordan and Maya Angelou are prefaced by a brief biographical sketch. Hurston is also represented with an extract.

C16. Bloom, Harold, ed. *Black American Women Fiction Writers*. New York: Chelsea House, 1995: 56-72. Entry contains a short biography of Hurston and critical extracts from previously published materials from authors such as H. I. Brock, Hedden, Wright, and Hurston herself.

C17. Boi, Paola. "Zora Neale Hurston's Autobiographies Fictive: Dark Tracks on the Canon of a Female Writer." In *The Black Columbiad: Defining Moments in African American Literature and Culture*. Ed. Werner Sollors. Cambridge: Harvard University Press, 1994. Argues that Dust Tracks on a Road is more fiction than self portrait of Hurston and posits that duplicity is an inherent part of autobiography. Defines "narrative fictive," and feels Hurston self-invents as she self-discovers/discloses. Concludes that autobiography is relevant more for its literary value than any realistic self portrait. Suggests that Hurston wrote about the woman she wanted to be.

C18. Bone, Robert. "Aspects of a Racial Past" *The Negro Novel in America*. New Haven: Yale University Press, 1965: 126-132. Also in *The Black Novelist*. Ed. Robert Hemenway. Columbus: Charles E. Merrill Publishing, 1970: 55-61. Article provides biographical information on Hurston, critical commentary on *Jonah's Gourd Vine*, and a critique of *Their Eyes Were Watching God*. Believes Hurston's use of folklore is too academic for fiction, but feels *Their Eyes Were Watching God* is one of the premiere novels of the Harlem Renaissance. Hurston also included in sub-essay entitled "George Wylie Henderson and Zora Neale Hurston."

C19. Bone, Robert. "Three Versions of the Pastoral." In *Down Home: A History of Afro-American Short Fiction From Its Beginning to the End of the Harlem Renaissance*. New York: Putnam, 1975: 141-150. Lists and summaries Hurston's major works. Believes Hurston worked best within the framework of what she knew best--settings such as her home town of Eatonville, Florida. Examines several of her short stories.

C20. Bontemps, Arna, ed. *The Harlem Renaissance Remembered*. New York: Dodd, Mead & Co., 1972: 190-214. Various sections mention Hurston and her participation in the era and her relationship with other writers.

C21. Brantley, Will. "Zora Neale Hurston: The Ethics of Self-Representation." In *Feminine Sense in Southern Memoir: Smith, Glasgow, Welty, Hellman, Porter, and Hurston*. Jackson: University Press of Mississippi, 1993: 185-239. Author discusses three women writers who have written book-length autobiographies or "self-studies." Says Hurston "deliberately works through disguises" in an attempt to define herself.

C22. Braxton, Joanne M. "Ancestral Presence: The Outraged Mother Figure in Contemporary Afra-American Writing." In *Wild Women in the Whirlwind: Afra-American Culture and the Contemporary Renaissance*. Eds. Joanne M. Braxton and Andree Nicola McLaughlin. New Brunswick: Rutgers University Press, 1990: 299-315. In brief reference to Hurston, claims that Nanny in *Their Eyes Were Watching God* is an "ancestral presence."

C23. Braxton, Joanne M. "Motherless Daughters and the Quest for Place: Zora Neale Hurston and Era Bell Thompson." In *Black Women Writing Autobiography: A Tradition Within a Tradition*. Philadelphia: Temple University Press, 1990: 44-180. Chapter five discusses Hurston's autobiography as a turning away from "slave narrative and extending the quest for a dignified and self-defining identity."

C24. Brock, Sabine and Ann Koenen. "Alice Walker in Search of Zora Neale Hurston: Rediscovering a Black Female Tradition." In *History and Tradition in Afro-American Culture*. Ed. Gunter Lenz. Frankfurt: Campus, 1984.

C25. Brown, Sterling. "Southern Realism." In *The Negro in American Fiction*. Sterling Brown. Washington, DC: The Associates in Negro Folk Education, 1937: 159-61. Summarizes and praises several Hurston works, but feels *Mules and Men* is "too pastoral" and *Their Eyes Were Watching God* is more love story than novel of protest.

C26. Bus, Heiner. "The Establishment of Community in Zora Neale Hurston's 'The Eatonville Anthology' (1926) and Rolando Hinojosa's 'Estampas del valle' (1973)." In *European Perspectives on Hispanic Literature of the United States*. Ed. Genieve Fabre. Houston: Arte Publico Press, 1988: 66-81. The article by Bus, a professor at the University of Mainz, is part of a collection of essays from the International Conference on Hispanic Cultures and Identities in the United States which was held in Paris in March 1986. Focuses on the role of the narrator and the urge for stability and continuity. Says Hurston's hometown "provides a positive mood and morality" but the "locality is never exposed to change and development."

C27. Callahan, John F. "'Mah Tongue Is in My Friend's Mouf:' The Rhetoric of Intimacy and Immensity in *Their Eyes Were Watching God*." *The African-American Grain: Call & Response in Twentieth-Century Black Fiction*. Middletown, CT: Wesleyan University Press, 1988: 115-149. Also in *Zora Neale Hurston's Their Eyes Were Watching God*. Ed. Harold Bloom. New York: Chelsea House, 1987. Essay examines and traces some of the "variations and adaptations of call and response patterns worked out in twentieth-century black fiction." The five-part article also examines voice and storytelling as each "collaborates" rather than competes.

C28. Candelaria, Cordelia-Chavez. "Difference and the Discourse of 'Community' in Writings by and About the Ethnic Other(s)." In *An Other Tongue: Nation and Ethnicity in the Linguistic Borderlands*. Ed. Alfred Arteaga. Durham, NC: Duke University Press, 1994. Looks at the works of Henry Roth, Rudolfo Anaya and Hurston. *Their Eyes Were Watching God* analyzed for a discussion of anthropological linguistics and intercultural communication.

C29. Cannon, Katie Geneva. *Katie's Canon: Womanism and the Soul of the Black Community*. New York: Continuum, 1995: 77-90, 91-100. Two essays on Hurston are included. In "Resources for a Constructive Ethnic: The Life and Work of Zora Neale Hurston," Cannon says the primary impetus for Hurston's work was to "capture the density of simple values" inherent in the "Negro farthest down." Believes all of Hurston's writings, including *Serape on the Suwanee,* incorporate the use of ethical habits, attitudes, and manners. "Unctuousness as Virtue--According to the Life of Zora Neale Hurston" discusses her "differentness" during the period 1920-1950 and how it affected reception of Hurston and her writing during this period. Believes Hurston was penalized for her unctuousness.

C30. Carby, Hazel. "The Politics of Fiction, Anthropology, and the Folk: Zora Neale Hurston." In *History and Memory in African-American Culture*. Eds. Genevieve Fabre and Robert O'Malley. New York: Oxford University Press, 1994: 28-44. Article deals with the contemporary "inclusion" of Hurston, her secure place in the academy, and Hurston as a profitable industry. Looks at the two societies of Hurston critics--her own contemporaries who viewed her one way, and the critics of the 1980s and 1990s who embrace her work and are responsible for her revival. Asks why *Their Eyes Were Watching God* is now one of the most frequently taught novels by an African-American, and cautions cultural critics to "question the extent of our dependence upon our re-creations" of Hurston.

C31. Christian, Barbara. "The Rise and Fall of the Proper Mulatta." *Black Women Novelists: The Development of a Tradition, 1892-1976*. Westport, CT: Greenwood Press, 1980: 56-61. Says that Hurston was different from other Harlem Renaissance writers because she "knew intimately rather than talked about folk speech and folk images." Believes Janie represents a "new black woman character." Says Hurston knew the beauty of folk language and used her cultural heritage to present a different view of the mulatta in fiction.

C32. Christian, Barbara. *Black Feminist Criticism: Perspectives on Black Women Writers*. New York: Pergamon Press, 1985: 7-11, 122-123, 174-175. Discusses *Dust Tracks on a Road* as an exception to the "image of the tragic mulatta" and Janie in *Their Eyes Were Watching God* as the exception to the self-alienated characters who peopled the fiction of Hurston's female contemporaries. Hurston also briefly discussed in chapters entitled "Images of Black Women in Afro-American Literature: From Stereotype to Character," and "Trajectories of Self-Definition: Placing Contemporary Afro-American Women's Fiction."

C33. *Contemporary Literary Criticism*. Vols. 7 and 30. Detroit: Gale Research, 1977 and 1984 respectively. These volumes have the standard *CLC* entries that include biographical information then critical excerpts from previously published materials. Volume seven (170-172) includes excerpts from Cheryl Wall, Robert Hemenway, June Jordan, Ellease Southerland, and Robert Bone. Volume 30 (207-229) presents excerpts from Fannie Hurst, Franz Boas, Worth Tuttle, Nick Aaron Ford, and Alice Walker, to name a few. The entry in volume 30 has a photograph.

C34. Cooke, Michael G. "Solitude: The Beginning of Self-Realization in Zora Neale Hurston, Richard Wright, and Ralph Ellison." *Afro-*

American Literature in the Twentieth Century: The Achievement of Intimacy. New Haven: Yale University Press, 1984: 71-109. Chapter three discusses the character Janie evolving from "materialism" to "self-realization" and finally to "self-reliance." Says that when *Their Eyes Were Watching God* was written in 1937, these were new qualities in the works of black women writers.

C35. Connor, Kimberly Rae. "Called to Preach." *Conversions and Visions in the Writings of African-American Women.* Knoxville: University of Tennessee Press: 110-169. This chapter examines the importance of sustaining and promoting African American culture in general and embracing femaleness in particular. Essay looks at Hurston's use of her cultural heritage, her glory in its differences, her need to "witness," and her anthropological work. Cites the work of numerous Hurston critics.

C36. Cooper, Jan. "Zora Neale Hurston Was Always a Southerner Too." In *The Female Tradition in Southern Literature.* Ed. Carol S. Manning. Urbana: University of Illinois Press, 1993: 57-69. Says Hurston is often omitted by scholars of the "Southern Renaissance" as they study authors of that era. Explains why she should be included.

C37. Curley, Dorothy Nyren, ed. "Zora Neale Hurston." *Modern American Literature.* Vol. 5. New York: Ungar, 1969: 198-202. The essay is a compilation of excerpts from previously published critical essays and reviews of Hurston's works.

C38. Dance, Daryl C. "Zora Neale Hurston." *In American Women Writers: Bibliographical Essays.* Eds. Maurice Duke, Jackson R. Bryer, and M. Thomas Inge. Westport, CT: Greenwood Press, 1983: 321-351. Hurston is the only "woman of color" included in this work that deals mainly with southern novelists. Her works are categorized by "full-length, short stories, essays and other writings, manuscripts and letters, and biography." Dance provides a fairly comprehensive look at Hurston, discusses each work individually, and includes a bibliography.

C39. Dandridge, Rita B. "On the Novels Written by Selected Black American Women: A Bibliographic Essay." In *But Some of Us are Brave.* Eds. Gloria T. Hull, Patricia Bell Scott, and Barbara Smith. Old Westbury: Feminist Press, 1982: 273-275. Provides a bibliographical survey of some of the early works "about" Hurston. Says Hemenway's literary biography of Hurston "will undoubtedly become the standard reference for information about Hurston's life and works."

C40.   Daniel, Walter C. "Zora Neale Hurston's John Pearson: Saint and Sinner." In *Images of the Preacher in Afro-American Literature.* Washington, DC: University Press of America, 1991: 83-109. This chapter begins with a brief biographical sketch and discusses Hurston's image of a preacher as depicted in *"Jonah's Gourdvine"* [sic]. Says the image she presents is "complex and authentic for the black experience in the Christian practice in America."

C41.   Davis, Arthur Paul. In *From the Dark Tower: Afro-American Writers (1900-1960).* Washington, DC: Howard University Press, 1974: 113-120. Hurston included in a chapter entitled, "First Fruits (1925-1940)." Bio-critical information summarizes her life and career, especially as a member of the "Negro literati," and examines her book-length works. Believes that *Dust Tracks on a Road* omits Hurston's connection to blacks but emphasizes Hurston's white friends, and says "Negro critics have tended to dismiss her" because of her racial attitude. Says *Jonah's Gourd Vine* is perhaps Hurston's best novel. A selective bibliography is included.

C42.   Davis, Thadious M. "Southern Standard-Bearers in the New Negro Renaissance." In *The History of Southern Literature.* Ed. Louis D. Rubin. Baton Rouge: Louisiana State University Press, 1985: 305-307. Says Hurston, unlike any other member of the Harlem Renaissance, was "irrepressibly Southern in her mannerism and speech." Section on Hurston briefly discusses her primary works, and notes that her main achievement was the use of language and voice.

C43.   Dearborn, Mary V. "Black Women Authors and the Harlem Renaissance." *Pocahonta's Daughters: Gender and Ethnicity in American Culture.* New York: Oxford University Press, 1986: 61-70. Hurston discussed in a chapter on "Black Women Authors and the Harlem Renaissance" because she is an "important force in black literature today." Dearborn ponders the question of Hurston's unique independence yet her dependence upon the support of others. The essay is bio-critical in nature and asks whether "mediation, authentication and authority, influence and patronage, and politics all fall away" when the reader confronts Hurston's important novel *Their Eyes Were Watching God.*

C44.   Deck, Alice A. "Zora Neale Hurston." In *Notable Black American Women.* Vol 1. Ed. Jessie Carney Smith. Detroit: Gale Research, 1992: 543-548. Hurston's photograph appears on the cover of this book, and Deck's article is accompanied by the same photograph. Hurston's life is summarized briefly and her major works are discussed and critiqued. A bibliography is appended, and a list of collections where Hurston papers are housed is provided.

C45. Dee, Ruby. Foreword to *Their Eyes Were Watching God*. Hurston, Zora Neale. Urbana: University of Illinois Press, 1991: v-xi. Says that Hurston was "theater, spectacle, controversy, harangue, promise," and *Their Eyes Were Watching God* is "romance, adventure, unforgettable people."

C46.   Dixon, Melvin. "Keep Me From Sinking Down: Zora Neale Hurston, Alice Walker, and Gayl Jones." In *Ride Out the Wilderness: Geography and Identity in Afro-American Literature*. Urbana: University of Illinois Press, 1987: 83-94. Believes Hurston's central subject is her depiction of life in her own hometown and that Hurston's positive portrayal of the South was the exception during the Harlem Renaissance. Feels she understands and uses the relationship between geography and identity in her work. Examines the "porch" theme in *Their Eyes Were Watching God* and follows Janie as she journeys to a "new baptism."

C47. Donaldson, Laura E. "Rereading Moses/Rewriting Exodus: The Post Colonial Imagination of Zora Neale Hurston." In *Decolonizing Feminism: Race, Gender & Empire-Building*. Ed. Sidonie Smith and Julia Watson. Minneapolis: University of Minnesota Press, 1992: 102-117. Thinks Hurston's fictional *Moses, Man of the Mountain* is a bold work which demands an intertextual reading of the Biblical Exodus story. Donaldson closely reads *Moses*; looks briefly at the "goddess movement," the pluralism of difference, "organic identity," nationalism, and the work of several scholars. Concludes that Hurston holds Moses together with "networks of difference which enmesh God with Goddess, Egypt with Hebrew" to produce a "radical pluralism."

C48.   Dorsey, Peter A. "The Varieties of Black Experience: Zora Neale Hurston's Dust Tracks on and Road and the Autobiography of Richard Wright." In *Sacred Estrangement: The Rhetoric of Conversion in Modern Autobiography*. University Park, PA: Pennsylvania State University Press, 1993: 166-189. An initial discussion of Hurston and Wright's attack on each other's portrayal of black life in the south is followed by an examination of both autobiographies where they use their early rejection of religion as a focal point. Discusses the "conversion discourse" used to write about self and focuses on the "deliberate subversion of the communal role in modern American autobiography."

C49. Dove, Rita. Foreword to *Jonah's Gourd Vine*. New York: Quality Paperback Books, 1990: vii-xv. Dove examines the character John Pearson and concludes what he learns on the ventures to find his fortune "form the trajectory of his life and the novel." Says Hurston's first novel is autobiographical but that she does not make the mistake of sticking too close to the true story--a mistake many first time novelists make.

C50. Doyle, Sister Mary Ellen. "The Heroines of Black Novels." In *Perspectives on Afro-American Women*. Ed. Willa D. Johnson. Washington, DC: ECCA Publications, 1975: 112-25. Says *Their Eyes Were Watching God* epitomizes the ideal relationship between a man and a woman.

C51. Draper, James P. ed. "Zora Neale Hurston." *Black Literature Criticism: Excerpts from Criticism of the Most Significant Works of Black Authors Over the Past 200 Years*. Detroit: Gale Research, 1992: 1068-1089. This article is the standard Gale entry which includes biographical information as well as excerpts from previously printed works about Hurston. Excerpts include works by Robert Bone, Cheryl A. Wall, Michelle Wallace, and Sherley Anne Williams. Also included is a photograph and an annotated list of further readings.

C52. duCille, Ann. *The Coupling Convention: Sex, Text, and Tradition in Black Women's Fiction*. New York: Oxford University Press, 1993: 80-84, 115-142. A section in chapter four includes the article "Hurstonism" and the Blues-Folk Moment;" *Seraph on the Suwanee* discussed is as a study in female psychology. In chapter six, "Stoning the Romance: Passion, Patriarchy, and the Modern Marriage Plot," duCille "explores the different aesthetic and political uses to which Hurston puts the coupling convention" in *Their Eyes Were Watching God*.

C53. DuPlessis, Rachel Blau. *Writing Beyond the Ending: Narrative Strategies of Twentieth-Century Women Writers*. Bloomington: Indiana University Press, 1985:157-58. Janie Crawford is discussed in a chapter entitled, "Beyond the Hard Visible Horizon," and the image of the horizon in *Their Eyes Were Watching God* is analyzed.

C54. Edwards, Lee R. "Makers of Art, Makers of Life: Creativity and Community in *Sula, Their Eyes Were Watching God*, and *The Dollmaker*." *Psyche as Hero: Female Heroism and Fictional Form*. Middletown, CT: Wesleyan University Press, 1984: 189-235. Hurston is included in a section called "The Road to Olympus: Women Heroes and Modern Texts."

Article compares the protagonists of three major works by African-American women and proclaims that Janie rebels against her community's rigid, prevailing norms and "reorganizes" her own world.

C55.   *The Florida Negro: A Federal Writers' Project Legacy*. Jackson: University Press of Mississippi, 1993. References to Hurston in many sections of the book as her involvement as editor and supervisor of the "Negro Unit" of the Florida WPA after 1938 is discussed. Hurston's pieces on Eatonville are published in this volume, and she conducted interviews, collected materials and wrote on a variety of topics and projects, including music and folklore. Also discusses weaknesses and problems in the final version of the Florida project.

C56.   Ford, Nick Aaron. *Contemporary Negro Novel: A Study in Race Relations*. Boston: Meador Publishing, 1936: 94-100. Recounts his detour from main highways to locate Hurston's home in Longwood, Florida and to see his second "live" Negro novelist. Relates a discussion with Hurston about Negro criticism of her book because she did not "make it a lecture on the race problem."   Believes Hurston's views posed "an unpleasant dilemma" for Negro novelists and was the reason *Jonah's Gourd Vine* was "received with small enthusiasm."

C57.   Fox-Genovese, Elizabeth. "My Statue, My Self: Autobiographical Writings of Afro-American Women."   In *Reading Black, Reading Feminist: A Critical Anthology*. Ed. Henry Louis Gates. New York: Meridian Book, 1990: 176-203, 63-89. Hurston is one of several writers of autobiography included in essay. Fox-Genovese examines *Dust Tracks on a Road* and concludes that the autobiography shows Hurston born as a woman of "wonderful reversals" who, as a writer, "refused the limitations of gender."   She feel, however, that Hurston's self-presentation was based upon "web upon web of deception" to augment her statue.

C58.   Fox-Genovese, Elizabeth. "To Write Myself: The Autobiographies of Afro-American Women."   In *Feminist Issues in Literary Scholarship*. Ed. Sharie Benstock. Bloomington: Indiana University Press, 1987. Hurston and her autobiography are discussed. Says her "obsession with self-concealment led her to veil the nature of her identification with her origins" and that Hurston's narrator is "the amused observer she wished to become."

C59.   Gabbins, Joanne V. "A Laying on of Hands: Black Women Writers Exploring the Roots of the Folk and Cultural Tradition." In *Wild Women in the Whirlwind: Afra-American Culture and the Contemporary Renaissance*. Eds. Joanne M. Braxton and Andree Nicola McLaughlin. New Brunswick: Rutgers University Press, 1990: 247-263. Says Hurston uses "language to push back the horizon," and that she "achieves a language and structure that evince her rooting in the Afro-American folk tradition." Discusses Hurston's use of folklore, including the "folksy vernacular" evident in *Their Eyes Were Watching God*.

C60. Gates, Henry Louis, Jr. "Color Me Zora: Alice Walker's (Re)writing of the Speakerly Text." In *Intertextuality and Contemporary American Fiction*. Baltimore: Johns Hopkins Press, 1989. Provides background information on the "double-voiced" narrative strategy employed in African American literary tradition; discusses Hurston's use of "free indirect discourse," and examines Walker's *The Color Purple* as a "revision" of *Their Eyes Were Watching God*. Says Walker was a master at conveying "the illusion of a (writing) narrative presence that records the actual words of a (speaking) subject."

C61. Gates, Henry Louis, Jr. "Zora Neale Hurston and the Speakerly Text." In *The Signifying Monkey: A Theory of Afro-American Literary Criticism*. New York: Oxford University Press, 1988: 170-216. Also In *Southern Literature and Literary Theory*. Athens: University of Georgia Press, 1990: 142-169. Calls "the Speakerly Text" Hurston's invention--her "rhetorical strategy." Gates traces the significance of blacks "assuming voices" back to the end of the Civil War, and uses Toomer's *Cane* as a primary example. Defines and refines the term "signifyin(g)," and cites numerous examples, including samples from H. Rap Brown and many from *Their Eyes Were Watching God*, to conclude that "signification is a complex rhetorical device." Says Hurston was a forerunner in the use of oral narration and influenced later writers such as Alice Walker and Ralph Ellison.

C62. Gates, Henry Louis, Jr. and Sieglinde Lemke, compilers. "Zora Neale Hurston: Establishing the Canon." Introduction to *The Complete Stories of Zora Neale Hurston*. New York: HarperCollins, 1995: ix-xxiii. Gates and Lemke introduce this volume of previously published and unpublished stories--part of an ongoing effort by Harper to bring Hurston back to the public and "establish Hurston's own canon of texts." Her stories are summarized and analyzed. Says most of her stories are "framed" tales-- a story within a story--and the speech is direct and alive. Says the published stories, printed in chronological order, allow readers to "examine the evolution of Hurston's skills at fiction-making."

C63. Gates, Henry Louis, Jr. "Zora Neale Hurston: 'A Negro Way of Saying.'" Afterword to *The Complete Stories of Zora Neale Hurston*. New York: HarperCollins, 1995: 285-294. Asks how a woman who was awarded two Guggenheim fellowships and who was a distinguished writer can disappear for three decades. Discusses Hurston's unprecedented rediscovery, her achievements with her writing, and the "legacy of fiction and lore" she left behind.

C64. Gates, Henry Louis, Jr. "A Tragedy of Negro Life." Introduction to *Mule Bone: A Comedy of Negro Life*. Eds. George Houston Bass and Henry Louis Gates, Jr. New York: HarperCollins, 1991: 5-24. Explains that the editors assembled and present archival and published materials in a kind of "casebook" so present day readers can follow the Hurston and Hughes debate about *Mule Bone*. Thinks one tragedy which grew out of the controversy is the "interruption of the impact it [publishing and producing *Mule Bone*] might have had on the shape and direction of Afro-American theatre."

C65. Gayle, Addison, Jr. "The Outsider." *The Way of the New World: The Black Novel in America*. Garden City, NJ: Anchor Press, 1975: 139-148. *Jonah's Gourd Vine* and *Their Eyes Were Watching God* are discussed; claims that publication of the latter marks the end of the Harlem Renaissance.

C66. Gilbert, Sandra M. and Susan Gubar. *No Man's Land: The Place of the Woman Writer in Twentieth Century*. New Haven: Yale University Press, 1988. "Sweat" is discussed in chapter entitled "Fighting for Life," and Janie Crawford briefly mentioned in the chapter "Sexual Linguistics."

C67. Gloster, Hugh Morris. "Negro Fiction of the Depression." In *Negro Voices in American Fiction*. Chapel Hill: University of North Carolina Press, 1948: 235- 237. Brief article in section on "Folk Realism" discusses *Jonah's Gourd Vine* and *Their Eyes Were Watching God* as studies in color. Notes that Hurston was more "interested in folklore and dialect than social criticism."

C68. Gordon, Deborah. "The Politics of Ethnographic Authority: Race and Writing in the Ethnography of Margaret Mead and Zora Neale Hurston." In *Modernist Anthropology: From Fieldwork to Text*. Ed. Marc Manganaro. Princeton: Princeton University Press, 1990: 146-162. Says *Tell My Horse* is part travelogue, part journalism, part political analysis, legend, and folklore in one. Examines why and how it violates ethnographic codes and discusses and the difficulty of "documenting a culture." Believes, however, that Hurston, like Mead, is a professional ethnographer, and that her work with *Tell My Horse* made her an etnographic authority for the period in which she wrote.

C69. Hapke, Laura. *Daughters of the Great Depression*. Athens: University of Georgia Press, 1995: Hurston's fiction discussed as part of a study that examines "the conflicts and tensions centering on the lives of women wage earners in the Depression."

C70. Hayes, Elizabeth T. "'Like Seeing You Buried': Persephone in *The Bluest Eye, Their Eyes Were Watching God*, and *The Color Purple*." In *Images of Persephone: Feminist Readings in Western Literature*. Ed. Elizabeth T. Hayes. Gainesville, FL: University Press of Florida, 1994. A comparative examination the relationship to Persephone found in the three novels. Treatment of women analyzed from a feminist perspective.

C71. Hemenway, Robert. "Are You a Flying Lark or a Setting Dove?" In *Afro-american Literature: The Reconstruction of Instruction*. Eds. Dexter Fisher and Robert B. Stepto. New York: Modern Language Association of America, 1979: 131-136. Discusses Afro-American literature as "powerful and distinctive," and not simply in its social or political content or context. Hurston used as an example of a trained folklorist who met two of Langston's Hughes' criteria for "determining the authenticity of folkloric representation" in literature. Discusses *Jonah's Gourd Vine* as one way to use folklore in literature. Wonderful notes appended.

C72. Hemenway, Robert, ed. Introduction to *Dust Tracks on a Road*. Urbana: University of Illinois Press, 1984. Call *Dust Tracks on a Road* "one of the most peculiar autobiographies in Afro-American literary history." Discusses omissions and discrepancies in the book and its "untrustworthiness." Ponders whether Hurston's tried to hide the "lost decade" since her actual year of birth is 1891. Hemenway also delves into other areas of Hurston's life--her biculturalism, her reluctance to offend possible future patrons, and her social and political views. He concludes that *Dust Tracks on a Road* "fails as autobiography" due to Hurston's "refusal to provide a second or third dimension to the flat surfaces of her adult image."

C73. Hemenway, Robert. "That Which the Soul Lives By." In *Mules and Men*. Bloomington: Indiana University Press, 1978. Hemenway wrote the introduction to this reprint of Hurston's collection of folklore. The article highlights Hurston's life and career, discusses her as a member of the Harlem Renaissance, and examines her use of dialect.

C74. Hemenway, Robert, ed. "Zora Neale Hurston." *The Black Novelist*. Columbus, OH: Charles E. Merrill Publishing, 1970: 55-61. This is a reprint of a previously published article that contends Hurston was interested in all things related to females, including their love lives.

C75. Hemenway, Robert. "Zora Neale Hurston and the Eatonville Anthology." In *The Harlem Renaissance Remembered*. Ed. Arna Bontemps. New York: Dodd, Mead, 1972. Says that Hurston's study and work with Franz Boas was significant to her inclusion of folklore in her writings. Discusses why Hurston is able to successfully incorporate her background and community yet absent herself from them in her work.

C76. Henderson, Mae Gwendolyn. "Speaking In Tongues." In *Changing Her Own Words: Essays on Criticism, Theory, and Writing by Black Women*. Ed. Cheryl A. Wall. New Brunswick: Rutgers University Press, 1989: 16-37. Wall notes in the introduction that the book's title is "derived from a recurrent figure in the prose of Zora Neale Hurston." Hurston is mentioned in several essays in this book, but especially in Henderson's essay where she defines "speaking in tongues" and uses Janie as one who used the "simultaneity of discourse" often found in the writings of black women writers.

C77. Henderson, Mae Gwendolyn. "Speaking In Tongues: Dialogues, Dialectics, and the Black Woman Writer's Literary Tradition." In *Aesthetics in Feminist Perspective*. Eds. Hilde S. Hein and Carolyn Korsmeyer. Bloomington: Indiana University Press, 1993:119-138. Says Janie in *Their Eyes Were Watching God* is an example of how both the "dialectics/dialogics of black and female subjectivity structure of black women's discourse."

C78. Hernandez, Graciela. "Multiple Subjectivities and Strategic Positionality: Zora Neale Hurston's Experimental Ethnographies." In *Women Writing Culture*. Ed. R. Behar and D.A. Gordon. Berkeley: University of California Press, 1995: 148-165. Discusses Hurston's significance to the mid-twentieth century and why she deserves a place in both contemporary literary history and anthropology. Believes in order to comprehend her life one must examine the environment in which she grew to adulthood and know the history of the periods in which she lived.

Hernandez closely examines *Mules and Men* which she feels is a "subjective narrative" but also a "methodological innovation" in ethnography. Concludes that Hurston's anthropological work in recording information on southern, rural communities made a significant and essential contribution to American history.

C79. Hite, Molly. "Romance, Marginality, and Matrilineage: *The Color Purple* and *Their Eyes Were Watching God*." In *Reading Black, Reading Feminist: A Critical Anthology*. Ed. Henry Louis Gates. New York: Meridian Book, 1990: 431-453. Authors suggests that "treating the marginal as central" in her novel allows Hurston to deal with "conventions that threaten to enslave [her] in a system of representation not of [her] own making.

C80. Holloway, Carla F. C. "Zora Neale Hurston. In *Oxford Companion to Women's Writing in the United States*. Eds. Cathy N. Davidson and Linda Wagner-Martin. New York: Oxford University Press, 1995: 408-410. This biographical entry also presents summaries of Hurston's primary works and provides critical comments about each.

C81. Holmes, Carolyn L. "Reassessing African American Literature Through an Afrocentric Paradigm: Zora Neale Hurston and James Baldwin." In *Language and Literature in the African American Imagination*. Ed. Carolyn Aisha Blackshire-Belay. Westport, CT: Greenwood, 1992: 37-51. Provides background information on the Black Arts and Black Power movements and discusses *Their Eyes Were Watching God* as a precursor of the critical Afrocentric approach. Believes Hurston's novel offers "myriad instructional avenues" for teaching African American youths, and that to fully appreciate Hurston and Baldwin, they must be "located" as individuals within the context of the broad African American experience.

C82. Holt, Elvin. "Zora Neale Hurston." In *Fifty Southern Writers After 1900: A Bio-Bibliographical Sourcebook*. Eds. Joseph M. Flora and Robert Bain. Westport, CT: Greenwood Press, 1987:259-269. Holt provides several pages of biographical information on Hurston's life and career, discusses the major themes of her works, and gives a "survey of criticism"--including Hurston critics Darwin Turner, Robert E. Hemenway, Ruthe T. Sheffey, and Daryl C. Dance. The section, "Studies of Zora Neale Hurston," includes periodical articles and books about Hurston.

C83. Holton, Sylvia Wallace.   *Down Home and Uptown: The Representation of Black Speech in American Fiction*.   Cranbury, NJ: Associated University Presses, 1984: 124-127. Hurston included in chapter on "Black English in Fiction, 1900-1945." Says that Hurston is at her best when she "shaped her folkloristic materials into fiction." Discusses black dialectal speech in *Their Eyes Were Watching God*, and examines techniques black writers use to present black speech.

C84. hooks, bell. "Saving Black Folk Culture: Zora Neale Hurston as Anthropologist and Writer."   *Yearning: Race, Gender and Cultural Politics*. Toronto: Between the Lines Press, 1990. Studies Hurston as subjective ethnographer and looks at her work at the " juncture of fiction and science." Believes Hurston deliberately resisted the call for scientific objectivity for cultural anthropologists.

C85.   Howard, Lillie P. "Zora Neale Hurston." In *Dictionary of Literary Biography: Afro-American Writers from the Harlem Renaissance to 1940*. Vol. 51. Ed. Trudier Harris. Detroit: Bruccoli Clark Layman, 1987: 133-145.   *DLB*'s usual excellent bio-critical review is written by Hurston scholar Lillie P. Howard and includes a photograph, awards and honors, bibliographical references, and a listing of Hurston's major works. Several periodical publications also included. Howard provides critical comments and notes that interest in Hurston had "diminished long before her death." She concludes, however, that the "Hurston renaissance is in full swing" today.

C86.   Hubbard, Dolan. "Recontextualizing the Sermon to Tell (Her)story: *Their Eyes Were Watching God*." *The Sermon and the African American Literary Imagination*. Columbia: University of Missouri Press, 1994: 47-63. Says the novel is divided into "three sections that correspond roughly to the modes of religious expression," and is a romantic love story that uses the church as a background. Believes the African American sermon is a folk narrative, and calls Janie's story sermon and testimony.

C87.   Huggins, Nathan.   *Harlem Renaissance*.   New York: Oxford University Press, 1971. Discusses Hurston's less than academic use of folklore, her relationship with Charlotte Osgood Mason, and gives some background on her relationship with other writers of the era.   Presents some negative views of Hurston and her work.

C88.   Hughes, Carl Milton. "Common Denominator: Man." In *The Negro Novelist, 1940-1950*. New York: The Citadel Press, 1953. Examines

Seraph on the Suwanee, provides several excerpts from reviews written at the time of its publication, and discusses Hurston's treatment of the character Arvay Henson.

C89.   Hughes, Carl Milton. *The Negro Novelist: A Discussion of the Writings of American Negro Novelists, 1940-1950*. New York: Citadel Press, 1970: 172-178, 238-240. Hurston called an author of "long standing and high attainment." *Their Eyes Were Watching God*--a "significant contribution" to American literature--is summarized and excerpts from critical reviews are included. Feels Hurston treats the character Arvay Henson from a psychological viewpoint. Article states that Hurston was a *graduate* of Columbia University.

C90.   Hughes, Langston. *The Big Sea*. New York: A. A. Knopf, 1940: 238-240. Hurston included in part three, "Black Renaissance" in a section entitled "Harlem Literati." Says Hurston was the "most amusing" of the "niggerati" of the 1920s. Provides brief information of Hurston's life in Harlem.

C91.   Ikonne, Chidi. "Affirmation of the Black Self: The Tom-Tom Cries and the Tom-Tom Laughs." In *From DuBois to Van Vechten: The Early Negro Literature, 1903-1926*. Westport, CT: Greenwood Press, 1981: 183-187. In the biographical commentary, Ikonne asserts that Hurston "was predisposed to identify more with whites than with blacks." (p. 183) The section also summarizes Hurston's short fiction, and indicates that she demonstrates "good knowledge of folkways" in "Color Struck."

C92.   Jackson, Blyden. Introduction to *Moses, Man of the Mountain*. Urbana: University of Illinois Press, 1984. Essay begins with the comment, "Zora Neale Hurston was an unusual women who lived an unusual life...that began in an unusual place." Traces Hurston's early movements says *Moses, Man of the Mountain* is her most ambitious work, especially for one needing a "demanding display of virtuosity." Says Hurston turned once more to folklore to tell an allegorical tale that relates the plight of the Biblical Moses to the plight that she witnessed in blacks at the time she wrote the book. Speculates as to the lesson meant to be learned from the work.

C93.   Johnson, Barbara. "Metaphor, Metonymy and Voice in *Their Eyes Were Watching God*." In *Textual Analysis: Some Readers Reading*. Ed. Mara Ann Caws. New York: Modern Language Association of America, 1986: 233-244. In *Black Literature and Literature Theory*. Ed. Henry

Louis Gates, Jr. New York: Methuen, 1984: 205-219. Also in *A World of Difference*. Baltimore: Johns Hopkins University Press, 1987. Article begins with background information on the "opposition between metaphor and metonymy." Examines the problems of rhetorical opposition as well as voice in *Their Eyes Were Watching*, and discusses Hurston use of this classical rhetorical device. Diagrams preface Johnson's discussion of Hurston's novel.

C94.   Johnson, Barbara. "Thresholds of Difference: Structures of Address in Zora Neale Hurston." In *"Race," Writing, and Difference*. Ed. Henry Louis Gates, Jr., Chicago: University of Chicago Press, 1986. Examines Hurston's rhetoric, especially in *Mules and Men,* and discusses "difference" as significant in a particular framework.

C95.   Jones, Gayl. "Dialect and Narrative: Zora Neale Hurston's *Their Eyes Were Watching God*." *Liberating Voices: Oral Tradition in African American Literature*. Cambridge: Harvard University Press, 1991 :125-139. Calls work a "transitional novel" in the dialect tradition. Provides background on pre-Hurston fiction writers' use of standard English for main characters, then examines dialect in Hurston's narrative and her technique of "framing" a story. Also looks at syntax and concludes that Hurston broke down barriers between narrative and dialect.

C96.   Jordan, Casper LeRoy, compl. *A Bibliographical Guide to African-American Women Writers*. Westport, CT: Greenwood Press, 1993: 133-140. Lists Hurston's articles, short stories, book-length works, and three pages of secondary sources which include journal articles and books written about Hurston.

C97.   Jordan, June. "Notes Toward a Black Balancing of Love and Hatred." In *Civil Wars*. Boston: Beacon Press, 1981: 84-89. (This article was first published in 1974 in *Black World*.) Believes Hurston's positive use of her experience in all black Eatonville is as valid as Richard Wrights's works of protest and confrontation. Says *Their Eyes Were Watching God* "affirms" and celebrates black life.

C98.   Kaplan, Carla. "'That Oldest Human Longing': The Erotics of Talk in *Their Eyes Were Watching God*." *The Erotics of Talk: Women's Writing and Feminist Paradigms*. New York: Oxford University Press, 1996: 99-122. Kaplan opens the chapter with this sentence: "Reduced to its basic narrative components, Zora Neale Hurston's *Their Eyes Were Watching God* is the story of a young woman in search of an orgasm." Kaplan breaks up the chapter with subheadings such as "Hungry Listening" to discuss the beginning of the novel or "Colored Women Sittin' on High" to deal with a reactionary Janie.

C99. Kaplan, Deborah. "Zora Neale Hurston." In *Critical Survey of Long Fiction*. Ed. Frank N. Magill. Englewood Cliffs, NJ: Salem Press, 1983. This long, comprehensive entry provides biographical information and critical commentary on Hurston's fiction--with emphasis on the use of folklore in *Jonah's Gourd Vine* and *Their Eyes Were Watching God*.

C100. Kennedy, Stetson. "Postscript: The Mark of Zora." In *Reading Black, Reading Feminist: A Critical Anthology*. Ed. Henry Louis Gates, Jr. New York: Meridian Book, 1990: 27-29. Kennedy was Florida state director of folklore for the Florida Writers' Project of the WPA, and his two page article discusses Hurston's involvement with the project. Said she was never supervisor of the "Negro Unit" nor editor of *The Florida Negro*; her title was "junior interviewer."

C101. King, Woodie J., ed. *New Plays for the Black Theatre*. Chicago: Third World Press, 1989: 137-152. A play entitled "Zora" by Laurence Holder, author of *When the Chickens Came Home to Roost*, debuted in 1981. Play begins with Hurston waiting for a bus and proclaiming, "I used to be somebody important in the big time." This drama provides a first person account of Hurston's life and the Harlem Renaissance.

C102. Kubitschek, Missy Dehn. "'Save de Text': History, Storytelling, and the Female Quest in *Their Eyes Were Watching God*." In *Claiming the Heritage: African-American Women Novelists and History*. Jackson: University Press of Mississippi, 1991: 52-68. Posits that sexism "influenced the novel's initial reviews" which were often negative or even damning. Says Hurston left a legacy to African-American female novelists who came after her, and many have met the challenge to use storytelling and oral narrative to create strong fictional heroines.

C103. Lewis, David Levering. "The Fall of the Manor." *When Harlem Was in Vogue*. New York: Alfred A. Knopf, 1981: 152-153, 260-261. Recounts the arguments between Hurston and Langston Hughes with regard to the authorship of *Mule Bone*. Notes that Hurston "eventually transferred her allegiance from Fannie Hurst to [Charlotte Osgood] Mason, the "Godmother/patron" of many Harlem Renaissance literati.

C104. Lionnet, Francois. "Autoethnography: The An-Archic Style of *Dust Tracks on a Road*." In *Reading Black, Reading Feminist: A Critical Anthology*. Ed. Henry Louis Gates, Jr. New York: Meridian Book, 1990: 382-414. And in Lionnet, Francoise. *Autobiographical Voices: Race, Gender, Self-Portraiture*. Ithica, N.Y.: Cornell University Press, 1989: 97-127. Also in *African American Autobiography: A Collection of Critical Essays*. Ed. William L. Andrews. Englewood Cliffs, N.J.: Prentice Hall, 1993. The essay studies female autobiography and examines bilingual or multilingual women of mixed races. Hurston is one of the African-American women discussed. Lionnet's article is written in two sections: "an-archy and community" and "history and memory." She examines Hurston's *Dust Tracks on a Road,* calling it a "powerful example of the braiding of cultural forms" that should be viewed as a self-portrait rather than as autobiography. Believes Hurston shows the reader who she is rather than simply recounting her life's story. Concludes the only events of Hurston's "private" life in her autobiography are those with "deep symbolic and cultural value."

C105. Lowe, John. "Hurston, Humor, and the Harlem Renaissance." In *The Harlem Renaissance Re-Examined*. Ed. Victor A. Kramer. New York: AMS Press, 1987: 283-313. This chapter on Hurston is presented in three parts. Part one is "Zora Comes to Harlem;" part two is "The Short Fiction, 1921-1933," and part three is "The Novels: 1934-1937." The last section discusses *Jonah's Gourd Vine* and *Their Eyes Were Watching God.* Believes that humor and laughter were significant in Hurston's life and her works.

C106. Lowe, John. "Zora Neale Hurston." In *American Playwrights, 1880-1945: A Research and Production Sourcebook*. Ed. William W. Demastes. Westport, CT: Greenwood Press, 1995: 206-213. Provides background information on Hurston, discusses her theatrical reception, and provides a summary and critical comments about each play. Says very little has been written on Hurston the dramatist and that her concentration on a "group culture" in her plays meant she sacrificed the strongly developed individual plots needed to succeed on the American stage.

C107. MacKethan, Lucinda H. "Prodigal Daughters: The Journeys of Ellen Glasgow, Zora Neale Hurston, and Eudora Welty." In *Daughters of Time: Creating Woman's Voice in Southern Story*. Athens: University of Georgia Press, 1990: 37-63. This book is one in the Mercer University Lamar Memorial Lecture series. Author looks at the three writers "living at home, leaving home and returning home." She says that Hurston returns home as a "new self."

C108. Magill, Frank N., ed. *Masterplots II: African American Literature Series*. Pasadena: Salem Press, 1994. Each essay on Hurston's novels provides a listing of principal characters, a summary of the novel and its themes and "meanings," "critical context," and a bibliography. Jeff Cupp wrote the notes on *Their Eyes Were Watching God*, vol. 3, 1418-1422. Cheri Louise Ross wrote the notes for *Moses, Man of the Mountain*, vol. 2, 823-828; Warren J. Carson wrote the essay for *Jonah's Gourd Vine*, vol. 2, 631-635, and Anita M. Vickers wrote the essay for *Seraph on the Suwanee*, vol. 3, 1257-1262. The notes for *Dust Tracks on a Road*--vol. 1, 390-393-- were written by Madelyn Jablon.

C109. McDowell, Deborah E. "New Directions for Black Feminist Criticism." *"The Changing Same": Black Women's Literature, Criticism, and Theory*. Bloomington: Indiana University Press, 1995. Hurston's *Their Eyes Were Watching God* and how female characters were portrayed during Hurston's era briefly discussed.

C110. McKay, Nellie Y. "Zora Neale Hurston." In *Encyclopedia of African-American Culture and History*. Eds. Jack Salzman, David Lionel Smith, and Cornel West. New York: Macmillan Library Reference, 1996: 1332-1334. McKay's three page article provides biographical information, summaries of Hurston's major works as well as critical comments. McKay also notes that Hurston received "mixed" review of her books during her own life time. Believes Hurston's "rediscovery" has led to critical acclaim as the "essential forerunner of black women writers who came after her."

C111. McKay, Nellie Y. "Race, Gender, and Cultural Context in Zora Neale Hurston's *Dust Tracts on a Road*." In *Life/Lines: Theorizing Women's Autobiography*. Eds. Bella Brodski and Celeste M. Schenck. Itacha, NY: Cornell University Press, 1988: 175-188. Discusses Hurston's autobiography as non-traditional in that it is the life story of an "individual" and not a "part of a group." Says Hurston "deliberately staged" *Dust Tracks on a Road* and she wrote "exactly what she wanted her readers to know."

C112. McKay, Nellie Y. "The Autobiographies of Zora Neale Hurston and Gwendolyn Brooks: Alternate Versions of the Black Female Self." In *Wild Women in the Whirlwind: Afra-American Culture and the Contemporary Renaissance*. Eds. Joanne M. Braxton and Andree Nicola

McLaughlin. New Brunswick: Rutgers University Press, 1990: 264-276. Claims Hurston "stepped outside the boundaries of conventional patterns of black autobiography." Discusses her silence and the fact that she often ignored the crucial events readers normally expect in autobiography. McKay says readers are "disappointed and even offended by her dispassionate presentations."

C113.   Meese, Elizabeth A.   "Orality and Textuality in Zora Neale Hurston's *Their Eyes Were Watching God.*" *Crossing the Double-Cross: The Practice of Feminist Criticism*. Chapel Hill: University of North Carolina Press, 1986: 41-53. Believes Hurston used language to empower Janie and that the novel is a "forceful resistance to black women's oppression in a sexist and racist society." Notes that Hurston transformed narrative from "temporality characteristic of oral tradition to the more enduring textuality required to outwit time's effect on memory," and thus influenced writers such as Alice Walker and other feminists.

C114.   Messent, Peter B.   "A Medley of Voices: Zora Neale Hurston's *Their Eyes Were Watching God.*" *New Readings of the American Novel: Narrative Theory and Its Application*. New York: St. Martin's Press, 1990: 243-287. Hurston's recognition of "different speech communities" and different voices as seen in *Their Eyes Were Watching God* is discussed.

C115.   Monroe, Barbara.   "Courtship, Comedy, and African American Expressive Culture in Zora Neale Hurston's Fiction." In *Look Who's Laughing: Gender and Comedy*. Ed. Gail Finney. Langhorne, PA: Gordon and Breach, 1994.   Looks at Hurston's fiction to examine the roles of comedy and humor in the courtship process.

C116.   Neal, Larry. Introduction to *Jonah's Gourd Vine*. Philadelphia: J.B. Lippincostt, 1971. Says one of the themes in this novel is the *real* romance found in the lives of rural black southerners. Believes however, that Hurston had not yet mastered the southern dialect when she wrote *Jonah's Gourd Vine*. Neal also discusses her treatment of attitudes toward spirituality.

C117.   North, Michael A. "'Characteristics of Negro Expression:' Zora Neale Hurston and the Negro Anthology." In *The Dialect of Modernism: Race, Language & Twentieth Century Literature*: New York: Oxford University Press, 1994: 175-195. Purports that "The *Negro* anthology is a very elaborate...act of modernist racial rebellion."   Concludes that the "Negro expression" used by James Weldon Johnson and defined by

Hurston "has exerted a profound influence, determining the course of literature written in English."

C118. Patterson, Tiffany R. "Zora Neale Hurston." In *Black Women in America: An Historical Encyclopedia*. Ed. Darlene Clark Hine. Brooklyn: Carlson, 1993: 598-603. This is a fairly comprehensive look at Hurston's life and work. Patterson examines each of her major works and calls *Dust Tracks on a Road* "a simulated story" of Hurston's life. She also discusses Hurston's views on the 1954 Supreme Court decision to desegregate public schools. The bibliography includes selected works by and about Hurston.

C119.   Perry, Margaret. "The Short Story." In *Silence to the Drums: A Survey of the Literature of the Harlem Renaissance*. Westport, CT: Greenwood Press, 1976: 110-111, 121-124. Notes that Hurston was "one of the better Harlem Renaissance writers of short fiction." Plot summaries are provided for "Drenched in Light," "Spunk," and "John Redding Goes tó Sea." Says "Sweat" is Hurston's strongest, most interesting, and intense story.

C120. Pettis, Joyce. "Zora Neale Hurston." In *American Women Writers: A Critical Reference Guide From Colonial Times to Present*. Vol. 2 Supplement. Ed. Lina Mainiero. New York: Continuum, 1980: 363-366. Each of Hurston's book-length works is summarized and discussed. Notes that Hurston was the only writer of the Harlem Renaissance who had a "southern background." Says the inclusion of "folk elements gives a uniquely southern flavor to character and setting."

C121.   Popkin, Michael, ed. *Modern Black Writers*. New York: Ungar, 1978: 242-247. This article reprints excerpts from previously published favorable and unfavorable reviews of Hurston's works. Included are excerpts from Nick Aaron Ford (1936), Sterling Brown (1937), Langston Hughes (1940), Fannie Hurst (1960), and Darwin Turner (1971), to name a few noted authors and critics who offer comments on both the works and life of Zora Neale Hurston.

C122. Pryse, Marjorie. "Zora Neale Hurston, Alice Walker, and the 'Ancient Power' of Black Women." In *Conjuring: Black Women, Fiction, and Literary Tradition*. Eds. Marjorie Pryse and Hortense J. Spillers. Bloomington: Indiana University Press, 1985: 1-24. This article discusses conjuring or "magical powers" as the legacies of black mothers to their daughters and examines how Alice Walker and Hurston use this "authority" to tell stories in their literary works.

C123. Puri, Usha. *Towards a New Womanhood: A Study of Black Women Writers*. Jaipur, India: Printwell Publishers, 1989: 32-68. This book looks at three authors whose fiction points to a new womanhood. The two chapters on Hurston examine her use of strong black female characters such as Janie and Lucy--a deviation from the traditional way such characters had been depicted. Feels that Hurston, Morrison and Petry portray negative family life, but that Hurston does portray "patriarchal family patterns in almost every novel."

C124. Quinby, Lee. *Anti-Apocalypse: Exercises in Genealogical Criticism*. Minneapolis: University of Minnesota Press, 1994: 97-112. Examines Hurston's use of "stereotypes as resistance" to "apocalyptic categories" such as sexuality, gender and race.

C125. Rampersand, Arnold. Foreword to *Mules and Men*. New York: Quality Paperbacks, 1990: xv-xviii. Discusses Hurston as a novice then a mature collector of southern folklore. Thinks there would have been no *Their Eyes Were Watching God* had Hurston not had the experience of collecting for and writing *Mules and Men*. Discusses her scholarships, growth and development, her comprehension of her roots, and her evolving as a "cultural nationalist."

C126. Raynaud, Claudine. "Autobiography as a 'Lying' Session: Zora Neale Hurston's *Dust Tracks on a Road*." In *Black Feminist Criticism and Critical Theory*. Eds. Joseph Weixlmann and Houston Baker, Jr. Greenwood, FL: Penkevill, 1988: 111-138. Essay examines how Hurston hides her "inner self" in *Dust Tracks on a Road*, an autobiography she did not want to pen and one in which she hides her own personal voice and fails to relate painful experiences--both personal and group. Concludes, "Everything in *Dust Tracks on a Road* points to the subversion of the autobiographical mode." Believes Hurston created "self in folklore" and that the book becomes mere commonplace generalizations that reveal little about the complex woman who was Zora Neale Hurston.

C127. Raynaud, Claudine. "'Rubbing a Paragraph With a Soft Cloth'? Muted Voices and Editorial Constraints in *Dust Tracts on a Road*." In *De/Colonizing the Subject: The Politics of Gender in Women's Autobiography*. Eds. Sidonie Smith and Julia Watson. Minneapolis: University of Minnesota Press, 1992: 34-64. Essay opens with an excerpt from *Dust Tracks on a Road* that was excised by editors from the published version of Hurston's autobiography. Discusses the history of the manuscript, which Lippincott asked Hurston to write; examines editorial intervention and alteration of language to present "polished acceptable" English. Also examines the alteration of Hurston 's erotic, "black woman," and political voices as well as omission of seemingly libelous materials and deletion of "extreme statements" that were considered politically incorrect. Questions why Hurston's "thank you" list was minimized. Concludes that omissions altered the structure and original chronology of the autobiography, and consequently "erases the psychological implications of Hurston's 'tangents.'" In other words, the excised portions go a long way in explaining Hurston's "ambivalence about race and self."

C128.   Reagon, Bernice Johnson.   In *Dictionary of American Negro Biography*. Eds. Rayford W. Logan and Michael R. Winston. New York: Norton, 1982: 340-341. Reagon provides a brief but comprehensive picture of Hurston, discussing several of her short stories as well as her book-length works.   Says Hurston was "mystical, impulsive, restless, and driven." Cites Darwin's Turner's *In a Minor Chord* and Arthur Davis's *From the Dark Tower* as sources of additional information.

C129.   Reed, Ishmael. "Zora Neale Hurston, Writer." *Airing Dirty Laundry*. Reading, MA: Addison-Wesley, 1993: 146-151. Reed has praise for Hurston's treatment of men--despite her being dubbed as a "radical feminist." Notes in the beginning of the essay, "It took the restless intellect of Zora Neale Hurston to make neo-African religion, and its gods, more than 'naught.'" He calls *Tell My Horse* a "major work of the voodoo bibliography" and feels Hurston wrote intelligently about a variety of subjects, including botany, sociology, geology and politics.

C130.   Reed, Ishmael. New foreword to *Tell My Horse*. New York: Harper Perennial, 1990: xi-xv.   Says the author of *Tell My Horse* is "skeptical, cynical, funny, ironic, brilliant, and innovative." Calls Hurston's account of Neo-African religion fascinating and believes her mix of techniques and genres is welcomed by post modernists.

C131.   Rosenblatt, Roger. *Black Fiction*. Cambridge: Harvard University Press, 1974: 84-90. An examination of *Their Eyes Were Watching God* is included in the chapter entitled "Eccentricities." Says Hurston breaks a pattern often found in characters in black fiction because Janie's journey and progress are toward personal emancipation.

C132.   Roses, Lorraine Elena and Ruth Elizabeth Randolph. "Zora Neale Hurston." In *The Harlem Renaissance and Beyond: Literary Biographies of 100 Black Women Writers, 1900-1945*. Boston: G.K. Hall, 1990: 181-

192. A photograph of a young Hurston is included, and the editors cite Hurston's birth year as 1891. A selected bibliography lists Hurston's primary works by genre, and each is discussed with critical comments. Notes that in her day, such critics as Sterling Brown, Alain Locke, and Richard Wright "missed the point" and criticized *Their Eyes Were Watching God* for its "absence of social content and a lack of militancy."

C133. Rubin, Louis D., Jr., ed. "The Southern Renascence, 1920-1950." *The History of Southern Literature*. Baton Rouge: Louisiana State University Press, 1985: 305-307. Writes of Hurston, "She alone of the writers who gathered in Harlem was irrepressible Southern in her mannerism and speech." Said she was "different in her audacious, down-home antics and her storytelling, or 'lying' as she called. it."

C134. Russell, Michele. "Black-Eyed Blues Connections: Teaching Black Women." In *But Some of Us are Brave*. Eds. Gloria T. Hull, Patricia Bell Scott, and Barbara Smith. Old Westbury: Feminist Press, 1982: 197-207. Chapter 18 discusses Hurston's ability to speak in tongues or to "specify" like Big Sweet.

C135. Russell, Sandi. "Jump at de Sun." *Render Me My Song: African-American Women Writers from Slavery to the Present*. New York: St. Martin's, 1990: 35-46. Chapter provides highlights of Hurston's life and writings. Discusses *Their Eyes Were Watching God* as a major literary undertaking.

C136. Schraufnagel, Noel. *From Apology to Protest: The Black American Novel*. Deland, FL: Everett/Edward, 1973: 16-17, 65-66. Hurston briefly discussed in relation to the novels that make use of "Negro folklore in settings conspicuous for the absence of whites." Hurston also included in the chapter, "The Revolt Against Wright" where the author claims that writers such as Attaway, Petry, West, and Hurston produced novels that were not in the "Wrightian protest vein." Examines *Seraph on the Suwanee* in light of this claim.

C137. Setterberg, Fred. "Zora Neale Hurston in the Land of 1,000 Dances." *The Roads Taken: Travels Through America's Literary Landscapes*. Athens: University of Georgia Press, 1993: 105-131. This whimsical and thoughtful essay is interspersed with discussions of Hurston's life and autobiographical stories and tidbits from the author's own life and musical upbringing. Book was the winner of the Associated Writing Programs Award for Creative Nonfiction.

C138. Sheffey, Ruthe T. "Behold the Dreamers: Katherine Dunham and Zora Neale Hurston Among the Maroons." *Trajectory: Fueling the Future and Preserving the African-American Past*. Baltimore: Morgan State University Press, 1989. Discusses the "life-long influences" of Jamaica on two young female anthropologists and their courage to not be boxed into scientific, objective observations. Says through her dance Dunham taught young blacks to love their bodies and Hurston through her craft taught survival; that both dreamers, despite "vilification and personal despair," sought to preserve a rich cultural heritage found in Jamaica.

C139. Shafer, Yvonne. *American Women Playwrights, 1900-1950*. New York: Peter Lang, 1995: 403-408. States that Hurston was a "flamboyant personality who achieved great fame, suffered disgrace, was forgotten." Highlights her life and summaries the plots of "The First One," "Color Struck," "Fast and Furious," and "Mule Bone." Says Hurston was never able to fully develop as a dramatist.

C140. Smith, Sidonie. "Diasporan Subjectivity and Identity Politics in Zora Neale Hurston's *Dust Tracks on a Road*." In *Subjectivity, Identity, and the Body: Women's Autobiographical Practices in the Twentieth Century*. Bloomington: Indiana University Press, 1993: 103-125. Essay cites the works of several Hurston scholars to conclude that the elusiveness in *Dust Tracks* is "purposeful, culturally specific, and subversive."

C141. Smith-Wright, Geraldine. "In Spite of the Klan Ghosts in the Fiction of Black Women Writers." In *Haunting the House of Fiction: Feminist Perspectives on Ghost Stories by American Women*. Eds. Lynette Carpenter and Wanda K. Kolmar. Knoxville: University of Tennessee Press, 1991: 142-165. Hurston included in this chapter with a brief discussion of *Mules and Men* and "Spunk."

C142. Southerland, Ellease. "The Influence of Voodoo on the Fiction of Zora Neale Hurston." In *Sturdy Black Bridge: Visions of Black Women in Literature*. Eds. Roseann P. Bell, Bettye J. Parker, and Beverly Guy-Sheftall. Garden City, NJ: Anchor Press, 1979: 172-183. Believes Hurston's years of personal study of voodoo naturally found expression in her writings. Discusses the voodoo influences found in her fiction. The recurrence of numbers, emphasis on colors, influence of trees and other voodoo representations as depicted Hurston are also examined. Says *Moses, Man of the Mountain* is written "completely within the form of the voodoo religion."

C143. Stadler, Quandra Prettyman. "Visibility and Difference: Black Women in History and Literature--Pieces of a Paper and Some Ruminations." In *The Future of Difference*. Eds. Hester Eisenstein and Alice Jardine. Boston: G.K. Hall, 1980: 239:246. Says *Their Eyes Were Watching God* is a novel about marrying and marriage, and uses Janie Crawford as an example of a feminist who means to live her own way.

C144. Stepto, Robert. *From Behind the Veil: A Study of Afro-American Narrative*. Urbana: University of Illinois Press, 1979: 164-166. Hurston's *Their Eyes Were Watching God* discussed in a chapter entitled, "Invisible Man." Disagrees with Hurston's use of a narrator to tell Janie's story rather than allowing Janie to use her own voice.

C145. Staub, Michael E. *Voices of Persuasion: Politics of Representation in 1930s America*. Cambridge, England: Cambridge University Press, 1994. Chapter provides a comprehensive discussion and analysis of *Mules and Men*. Says Hurston as ethnographer and folklorist who documented the speech and "folkways of Black Americans" was the exception in her day.

C146. Sunquist, Eric J. "The Drum With the Man Skin." *The Hammers of Creation; Folk Culture in Modern African-American Fiction*. Athens: University of Georgia Press, 1992: 49-91. Discusses Hurston's use of the "call and response" format as well as her use of songs and drumming in *Jonah's Gourd Vine* and *Their Eyes Were Watching God* and in her essays. Notes especially her 1934 essay, "Spirituals and Neo-Spirituals."

C147. Tate, Claudia. "To Vote and to Marry: Locating a Gendered and Historicized Model of Interpretation." In *Domestic Allegories of Political Desire: The Black Heroine's Text at the Turn of the Century*. New York: Oxford University Press, 1992: 70-96. This chapter examines *Their Eyes Were Watching God* as one of the "domestic novels of post-Reconstruction black women," a work which deals with racial and sexual desire.

C148. Traub, Valerie. "Rainbows of Darkness: Deconstructing Shakespeare in the Works of Gloria Naylor and Zora Neale Hurston." *Cross-Cultural Performances: Differences in Women's Re-Visions of Shakespeare*. Urbana: University of Illinois Press, 1993: 150-164. Examines intertextuality between Shakespeare, Naylor and Hurston and discusses how African American authors deal with "plots, conventions, and politics of Anglo-European cultural traditions." Briefly discusses how "Spunk" rewrites Gertrude's marriage to Hamlet's uncle.

C149. Turner, Darwin T. "Zora Neale Hurston: The Wandering Minstrel." In *In a Minor Chord: Three Afro-American Writers and Their Search for Identity*. Carbondale: Southern Illinois University Press, 1971:89-120. Chapter three entitled, "Zora Neale Hurston - The Wandering Minstrel," begins with two pages of biographical information. Turner theorizes that an understanding of Hurston the writer begins with a study of Hurston the wanderer. He examines her autobiography and discusses Hurston's tolerance for whites and is critical of her lack of involvement in the black struggle for racial justice. Hurston's novels are also discussed, and Turner concludes that she regarded folklore from the viewpoint of a "novelist" rather than a "scholar."

C150. Vottler, Thomas, ed. *Short Story Criticism, Excerpts from Criticism of the Works of Short Fiction Writers*. Vol. 4. Detroit: Gale Research, 1990: 132-161. Several photographs of Hurston throughout her career accompany this article. Excerpts from Gates, Hemenway, Willis, Boas and others discuss *Mules and Men*, and Lillie Howard discusses selected short fiction.

C151. Wainwright, Mary Katherine. "The Aesthetics of Community: The Insular Black Community as Theme and Focus in Hurston's *Their Eyes Were Watching God*." In *The Harlem Renaissance: Revaluations*. Eds. Amritjit Singh, William S. Shiver, and Stanley Brodwin. New York: Garland, 1989: 233-243. Essay is from a paper presented at 1985 Hofstra University conference on "Heritage: A Reappraisal of the Harlem Renaissance."

C152. Walker, Alice. "Looking for Zora." In *Chant of Saints: A Gathering of Afro-American Literature, Art, and Scholarship*. Eds. Michael S. Harper and Robert B. Stepto. Urbana: University of Illinois Press, 1979: 377-392. In *In Search of Our Mother's Gardens: Womanist Prose*. New York: Harcourt Brace Jovanovich, 1983: 93-116. Also in *Between Women: Biographers, Novelists, Critics, Teachers, and Artists Write About Their Work on Women*. Eds. Carol Ascher, Louise DeSalvo, and Sara Ruddick. Boston: Beacon, 1984: 431-447. These are reprints of an article written in 1975 in *Ms.* magazine which focuses on Hurston as a forgotten black artist and describes Walker's pilgrimage to Hurston's burial site to mark her grave with a stone.

C153. Walker, Alice. "Zora Neale Hurston: A Cautionary Tale and a Partisan View." In *In Search of Our Mother's Gardens: Womanist Prose*. New York: Harcourt Brace Jovanovich, 1983: 83-92. And Foreword to

Zora Neale Hurston, A Literary Biography. Robert Hemenway. Chicago: University of Illinois Press, 1977: xi-xxiii. This reprint of an article that originally appeared in *Ms.* magazine in 1975 focuses on Hurston the feminist and as a symbol of black women looking for a "voice" in a gender-conscious and racially biased world.

C154. Walker, Alice. "On Refusing to Be Humbled by Second Place in a Contest You Did Not Design: A Tradition by Now." In *I Love Myself When I Am Laughing... A Zora Neale Hurston Reader*. Old Westbury: Feminist Press, 1979: 1-5. This short essay, the *dedication* for the book, applauds Hurston for her devotion to and appreciation of her own culture. It asks if Hurston is the "messenger who brings the bad news, or is she the bad news herself?" Then answers that she should simply ve viewed as an artist rather than the "artist/politician most black writers are required to be."

C155. Wall, Cheryl A. "Zora Neale Hurston: Changing Her Own Words." In *American Novelists Revisited: Essays in Feminist Criticism*. Ed. Fritz Fleischmann, Boston, 1982: 371-393. Wall asserts that though Hurston was not the first Afro-American female to publish a novel, she was the "first to create language and imagery that reflected the reality of black women's lives." The articles examines Hurston's major works and provides critical commentary. Says Hurston's writing excels when she uses folklore and her racial heritage.

C156. Wall, Cheryl A. "Zora Neale Hurston." In *African-American Writers*. Eds. Valerie Smith, Lea Baechler, and A. Walton Litz. New York: Charles Scribner's Sons, 1991: 205-218. A long, comprehensive article provides biographical detail of Hurston and discusses at length her primary works and several of her short stories and articles. Discusses Hurston's political views and how they alienated her from her race. Lists selective works by and about Hurston at end of article.

C157. Washington, Mary Helen. Forward to *Their Eyes Were Watching God*. New York: Harper & Row, 1990: vii-xiv. This Hurston scholar says what she loves about this novel is "its investment in black folk traditions." She comments upon reactions of women who see Janie representing them, and notes that males were often harsh in their criticism of the novel. Washington also discusses the Hurston "renaissance."

C158. Washington, Mary Helen. "Zora Neale Hurston: A Woman Half in Shadow." Introduction to *I Love Myself When I Am Laughing... A Zora Neale Hurston Reader*. Old Westbury: Feminist Press, 1979: 7-25.

Provides biographical highlights of Hurston's life and career; discusses why her unusual personality often meant her work was not well received by critics, and delves into her relationship with Charlotte Osgood Mason, her patron. Also discusses gender bias evident toward black female artists in Hurston's time. Says Hurston was a prolific writer who, despite poverty, homelessness, and ill-health, continued to work until her death. Ends by stating, "We should be grateful for her survival."

C159. Washington, Mary Helen. "'I Love the Way Janie Crawford Left Her Husbands': Zora Neale Hurston's Emergent Female Hero." In *Invented Lives: Narratives of Black Women, 1986-1960*. Garden City, NY: Doubleday/Anchor, 1987. Looks at *Their Eyes Were Watching God* and Janie through the eyes of females relating to the community they inhabit. Discusses Hurston's the use of language to express growth and power.

C160. Watson, Carol McAlpine. "Race Consciousness and Self-Criticism, 1921-1945." In *Prologue: The Novels of Black American Women, 1891-1965*. Westport, CT: Greenwood Press, 1985: 3-5, 7-8, 139-40, 147-48. Watson's annotated bibliography includes critical abstracts for *Jonah's Vine Gourd* and *Their Eyes Were Watching God*. Examines Hurston's use of anthropology and discusses *Moses, Man of the Mountain* in detail .

C161. Werner, Craig. "Zora Neale Hurston." In *Modern American Women Writers*. Eds. Elaine Showalter, Lea Baechler, and A. Walton Litz. New York: Scribner, 1990: 221-233. This lengthy bio-critical article provides a comprehensive look at Hurston's life and works. Werner discusses the influences of blues, jazz, gospel, the black church, cultural anthropology, and folklore on Hurston's work and outlook on life. A selected bibliography includes Hurston's works--cited by genre, as well as secondary biographical and critical works related to Hurston.

C162. Whitlow, Roger. "1920-1940: The Harlem Renaissance and Its Influence." *Black American Literature: A Critical History*. Chicago: Nelson Hall, 1973: 103-106. Hurston included in the chapter, "1920-1940: The Harlem Renaissance and Its Influence" and briefly discussed in the "End of the Harlem Renaissance." Calls Hurston the "last major figure of the period."

C163. Wilentz, Gay. "Defeating the False God: Janie's Self-Determination in Zora Neale Hurston's *Their Eyes Were Watching God*." In *Faith of a (Woman) Writer*. Eds. Alice Kessler-Harris and William McBrien. Westport, CT: Greenwood Press, 1988: 285-291. An insightful treatment

of Janie whom she believes "pays the price for finding her humanity."
Wilentz further states, "But by negating a false system of values, she
becomes one of the few women characters in early Afro-American fiction
to emerge whole."

C164. Williams, Delores S. "Black Women's Literature and the Task of
Feminist Theory." In *Immaculate & Powerful: The Female in Sacred
Image and Social Reality*. Boston: Beacon, 1985: 88-110. Examines
"imaginative literature as a source for theology" and explaining the "nature
of women's experiences." "Lucy's Story" from *Jonah's Gourd Vine* is
discussed; says Hurston uses the language of African American folk culture
to tell the story. Also analyzes Hurston's use of ritual and conflicting
religious systems.

C165.   Williams, Sherley Anne.   Introduction to *Their Eyes Were
Watching God*. Zora Neale Hurston. Urbana: University of Illinois Press,
1978. Williams' bio-critical essay introduces a text illustrated by Jerry
Pickney. Believes Hurston's use of diction, metaphor and syntax of the
black rural South is almost unparalleled.   Bibliographical notes are
included.

C166. Willis, Susan. "Wandering: Zora Neale Hurston's Search for Self
and Method." *Specifying: Black Women Writing the American Experience*.
Madison: University of Wisconsin Press, 1987: 26-52. Discusses many of
the "tricks" found in Hurston's writing, the narratives in *Mules and Men*,
and provides a lengthy discussion of *Their Eyes Were Watching God*.
Discusses Hurston's use of the journey, "wandering," as a "quest for self."

C167. Wintz, Cary D. *Black Culture and the Harlem Renaissance*.
Houston: Rice University Press, 1988: 213-216. Discusses Hurston's life
and career, her relationship with her patron, and provides a summary and
analysis of *Their Eyes Were Watching God* which depicts poor, uneducated
southern blacks. Says Hurston did her best writing in the 1930s, and like
Larsen and Fauset, she looked at the "limits confronting contemporary
women."

C168. Young, James O. *Black Writers of the Thirties*. Baton Rouge:
Louisiana State University Press, 1973: 203-235. Hurston included in
chapter "Black Reality and Beyond" where her use of imagery to "specify"
in *Their Eyes Were Watching God* is analyzed. Summarizes the novel and
concludes that it was "one of the better novels produced by a black writer
during the 1930s." Lauds her use of Negro folk culture.

C169.   Ziadman, Laura M. "Zora Neale Hurston." In *Dictionary of Literary Biography: American Short Story Writers 1910-1945*. Vol. 86. Ed. Bobby Ellen Kimbel. Detroit: Bruccoli Clark Layman, 1989: 159-171. University of South Carolina professor Ziadman writes the article on Hurston for the period indicated in title. In addition to a photograph and bibliographical references, Hurston's primary works are listed by genre. A paragraph telling where major depositories of Hurston's manuscripts may be found is appended to the article. Hemenway's biography is noted as a "comprehensive appraisal" of her life and work. Notes that she "produced a substantial body of literature of intense human emotion."

C170.   "Zora Neale Hurston." In *Modern American Literature*. Eds. Dorothy Nyren Curley, Maurice Kramer, and Elaine Fialka Kramer. New York: Ungar, 1969: 199-202. This entry has excerpts from previously published works such as Langston Hughes' *The Big Sea* and Lillie P. Howard's book *Zora Neale Hurston*.

D

Periodical Literature about Zora Neale Hurston

"Old Maker, please take my guilt away and cast it into the sea of forgetfulness where it won't never rise to accuse me in this world, nor condemn me in the next."

"The Conscience of the Court"

<u>1997</u>

DO1. Pierpont, Claudia Roth. "A Society of One: Zora Neale Hurston, American Contrarian." *New Yorker* 73, 1 (February 17, 1997): 80-90. Pierpont provides background information on Hurston and the Harlem Renaissance, and notes the *industry* surrounding Hurston, including re-issue of all her works. Believes that despite the "canonization by the black- and women's- studies departments," Hurston's views are as "obstreperous today" as they were when she wrote. Summarizes and analyzes several Hurston works, including looking closely at Janie in *Their Eyes Were Watching God*; wonders why she does not find her "voice" earlier.

D01A. Bordelon, Pam.   "New Tracks on Dust Tracks: Toward a Reassessment of the Life of Zora Neale Hurston." *African American Review* 11 (Spring 1997): 5-21. Examines issues related to gender and race as they relate to the accuracy of Hurston's autobiography and looks at "pivotal events" in her life to examine her feelings about her father and other issues.

1996

DO2. Ambrose, D. Lena M. "Encouraging Black Writers." *Chronicle of Higher Education* 42 (June 14, 1996): A45-A46. Discusses the Zora Neale Hurston/Richard Wright Foundation which makes awards to black fiction writers.

D03. Anokye, Akua Duku. "Private Thoughts, Public Voices: Letters from Zora Neale Hurston." *Women: A Cultural Review* 7, 2 (Fall 1996): 150-159. Uses some excerpts from Hurston's letters to provide an intimate portrait of a complex woman who lived by her wits during a difficult time. Discusses Hurston's use of her own cultural roots and examines the many voices--folk, political, racial, and "trickster" --she uses to write.

D04. Collins, Derek. "The Myth and Ritual of Ezili Freda in Hurston's *Their Eyes Were Watching God*." *Western Folklore* 55, 2 (Spring 1996): 137-154. Author examines Janie Crawford in the novel to "demonstrate the complexities of Hurston's art." The similarities between Janie and the mythical Ezila are also discussed.

D05. Corkin, Stanley and Phyllis Frus. "An Ex-Centric Approach to American Culture Studies: The Interesting Case of Zora Neale Hurston as a Non-canonical Writer." *Prospects* 21 (1996): 193-228. Authors think Hurston is a writer who does not fit into the traditional literary canon of women or African American, or American write. They argue for an examination of her works using a multicultural focus because to categorize her is to see her as fitting into the canon most appealing for the argument being defended or studies. Use Hurston in their study because her works allow a discussion "about what we feel are focal terms in literary and cultural studies: race, culture, and national or group, rather than individual, identify."

D06. Dubek, Laura. "The Social Geography of Race in Hurston's *Seraph on the Suwanee*." *African American Review* 30 (Fall 1996): 341-351. Author provides some foundational information on poor white women and notes some of the "structural advantages" enjoyed by some middle class white women. Believes Hurston's last novel "examines white women's social positioning by showing how race and class privilege" shape their lives. Concludes that as long as white women such as Arvay interact only with their husbands, they will be remain victims to social forces "intent on maintaining white male supremacy."

D07. Harrison, Beth. "Zora Neale Hurston and Mary Austin: A Case Study in Ethnography, Literary Modernism, and Contemporary Ethnic Fiction." *MELUS* 21 (Summer 1996): 89-106. Discusses Hurston's knowledge of anthropology and use of folklore to write her fiction. Says Hurston's literature links modern regional literature and post-modern multicultural texts and that she understands the relationship among narrator, subject, and audience. Says both authors benefitted from their training in cultural relativism and both had an interest in the stories of neglected groups.

D08. Jones, Evora. "Ascent and Immersion: Narrative Expression in *Their Eyes Were Watching God*." *CLA Journal* 39 (March 1996): 369-379. Discusses Hurston's use of cyclic action in the novel which she feels is used to give meaning to Janie's experiences. Examines Janie's "ritualized journey"--her symbolic trip to herself.

D09. Kunishiro, Tadao. "'So Much of Life in Its Meshes!': Alice Walker's *The Color Purple* and Zora Neale Hurston's *Their Eyes Were Watching God*." *Marjorie Kinnan Rawlings Journal of Florida Literature* 7 (1996): 67-83. Compares the two novels and discusses the treatment of heterosexuality in each.

D10. Meisenhelder, Susan. "Conflict and Resistance in Zora Neale Hurston's *Mules and Men*." *Journal of American Folklore* 109 (Summer 1996): 267-288. Looks at *Mules and Men* and discusses the use of folklore by Hurston and other African American writers. Abstract states that Hurston "carefully arranged her folktakes...to reveal complex relationships between race and gender in Black life."

D11. Puckrein, Gary. "Eat Your Heart Out, Tina Brown!" *American Visions* 11, 6 (December/January, 1996): 4. Brief article explains how *American Vision* was selected to publish "Under the Bridge," the Hurston short story found in her old Zeta Phi Beta Sorority notebook by collector Wyatt Houston Day.

D12. Stein, M. "Remembering the Sacred Tree, Black Women, Nature and Voodoo in Hurston's *Tell My Horse* and *Their Eyes Were Watching*

God." Women's Studies, An Interdisciplinary Journal 25 (1996): 465-482.
Says *Tell My Horse* is a pioneering study of Afro-Caribbean society and
shows that Hurston understood the influence of colonialism upon black
women and their treatment as animals--as mules. Feels her study of
religious beliefs challenges the denigration of black females, and in *Their
Eyes Were Watching God,* Janie's pear tree is synonymous to a "voodoo-
informed vision" that allows an "alternate image of freedom and self-love."
Taken together, these two works "articulate Hurston's analysis of the
conjunction of colonial conceptions of race, sex, and nature."

D12A. Chinn, Nancy and Elizabeth E. Dunn. "'The Ring of Singing Metal
on Wood': Zora Neale Hurston's Artistry in 'The Gilded Six-Bits.'"
Mississippi Quarterly 49 (Fall 1996): 775-790. Believes Hurston uses
"history, folk culture, and subtle but complex characterizations to mix fact
and fiction in a story that generalizes from the particular." Article also
discusses what Hurston perceived as her role as an author, how she
reconciled her " rural Florida childhood with her liberal arts education,"
and how she used her training as an anthropologist to be a fiction writer,
folklorist, and historian.

1995

D13. Anokye, Akua Duku. "A Report on the Fifth Annual Zora Neale
Hurston Festival of the Arts and Humanities: An International
Celebration." *Sage: A Scholarly Journal on Black Women* 9 (Summer
1995): 92-94. Reports on the fifth conference and notes that one significant
session was a discussion of Hurston's influence on African American
feminist literature.

D14. Ashe, Bertram D. "'Why Don't He Like My Hair?': Constructing
African-American Standards of Beauty in Toni Morrison's *Song of
Solomon* and Zora Neale Hurston's *Their Eyes Were Watching God*."
African American Review 29 (Winter 1995): 579-592. Looks at black
female hairstyles in the two novels and the hair preferences of men and
women.

D15. Beito, David T. "Zora Neale Hurston: Alternative Afrocentrisms:
Three Paths Not Taken - Yet!" *American Enterprise* 6, 5 (September-
October 1995): 61-63. Thinks Hurston's writing can be categorized as

"individual feminism," and that her independence was framed by the environment and culture in which she grew up.

D16. Boyd, Lisa. "The Folk, the Blues, and the Problems of Mule Bone." *Langston Hughes Review* 13, 1 (Fall/Spring 1995): 33-44. Believes critics have looked in the wrong places for answers to the question of why Hughes and Hurston "fell out" over *Mule Bone: A Comedy of Negro Life*. Feels that a "complex critical" examination of the play will explain some of the debate about the dispute. Calls the play a "divided work" whose acts are not balanced or well integrated. Points out that the 1991 production was negatively reviewed and not well received, and one reason is its fragmentation.

D17. Cairney, Paul. "Writings About Zora Neale Hurston's *Their Eyes Were Watching God*." *Bulletin of Bibliography* 52 (June 1995): 121-132. Bibliographic essay includes numerous interpretations of Hurston's writings. Annotated bibliography by year follows for 1987-1993 with a listing of new editions of Hurston's primary works released during those years.

D18. Capetti, Carla. "Zora Neale Hurston: La mitologia e la storia." *Acoma: Revista Internationale di Studi Nordameraicani* 2, 4 (Spring 1995): 76-87. Analyzes *Their Eyes Were Watching God* and discusses the use and treatment of myth and history in the novel.

D19. Chinn, Nancy. "Like Love, 'A Moving Thing': Search for Self and God in *Their Eyes Were Watching God*." *South Atlantic Review* 60 (January 1995): 77-95. Believes God is represented throughout the novel and that Janie moves toward individualism and toward God because she learns to "accept and affirm."

D20. Curren, Erik D. "Should Their Eyes Have Been Watching God?: Hurston's Use of Religious Experience and Gothic Horror." *African American Review* 29 (Spring 1995): 17-25. Believes the title Hurston gives the novel provides a "clue to the complexity of her narrative." Examines the role of religion in *Their Eyes Were Watching God* and looks as Hurston's inclusion of horror in the last quarter of the novel. Feels she uses the gothic "to inoculate blacks America against the infection of white prejudices."

D21. Kaplan, Carla. "The Erotics of Talk: 'That Oldest Human Longing' in *Their Eyes Were God*." *American Literature* 67 (March 1995): 115-142. Discusses how the story is "framed" and argues that Janie did not need to search for a voice because she had one already. Believes Janie is seeking a *listener* to confirm the voice she already has. Says the bottom line is *Their Eyes Were Watching God* is about a woman looking for an orgasm.

D22. Lowe, John. "From Mule Bones to Funny Bones: The Plays of Zora Neale Hurston." *Southern Quarterly* 33, 2-3 (Winter 1995): 65-. Believes Hurston the dramatist has not been studied enough. The article summarizes her plays and lists her published and unpublished works. Also adds archival sources and performances about Hurston.

D23. Meisenhelder, Susan. "'Sisters Under the Skin': Race and Gender in Zora Neale Hurston's *Tell My Horse*." *Western Journal of Black Studies* 19 (Fall 1995): 181-188. Looks at Hurston's views on gender and race and concludes that her examination of black life in the Caribbean proves similarities with black life in the United States.

1994

D24. Brigham, Cathy. "The Talking Frame of Zora Neale Hurston's Talking Book: Storytelling as Dialectic in *Their Eyes Were Watching God*." *CLA Journal* 37 (June 1994): 402-419. Believes if readers focus on the narrative structure as a "multivocal storytelling dialectic" in the novel, the problems with narration and voice disappear. Explains the "talking frame"--a rhetorical strategy used by Hurston.

D25. Bush, Roland E. "Narrative Strategy and Purpose in Zora Neale Hurston's *Mules and Men*." *Zora Neale Hurston Forum* 8, 2 (Spring 1994): 14-23. Argues for a very specific narrative purpose and strategy in *Mules and Men,* and claims that in her role as subjective ethnographer, Hurston is both a direct participant and an investigative anthropologist. Concludes that the purpose of Hurston's narrative is to balance and reconcile narrative voice and linguistic style. Thinks Hurston's deviation from a standard, objective, ethnographic style is radical and innovative.

D26. Cobb-Moore, Geneva. "Zora Neale Hurston as Local Colorist." *Southern Literary Journal* 26 (Spring 1994): 25-34. Believes Hurston not only a regionalist, but a "local colorist"--a native "equipped to write successful local fiction," one intimate with the "mannerisms, mind-set, dialect, and mode of existence" of a distinctive group of people. Discusses how Hurston crafts the characters in *Their Eyes Were Watching God* and *Jonah's Gourd Vine*.

D27. Crosland, Andrew. "The Text of Zora Neale Hurston: A Caution Essay." *CLA Journal* 37 (June 1994): 420-424. Discusses some examples of missing or excised portions of Hurston texts, and cautions editors who publish her works to add explanatory notes so readers have a fuller understanding of and greater appreciation for a writer in whom so much interest has been shown in recent decades.

D28. Hattenhauer, Darryl. "The Death of Janie Crawford: Tragedy and the American Dream in *Their Eyes Were Watching God*." *MELUS* 19 (Spring 1994): 45-56. Looks at all the ironies and denials associated with Janie's actions in the novel. Feels she is a tragic heroine whose quest has been "more psychological than geographical."

D28A. Holmes, Gloria. "Zora Neale Hurston's Divided Vision: The Influence of Afro-Christianity and the Blues." *Zora Neale Hurston Forum* 8, 2 (Spring 1994): 26. Feels recent criticism of Hurston's work has not focused on the "complex and contradictory meanings that she associates with the concept of God." Essay is a non-theological study which uses cultural anthropology to examine Hurston's "literary treatment of the concept of God." Discusses Hurston's emphasis on self-reliance and self-determination as a way out of oppression rather than waiting for a liberating afterlife. Also studies the "blues conditions" of blacks as translated by Hurston to interpret the experiences of a community.

D29. Lee, Thonnia. "A Literary Sojourn." *Black Enterprise* 24 (February 1994): 213. Discusses the annual Zora Neale Hurston Festival for the Arts and Humanities held in Eatonville, Florida.

D30. Levecq, Christine. "'Mighty Strange Threads in Her Loom': Laughter and Subversive Heteroglossia in Zora Neale Hurston's *Moses, Man of the Mountain*." *Texas Studies in Literature and Language* 36 (Winter 1994): 436-461. Examines *Moses, Man of the* Mountain, Hurston's use of laughter and subtle, latent "poking fun" at oppressors--the "polyvocality" evident in many Hurston characters. Also examines her views on social class.

Believes the book establishes parallel historical and social contexts for the actions of characters.

D31. Levecq, Christine. "'You heard her, you ain't blind': Subversive Shifts in Zora Neale Hurston's Their Eyes Were Watching God. *Tulsa Studies in Women's Literature* 13, 1 (Spring 1994): 87-111. Looks at the novel as a exploration of the "sophistication and complexity of black female identity" in a society set on putting them in limiting roles. Levecq examines Hurston's use of paradoxes, subversive humor, and subtle shifts as she converts Janie's "romantic journey into a realistic quest."

D32. Morgan, Kathleen. "'An Ox Upon the Tongue': An Allusion to Aeschylus' Agamemnon in Zora Neale Hurston's *Their Eyes Were Watching God*." *Classical and Modern Literature, A Quarterly* 15, 1 (Fall 1994): 57-65. Analyzes the novel to discover and discuss Agamemnon as a source of inspiration for Hurston's novel.

D33. Orlow-Klein, Ingrid M. "'Witnessing the Ceremony' The Writing of Folklore and Hoodoo in Zora Neale Hurston's *Mules and Men*." *Bulletin of the Faculty of Commerce* 38, 2 (March 1994): 33951. Article discusses Hurston's treatment of Voodoo and her representation of folklore in *Mules and Men*.

D34. Peters, Pearlie M. "'I Got the Law in My Mouth': Black Women and Assertive Voice in Hurston's Fiction and Folklore." *CLA Journal* 37 (March 1994): 293-302. Looks at Hurston's novels and non-fiction/folklore to discuss the use of African American, southern oral tradition in her writings.

D35. Racine, Maria J. "Voice and Interiority in Zora Neale Hurston's *Their Eyes Were Watching God*." *African American Review* 28 (Summer 1994): 283-292. Discusses Janie's quest to find her voice; believes Janie's voice improves as the voices of her men improve. Defines *interiority* as "an author's relatively full and non-judgmental rendering of the internal consciousness of a character."

D36. Ramsey, William M. "The Compelling Ambivalence of Zora Neale Hurston's *Their Eyes Were Watching God*." *Southern Literary Journal* 27 (Fall 1994): 36-50. Though provocative and original, feels the novel is not a finished product; notes that Hurston herself said she wished she could write it again. Believes text is ambivalent, often self-contradictory, and literary critics tend to "gloss over, evade, or ingeniously explain away the novel's most troubling problems."

D37. Thompson, Gordon E. "Projecting Gender: Personification in the Works of Zora Neale Hurston. *American Literature* 66 (December 1994): 737-763. Discusses Hurston's use of "projection" to achieve voice in *Dust Tracks on a Road* and *Their Eyes Were Watching God*. Believes Hurston created "tales" and adopted the "role of teller-of-tall-tales" in order to impersonate or masquerade as male. Theorizes that Hurston's use of personification allowed her to enter a previously all-male domain--one where stories are told from a male point of view.

D38. Vickers, Anita M. "The Reaffirmation of African-American Dignity Through Oral Tradition in Hurston's *Their Eyes Were Watching God*." *CLA Journal* 37 (March 1994): 303-315. Believes to see the novel simply as a "love story" is to miss the "nested narrative structure," the wonderful use of nature and landscape, and the oral storytelling strategy Hurston uses to "frame" a work of fiction. Believes that in using the "motif of the oral tradition," Hurston has "chronicled and reaffirmed the dignity of all audiences."

D39. Vidal, Bernard. "Le Vernaculaire noir américan: Ses enjeux pour la traduction envisages à travers deux œuvres d'écrivaines noires, Zora Neale Hurston et Alice Walker." *TTR: Traduction, Terminologie, Rédaction: Études Sur le Texte et Ses Transformations* 7, 2 (1994): 165-207. Examines the French language translations of Hurston's *Their Eyes Were Watching God* and Walker's *The Color Purple* to analyze how the Black English dialect used in both novels stands up in translation.

D40. Williams, Donna M. "Our Love/Hate Relationship With Zora Neale Hurston." *Black Collegian.* 24 (January-February 1994): 86-89. Discusses the recent "revival" of interest in Hurston's literary career. Says folks either love Hurston or hate her, and that her life and works have been "dissected, psycho-analyzed, apologized for, rationalized, applauded and decried" and she would love every minute of it.

D41. Woodward, Helena. "Expressions of 'Black Humor': Laughter as Resistance in Alice Walker's *The Color Purple* and Zora Neale Hurston's *Moses, Man of the Mountain*." *Texas Studies in Literature and Language*

36 (Winter 1994): 431-435. The humor in Walker and Hurston is a subversive humor which permits opposition to abuse. In Walker, humor is a resisting force; Hurston uses it intertextually as a means of weaving African American cultural identity into the novel.

1993

D42. Adams, Tony Michelle. "The Mark of Zora." *Essence* 23 (January 1993): 101. Brief entry announces the annual Zora Neale Hurston Festival of the Arts and Humanities. The 1993 theme was "Zora Neale Hurston and Folk Culture: Their Influence on African American Theater."

D43. Bauer, Margaret D. "The Sterile New South: An Intertextual Reading of *Their Eyes Were Watching God* and *Absalom, Absalom!*" *CLA Journal* 36 (June 1993): 384-405. Examines the similarities between characters in the two novels written by southerners. Feels Joe Starks is a "sterile" character because of his lust for a "bourgeois" way of life. Feels that Hurston's novel fails to develop some critical themes.

D44. Cassidy, Thomas. "Janie's Rage: The Dog and the Storm in *Their Eyes Were Watching God.*" *CLA Journal* 36 (March 1993): 260-269. Discusses the symbolism evident in Hurston's use of the rabid dog and the storm.

D45. Davie, Sharon. "Free Mules, Talking Buzzards, and Cracked Plates: The Politics of Dislocation in *Their Eyes Were Watching God.*" *PMLA* 108 (May 1993): 446-459. Looks at the physical imagery in the novel, the free mule story, and the buzzard in the novel. Examines Hurston's inversion of hierarchy (dislocation), multiple conversations, and her failure to question the dualism inherent in a culture that perpetuated categorizations.

D46. Dolby-Stahl, Sandra. "Literary Objectives: Hurston's Use of Personal Narrative in *Mules and Men.*" *Western Folklore* 51 (January 1993): 51-63. Looks at this work as literature rather than as simple folklore. Says Hurston's use of a personal narrative format is effective and that book gives readers an intimate portrait of Hurston's values.

D47. Dutton, Wendy. "The Problem of Invisibility: Voodoo and Zora Neale Hurston." *Frontiers: A Journal of Women Studies* 13, 2 (1993): 131. Dutton provides some history of voodoo and discusses its impact on

Hurston's writing. Says Hurston's experimenting with voodoo and creating black women in conjure pioneered the tradition often seen in the works of black women writers who came after her.

D48. Hale, David G. "Hurston's 'Spunk' and *Hamlet*." *Studies in Short Fiction* 30 (Summer 1993): 397-398. This brief article in the "Notes" section explains that "Spunk," a story of "lust, killing, and supernatural revenge," is "something of a prequel to *Hamlet*." Explains the parallels between the two works and lists other elements of *Hamlet* that are recognizable in "Spunk."

D49. Hubbard, Dolan. "'...Ah said Ah'd save de text for you': Recontextualizing the Sermon to Tell (Her)story in Zora Neale Hurston's *Their Eyes Were Watching God*." *African American Review* 27 (March 1993): 167-178. Examines religious modes of expression in the novel. Feels that Janie telling her story is a kind of sermon and that she is liberated as a result of the telling.

D50. Hurd, Myles Raymond. "What Goes Around Comes Around: Characterization, Climax, and Closure in Hurston's 'Sweat.'" *Langston Hughes Review* 12, 2 (Fall 1993): 7-15. Says "Sweat," despite its flaws and that it is a product of Hurston's early literary career, holds readers' interests and "ultimately withstands close scrutiny." Analyzes the story and Hurston's use of New Testament allusions and other techniques.

D51. Patterson, Gordon. "Zora Neale Hurston as English Teacher." *Zora Neale Hurston Forum* 8, 2 (Spring 1993): 39-50. Relates the story of Hurston getting a job in 1958 as an English teacher at Lincoln Park Academy in Fort Pierce, Florida. Says she still had a "talent for generating controversy."

1992

D52. Boxwell, D. A. "'Sis Cat' as Ethnographer: Self-Presentation and Self-Inscription in Zora Neale Hurston's *Mules and Men*." *African American Review* 26 (Winter 1992): 605:617. Says Hurston's self-inscription--the "author image"--in *Mules and Men* is the reason for the lack of sympathy for her achievement as an ethnographer. Boxwell believes however, that as an anthropologist, Hurston resolved the conflict of "self-presentation" in this work and was far ahead of her time. Feels "writing social-scientific text was not an impersonal, value-free form of claiming authority."

D53. Carr, Pat and Lou Ann Crouther. "Pulling in the Horizon: Death, Sacrifice, and Rabies in Zora Neale Hurston's *Their Eyes Were Watching God*." *Marjorie Kinnan Rawlings Journal of Florida Literature* 4 (1992): 51-57. Carr feels *Their Eyes Were Watching God* is a tragedy and at the book's end, Janie does not live as a liberated woman, but as one dying of rabies. In Janie, Hurston not only develops a character who blossoms and matures but one who is destined for a tragic end.

D54. Dalgarno, Emily. "'Words Walking Without Masters': Ethnography and the Creative Process in *Their Eyes Were Watching God*." *American Literature* 64 (September 1992): 519-541. Carefully examines the novel as finally published with the manuscript copy to provides foundation for her argument that Hurston accepted that a final draft was a compromised draft. Looks at revisions and additions to original text that tend to show that Hurston's views about folk life are different from the narrator in the novel.

D55. Davies, Kathleen. "Zora Neale Hurston's Poetics of Embalmment: Articulating the Rage of Black Women and Narrative Self-Defense." *African American Review* 26 (March 1992): 147-160. Davies provides background information on the "doubleness" in *Dust Tracks on a Road* and a rationale for her use of the word *embalm* to describe Hurston's "strategy for signifyin' on oppressive black men." Looks at Hurston's "punishments" of men in *Their Eyes Were Watching God* and how the "double voice of one black woman provided a way for her to speak, to write...to survive."

D56. Dolby-Stahl, Sandra. "Literary Objectives: Hurston's Use of Personal Narrative in *Mules and Men*." *Western Folklore* 51, 1 (January 1992): 51-63. Included in a special issue on the personal narrative in literature, Dolby-Stahl's article looks at *Mules and Men* as an example of "self-reflexive, literary ethnography." Thinks Hurston's use of the personal narrative format to present her collection helps hide her manipulation of the folkloric material she collected. This has led to some confusion as to what genre the collection really belongs.

D57. Hattenhauer, Darryl. "Hurston's *Their Eyes Were Watching God*." *Explicator* 50 (February 1992): 111-112. Believes most critics fail to see that Janie's and Tea Cake's deaths are foretold, that Janie is guilty of murder, and that she does not live to become a liberated, independent woman because nothing in the novel suggests she goes to get antirabies shots.

D58. Hemenway, Robert. "Zora Neale Hurston et L'Ethnologie d' Eatonville (Florida)." *Cahiers de Litterature Orale* 31 (1992): 17-445. Provides a fairly comprehensive biography of Hurston's life, education, career, and her participation in the Harlem Renaissance. Summaries her major works and discusses her involvement with the magazines *Fire!* and *Opportunity*.

D59. Jackson, Tommie. "Authorial Ambivalence in Zora Neale Hurston's *Dust Track on a Road* and *Their Eyes Were Watching God*." *Zora Neale Hurston Forum* 7 (1992): 17-39. Examines these two works for an analysis of authorial ambivalence and Hurston's eschewal of popular rhetoric and causes. Says her irreverence, attitude, "ambivalence on the black female and on race relations set her work apart."

D60. Jones, Evora W. "The Pastoral and Picturesque in Zora Neale Hurston's 'The Gilded Six-Bits.'" *CLA Journal* 35, 1 (March 1992): 316-124. Investigates the four characteristics of the *pastoral* as found in the story, and discusses each in detail as a preface to her discussion of of the short story.

D61. Jordan, Rosan Augusta. "Not in Cold Space: Zora Neale Hurston and J. Frank Dobie as Holistic Folklorists." *Southern Folklore* 49 (1992):109-131. Both authors use a fiction or "semi-fiction" narrator/collector who reports folklore activities. Says Hurston backed away from a scholarly approach to actually going to "the folks" for her stories, but believes she was not above "fixing" a tale to suit her needs.

D62. Mackey, Nathaniel. "Other: From Noun to Verb." *Representations* 39 (Summer 1992): 51-70. Says Hurston was a pioneer practitioner of black linguistics; discusses her use of "verbal nouns."

D63. O'Connor, Mary. "Zora Neale Hurston and Talking Between Cultures." *Canadian Review of American Studies* (Special issue, part 1,1992): 141-162. Discusses Hurston's adaptation to particular settings in order to collect folklore, and her talent in finding a place in popular culture for her ethnography. Believes, in hindsight, that Hurston founded a "new literary tradition for African-American women writers" who "talked" and learned ways to integrate race and gender and southern culture into their works.

D64. Sanchez-Eppler, Benigno. "Telling Anthropology: Zora Neale Hurston and Gilberto Freye--Disciplined in Their Field, Home, Work." *American Literary History* 4 (1992): 464-480. Examines two students of anthropology and focuses on their "attempt to function as participant-observers back home." Also looks at the way both used what they collected in their home towns to make their narratives unique. Both were disciples of Franz Boas.

D65. Schamburger, Nancy. "Beyond *Jane Eyre*: The Maturity of Tea Cake and Janie in *Their Eyes Were Watching God*." *Zora Neale Hurston Forum* 6 (1992):1-8. Begins the article with the Freudian observation that love and work are the two "great spheres of human activity" and uses this observation to scrutinize characters in Hurston's "greatest novel." Says Joe Starks and Mrs. Turner are just two examples of "people who are failures at becoming human beings." Believes the union between Janie and Tea Cake is a simple, "almost seamless form of living together" that is a model for the ideal marriage.

D66. Setterberg, Fred. "Zora Neale Hurston in the Land of 1,000 Dances." *The Georgia Review* 46 (1992): 627. An interesting discussion of who Hurston is and her works is juxtaposed against a trip down "memory lane" for the author.

D67. Sheppard, David M. "Living By Comparisons: Janie and Her Discontents." *English Language Notes* 30 (December 1992): 63-75. Says *Their Eyes Were Watching God* is a dream and believes Freudian psychoanalytic ethnography yields a better interpretation and analysis of the novel than literary conventions.

D68. Turner, Darwin T. "Zora Neale Hurston: One More Time." *Langston Hughes Review* 11 (1992): 34-37. Turner breaks the silence about his analysis of Hurston in his earlier work, *In a Minor Chord*. Discusses his familial background and how it influenced his stance on Hurston. Does not apologize for nor modify his earlier conclusions.

D69. Woodson, Jon. "Zora Neale Hurston's *Their Eyes Were Watching God* and the Influence of Jens Peter Jacobsen's *Marie Grubbe*." *African American Review* 26 (Winter 1992):19-35. Explores the possibility that Jacobsen's 1876 work, *Marie Grubbe: A Lady of the Seventeenth Century*, influenced Hurston to write *Their Eyes Were Watching God*. Provides a summary of Jacobsen's historical novel and a comparative reading--cross matching characters, themes, and narrators--to show the "remarkable textual parallelism between the two novels."

1991

D70. Abbott, Dorothy. "Rediscovering Zora Neale Hurston's Work." *Frontiers: A Journal of Women's Studies* 12 (1991):174-191. Discusses her research on Hurston and reprints for the first time "Florida Migrant Farm Labor" as reconstructed from burnt papers. Photos by Ernie Tyner accompany Hurston's article. Also includes Hurston's essay "Folklore and Music."

D71. Beardslee, Karen E. "Self-Actualization in *Their Eyes Were Watching God* and *The Color Purple*." *Zora Neale Hurston Forum* 6 (1991): 56-73. This paper, presented to the American Women of Color Conference, examines the origin and meaning of "self-actualization." Says both novels are structured around the "fulfillment of Maslow's Basic Human Need Theory" and that Hurston and Walker actually rewrite his theory to "reflect and validate" their own portrayals of self-actualization and those of voiceless African American women everywhere.

D72. Berrian, Brenda F. "The Evolution of Janie From *Their Eyes Were Watching God* Into Three Characters from Marita Golden's *A Woman's Place*." *Zora Neale Hurston Forum* 6 (1991): 18-48. Says Hurston is a "literary foremother for writers like Marita Golden" and that one must not read her novel *A Woman's Place* without seeing Hurston's novel reflected in it. Believes Janie continues in Golden's character and that Hurston must be smiling about having her line continued.

D73. Bush, Ronald. "'Ethnographic Subjectivity' and Zora Neale Hurston's *Tell My Horse*." *Zora Neale Hurston Forum* 5 (1991): 11-17. Says Hurston anthropological work is a "radical departure" from that of other scientifically trained ethnographers of her time because she does not distance herself as a normal outside investigator. Believes that as an artist,

Hurston consciously chose to interweave fiction and other "modes of discourse" into *Tell My Horse*.   Concludes that she "rehumanized anthropological writing."

D74. Byrd, Rudolph P. "Shared Orientation and Narrative Acts in *Cane, Their Eyes Were Watching God*, and *Meridian*." *MELUS* 17 (Winter 1991/92): 41-56. Discusses the "literary line of descent" from Toomer and Hurston to Alice Walker. All three are southerners, and they all embrace and appreciate African American folk culture. Discusses the impact of Hurston and Toomer's work on Alice Walker's fiction, and uses *Meridian* to discuss the "shared orientation." Argues that although Walker said *Their Eyes Were Watching God* is on her top ten list, its direct impact upon Walker's fiction seems to be minimal. Spirituality is also examined.

D75. Daniel, Janice. "'De Understanding' to go 'Long Wid it' Realism and Romance in *Their Eyes Were Watching God*." *Southern Literary Journal* 24 (Fall 1991): 66-76. Says a close examination of the novel shows that "Janie's experiences closely parallel that of the traditional literary romance." Uses Northrop Frye's explanation of the romance quest to frame Hurston's presentation of Janie's journey "tuh de horizon." Also examines the psychological realism that Hurston weaves into the story, and concludes that she endows Janie with all the heroic qualities she needs to "survive with her identity intact."

D76. Dickerson, Vanessa D. "'It Takes Its Shape From de Shore it Meets': The Metamorphic God in Hurston's *Their Eyes Were Watching God*." *Lit: Literature, Interpretation, Theory* 2 (1991): 221-230. Examines Hurston's use of God in the novel. Concludes that Janie devises her own concept of god.

D77. Faulkner, Howard J. "*Mules and Men*: Fiction as Folklore." *CLA Journal* 34 (March 1991): 331-339. Believes collection is "valuable fiction" and that Hurston's narration and analysis go beyond anthropological presentation. Feels the work is not easy to categorize because its "theme is the nature of fiction" and there is "constant movement between the fictive tale...and the nonfiction commentary."

D78. Holloway, Carla F. C. "Holy Heat: Rituals of the Spirit in Zora Neale Hurston's *Their Eyes Were Watching God*." *Religion and Literature*

23 (Autumn 1991): 127-141. Essay is a concluding argument to a 1987 essay linking spirituality to narrative verse.

D79. Jablon, Madelyn. "The Zora Aesthetic." *Zora Neale Hurston Forum* 6 (1991): 1-15. Feels not much as been written about Hurston the literary theorist and studies her aesthetics to shed light on her as a researcher and storyteller and novelist who accurately represented reality. Believes her aesthetic differed from "black aesthetic because it did not aim to reform white folks by painting portraits of black folks who looked just like them."

D80. Kauffman, Bill. "Zora Neale Hurston and Clarence Thomas." *Lincoln Review* 10 (1991): 11-13. Says Clarence Thomas and Hurston share a common heritage--both were shaped by rural childhood experiences. Said Hurston, a conservative Republican who was stubborn, independent and not easily categorized, would have loved Thomas.

D81. Kharif, Wali Rashash. "Rediscovering Zora Neale Hurston." *Griot* 10 (Spring 1991): 20-22. Reviews *Jonah's Gourd Vine, Their Eyes Were Watching God*, and *Tell My Horse*. Says a knowledge of French and the ability read music are necessary for an appreciation of *Tell My Horse*.

D82. Rosenblatt, J. "Charred Manuscripts Tell Zora Neale Hurston's Poignant and Powerful Story." *Chronicle of Higher Education* 37, 38 (June 5, 1991): B4-B5. Accompanied by a photograph, this feature article profiles Hurston's life and career.

D83. Sheffey, Ruthe T. "Behold the Dreamers: Katherine Dunham and Zora Neale Hurston Among the Maroons." *Zora Neale Hurston Forum* 5 (1991): 20-29. Article originally published in Sheffey's book, *Trajectory: Fueling the Future and Preserving the African-American Past*. Discusses the "life-long influences" of Jamaica on two young female anthropologists and their courageous decision not be boxed into scientific, objective observations. Says, through her dance, Dunham taught young blacks to love their bodies and Hurston, through her craft, taught survival; that both dreamers, despite "vilification and personal despair," sought to preserve the rich cultural heritage they found in Jamaica.

D84. Thomas, Marion A. "Reflections on the Sanctified Church as Portrayed by Zora Neale Hurston." *Black American Literature Forum* 25 (Spring 1991): 35-41. Reviews Hurston's use of a sanctified church that is more African than Christian, and examines several Hurston essays, including "Conversion and Vision," "The Spirituals," "Shouting," and "Preaching." Lauds her celebration of a sanctified church, but feels inclusion of "high brow" church has strengths as well.

D85. Urgo, Joseph R. "'The Tune is the Unity of the Thing': Power and Vulnerability in Zora Neale Hurston's *Their Eyes Were Watching God*." *Southern Literary Journal* 23 (Spring 1991): 40-54. Believes the need to *explain* the novel "only emphasizes the assumption of textual weakness;" however, feels that any weakness is in the reading, not in the text itself. Discusses Hurston's achievements in the novel: how she took a "marginal or noncanonical cultural form" and successfully used it in written fiction, and her handling of the relationship between "folk and literate culture." Feels novel successfully sings Hurston's tune of "power and survival."

1990

D86. Anderson, Kamili. "Report from the Zora Neale Hurston Society Conference." *Zora Neale Hurston Forum* 5 (1990): 38-39. Brief article reports on the sixth national conference of the Society; the theme for the 1990 conference was "Breaking the Silence: Black Voices in the Diaspora: African-American, Caribbean, and African Literature." Paule Marshall made the keynote address, and Hurston's niece and executor of her estate also participated.

D87. Blickle, Peter. "Reading Zora Eyes: Vision and Perspective in Zora Neale Hurston's *Their Eyes Were Watching God*." *Zora Neale Hurston Forum* 5 (1990): 1-8. Looks closely as Hurston's use of visual imagery throughout the novel. Compares Hurston to a photographer who constantly makes decisions about "visual approaches." Discusses her visual metaphors; says she plays with numerous "levels of seeing." Lauds Hurston's "inner vision" because without Phoeby, readers would not see the story.

D88. Caputi, Jane. "'Specifying' Fannie Hurst: Langston Hughes's 'Limitations of Life,' Zora Neale Hurston's *Their Eyes Were Watching God*, and Toni Morrison's *The Bluest Eye* as 'Answers' to Hurst's *Imitation of Life*." *Black American Literature Forum* 24, 3 (Winter 1990): 696-716. Article traces the responses of three African American writers to Hurst's *Imitation of Life*, which was made into a motion picture. Hughes's response is a satire set in Harlem. Hurston praises the novel, though speculation is she responded to her dislike for Sterling Brown whose review bashed the novel. Caputi believes *Their Eyes Were Watching God* is a "subtle and complete retort" to Hurst's novel. Pecola Bredlove is an ugly black girl in *The Bluest Eye*, and Morrison is thumbing her nose at traditional standards of white beauty as depicted in Hurst's novel.

D89. duCille, Ann. "The Intricate Fabric of Feeling: Romance and Resistance in *Their Eyes Were Watching God.*" *Zora Neale Hurston Forum* 5 (Spring 1990): 1-16. The author examines the treatment of love and romance in the novel and also takes a look at the theme of resistance.

D90. Foreman, P. Gabrielle. "Looking Back from Zora, or Talking Out Both Sides My Mouth for Those Who Have Two Ears." *Black American Literature Forum* 24, 3 (Winter 1990): 649-666. Looks at the works of Harper, Fauset, Larsen and Hurston as being built on a female literary tradition that is often disputed in African American women's writings. Believes Hurston's representation of race, class and gender are built, in part, upon the work of predecessors, but that she rejected the middle and upper-middle class values often represented in works of other African-American women writers.

D91. Jacobson, Lynn. "The Mark of Zora: The Queen of the Harlem Renaissance Stages a Comeback." *American Theatre* 7 (July 1, 1990): 24-30. Article looks at four Hurston-related works that have played or will debut in near future. Discusses Laurence Holder's play *Zora Neale Hurston* as a "bare bones depiction" of Hurston's life. Also discusses George C. Wolfe's adaptation of "Spunk," Ellen Sebastian's *Sanctified Church*, and *Mule Bones* set to open at Lincoln Center.

D92. Johnson, Lonnell. "The Defiant Black Heroine: Ollie Miss & Janie May, Two Portraits from the '30s." *Zora Neale Hurston Forum* 4, 2 (Spring 1990): 41-46. Johnson looks at the heroines of two Harlem Renaissance authors--Hurston's Janie and George Wylie's Ollie Miss.

D93. Kim, Myung Ja. "Zora Neale Hurston's Search for Self: *Their Eyes Were Watching God.*" *Journal of English Language and Literature* 36 (Autumn 1990): 491-512. Written in Korean, the article has an English abstract and excerpts from Hurston's works are provided in English. Abstract states, "Hurston believed that Afro-American liberation and freedom were dependent on the black community's recognition of the folk heritage that sustains and binds it together." Concludes that her writing was a precursor to black women's fiction of the 1970s.

D94. King, Sigrid. "Naming and Power in Zora Neale Hurston's *Their Eyes Were Watching God*." *Black American Literature Forum* 24 (1990): 683-696. Discusses "naming as power" as a major element in novel. Believes Janie moves from being nameless to being in control.

D95. Kroll, Jack. "Marching to Her Own Tune." *Newsweek* 115 (May 7, 1990): 62. Brief theater review of George Wolfle's adaptation of "Spunk" which played at Public Theatre in New York City. Says Hurston is a "welcome presence on stage" and that she remains a "fountainhead of African-American writing."

D96. LeSeur, Geta. "Janie as Sisyphus: Existential Heroism in *Their Eyes Were Watching God*." *Zora Neale Hurston Forum* 4, 2 (Spring 1990): 33-40. Explains existentialism as used by Hurston in the novel and discusses Janie Crawford in light of the existential myth.

D97. Mason-Grant, Joan. "Zora Neale Hurston: Writing Culture." *Culture* 10 (1990): 49-60. Argues that Hurston's anthropological work is done strictly as a scientific, objective collector. Believes Hurston "writes culture" and constantly moves back and forth between fiction and non-fiction, between social classes, between urban and rural to present heterogeneous texts. Concludes that she is neither objective nor subjective; she plays "both sides of the field."

D98. Norman, Wilbert Reuben, Jr. "The Use of African-American Culture as a Foundation for Community Cohesion and Self-Esteem in *Their Eyes Were Watching God*." *Zora Neale Hurston Forum* 5 (1990): 30-36. Says the novel is a book about women's rights to "equality and personal development" and about the sense of community found in an all-black town. Believes Hurston embraced African American folklore--though she may have arrived too soon for many to understand what she was doing.

D99. Olaniyan, Tejumola. "God's Weeping Eyes: Hurston and the Anti-Patriarchal Form." *Obsidian II: Black Literature in Review* 5 (Summer 1990): 30-45. Feels the feminists' rejection of *Their Eyes Were Watching*

God is unfair and that a close reading of the novel reveals that it does have a definite message and theme.

D100. Oliver, Edith. "The Theatre: Hurston & Wolfe." *New Yorker* 66 (May 7, 1990); 83. Discusses George Wolfe's translation of several Hurston stories into unique theatrical sketches that use jazz and blues songs.

D101. Paquet, Sandra Pouchet. "The Ancestor as Foundation in *Their Eyes Were Watching God* and *Tar Baby*." *Callaloo* 13 (Summer 1990): 499-515. Discusses "cultural rootedness" and contrasts Janie with Jadine in *Tar Baby*. Says Janie has "cultural stability."

D102. Robey, Judith. "Generic Strategies in Zora Neale Hurston's *Dust Tracks on a Road*." *Black American Literature Forum* 24, 3 (Winter 1990): 667-682. Examines the way the "author-reader relationship" is constructed in Hurston's autobiography. Analyzes the work by a black female writing for a "largely white audience" and discusses each of the shifts in generic modes Hurston employs--"myths, the picaresque, and the essay."

D103. Sundahl, Daniel J. "Zora Neale Hurston: A Voice of Her Own/an Entertainment in Herself." *Southern Studies* 1 (1990): 243-256. Looks at several Hurston works to support his belief that Hurston was primarily interested in the portrayal of individual characters, not characters who could be "categorized." Discusses her use of realistic folk life, and her decision to write from a different "racial perspective."

D104. Thielke, Rosemary. "A Map of Zora's Florida." *Zora Neale Hurston Forum* 5 (1990); 43-47. The notes say Thiekle's map identifies places where Hurston's characters traveled. She said being able to see these places added to her enjoyment of Hurston's books.

D105. Wald, Priscilla. "Becoming 'Colored': The Self-Authorized Language of Difference in Zora Neale Hurston." *American Literary History* 2 (1990): 79-100. Purports that Hurston invented a strategy of "double-consciousness" which allowed her to speak her own language in opposition to a liberal American dogma that offered no freedom at all.

D106. Clark, W. Jean. "Zora Neale Hurston's *Their Eyes Were Watching God*: The Ephesian Love Mystery." *MAWA Review* 4 (December 1989): 51-54. Looks at Janie's marriages in view of the love found in Ephesians 5:22. Draws several parallels between the Biblical admonition about a wife's responsibility and Janie's first two marriages. Similarities to other Biblical scriptures in Janie's relationships are also noted.

D107. Flores, Toni. "Claiming and Making: Ethnicity, Gender, and the Common Sense in Leslie Marmon Silko's *Ceremony* and Zora Neale Hurston's *Their Eyes Were Watching God*." *Frontiers: A Journal of Women Studies* 10, 3 (1989): 52-58. Says "power-wielding and autonomy" are the main concerns of the novels. Believes women in both works are nurtured by the women in their culture.

D108. Hamilton, William H., Jr. "*Dust Tracks on a Road*: A View From the Audience." Paper presented at the annual meeting of the 40th Conference on College Composition and Communication. Seattle, Washington (March 1989). This 12-page ERIC document discusses *Dust Tracks on a Road* as "atypical" of black autobiography. Says it is a complex account of a black woman who did not require an "explicit reference to anything but her own work in order to articulate her sense of self."

D109. Hite, Molly. "Romance, Marginality, Matrilineage: Alice Walker's *The Color Purple* and Zora Neale Hurston's *Their Eyes Were Watching God*." *Novel: A Forum on Fiction* 22 (1989): 257-273. Believes that the complexity of treating the marginal as central and reversing the normal hierarchy are keys to understanding the novel's romance and system of values.

D110. hooks, bell. "Zora Neale Hurston: A Subversive Reading." *Matatu: Journal for African Culture and Society* 3 (1989): 5-23. Article looks at Hurston's development of the character Janie Crawford in *Their Eyes Were Watching God* and analyzes her use of imagination.

D111. Hudson-Weems, Clenora. "The Tripartite Plight of African-American Women as Reflected in the Novels of Hurston and Walker." *Journal of Black Studies* 20 (December 1989): 192-207. Analyzes two novels which depict women as victims because of their race, class and gender.

D112. Krasner, James. "The Life of Women: Zora Neale Hurston and Female Autobiography." *Black American Literature Forum* 23 (1989): 113-126. States that in *Dust Tracks on a Road* and *Their Eyes Were Watching God*, Hurston structures her "narratives in a distinctly black, and distinctly subversive, anti-narrative form." Discusses her visions and the symbolism in the novel. Feels that Hurston's autobiography is the telling of a "constructed past," and questions whether the novel is an example of female autobiography which is also "constructed."

D113. McKay, Nellie Y. "Black Women's Literary Scholarship: Reclaiming an Intellectual Tradition." *Sage: A Scholarly Journal on Black Women* 6 (Summer 1989): 89-91. Discusses a renewed interest/revival in Hurston and reissue of works by Zora Neale Hurston and other African American women writers. Thinks that by the 1970s Black women knew that gender, race and class bias of black men and white women would "continue to exclude the Black female experience from more than token representation withing the literary canon." The multi dimensionality of African American women writings helped them find an audience larger than that of Black men who focused primarily on race. And the women who wrote about them helped establish a tradition worthy of continuing. Thinks there are too few African Americans going into academe, especially in the humanities, to help carry on that tradition.

D114. Plant, Deborah G. "Narrative Strategies in Zora Neale Hurston's *Dust Tracks on a Road.*" *Sage: A Scholarly Journal on Black Women* 6 (Summer 1989): 18-23. Believes that Hurston wrote her autobiography for two audiences--the overt, surface discourse aimed at white readers and the subtle, suggested discourse for black readers.

D115. Roemer, Julie. "Celebrating the Black Female Self: Zora Neale Hurston's American Classic (Reclaiming the Canon)." *English Journal* 78 (November 1989): 70-72. Discusses the "importance of reading female," and includes excerpts from her students papers in a class at Alameda High School. Feels that *Their Eyes Were Watching God* is suitable reading for a high school class.

D116. St. Clair, Janet. "The Courageous Undertow of Zora Neale Hurston's *Seraph on the Suwanee.*" *Modern Language Quarterly* 50 (1889): 38-57. Looks at the "substory" of resistance and self-discovery in this novel which is often ignored and dismissed by critics. Encourages a close reading of the novel in order to see the "undertow" not readily evident.

D117. Story, Ralph D. "Gender and Ambition: Zora Neale Hurston in the Harlem Renaissance." *Black Scholar* 20 (Sum-Fall 1989): 25-31. Examines several views of Hurston the scholar and discusses her personality during Harlem Renaissance. Investigates her relationship with Hughes, Wright and others who scorned her work and ridiculed her personality.

D118. Wall, Cheryl A. "*Mules and Men* and Women: Zora Neale Hurston's Strategies of Narration and Visions of Female Empowerment." *Black American Literature Forum* 23 (Winter 1989): 661-680. Believes *Mules and Men* to be an "underdiscussed classic in Afro-American anthropology." Discusses ways Hurston represents gender roles, women on the "porch," hoodoo, and the formal devices she uses to unify her narrative. Feels Hurston "presents" rather than analyzes, and that women are empowered in her works.

<u>1988</u>

D119. Benesch, Klaus. "Oral Narrative and Literary Text: Afro-American Folklore in *Their Eyes Were Watching God.*" *Callaloo* 11, 3 (Summer 1988): 627-635. Discusses use of black English, black representation, and communication (or lack of communication) in the novel. Sees Janie's journey as a search of "blackness."

D120. Bush, Trudy Bloser. "Transforming Vision: Alice Walker and Zora Neale Hurston. *Christian Century* 105 (1988): 1035-1039. Believes that despite the forty-five years that separate the two novels, they still have common concerns and methods. Both use folk language, and both use the "experience of uneducated rural southern women." Compares and contrasts the two main characters--Janie and Celie and notes that *The Color Purple* takes up the "project of self-definition" where it ends in *Their Eyes Were Watching God.*

D121. Jordan, Jennifer. "Feminist Fantasies - Hurston's *Their Eyes Were Watching God*." *Tulsa Studies in Women's Literature* 7 (Spring 1988): 105-117. Believes that the novel fails to meet several established criteria for black feminist criticism. Though critics may view Janie as moving toward self-empowerment, feels her character is not aware of her own journey.

D122. Kalb, John D. "The Anthropological Narrator in Hurston's *Their Eyes Were Watching God*." *Studies in American Fiction* 16 (Autumn 1988): 169-180. Feels that Janie's character is anthropologically correct in that she moves away from her community in order to successfully observe the action and that her "reporting" is not a negative in the novel but a technique used to tell her story. A close examination of narration is provided.

D123. Plant, Deborah G. "Narrative Strategies in Zora Neale Hurston's *Dust Tracks on a Road*." *Sage: A Scholarly Journal on Black Women* 6 (Summer 1988): 18-23. Believes Hurston excelled at "masking as a subversive strategy." Unlike critics who object to her failure to deal with racism, Plant examines the narratives strategies that allow Hurston to "accommodate" sponsors and still show her admiration for her own race. Discusses her narrator who often "wittingly toys with white narratee(s)" and admonishes readers to dig deeper in order to get a fuller understanding of this complicated woman.

D124. Ryan, Bonnie C. "Zora Neale Hurston - A Checklist of Secondary Sources." *Bulletin of Bibliography* 45 (1988); 122-139. A fairly comprehensive bibliography of articles written about *Their Eyes Were Watching God* between 1987 and 1993. Also lists editions of the novel released between these dates.

D125. Saunders, James Robert. "Womanism as the Key to Understanding Zora Neale Hurston's *Their Eyes Were Watching God* and Alice Walker's *The Color Purple*." *Hollins Critic* 4 (October 1988): 1-11. Examines the woman's "place" and role in the two novels and looks at sexism against the deliberately "willful" females who journeyed toward autonomy in a male-dominated culture. Provides a few definitions of "womanism," one of which is a woman's right to choose her own direction in life.

D126. Speisman, Barbara. "A Tea With Zora and Marjorie." *Rawlings Journal* (1988): 67-100. This is a series of vignettes based on the unique friendship of Zora Neale Hurston and Marjorie Kinnan Rawlings. Act one is set in August 1942 in Rawlings' Florida apartment and on Hurston's houseboat. Act two is set on the front porch at Cross Creek. Includes scene where Hurston talks about her time in jail.

D127. Thornton, Jerome E. "'Goin on de Muck': The Paradoxical Journal of the Black American Hero." *CLA Journal* 31 (March 1988): 261-280. *Their Eyes Were Watching God* is one of three novels examined in this article. Discusses the paradox of ascension and descension often associated with the "black hero." Also looks at the "quest pattern" in *Their Eyes Were Watching God* to discuss the "Muck" in other black novels.

D128. Wallace, Michelle. "Who Dat Say Who Dat When I Say Who Dat? Zora Neale Hurston Then and Now." *Village Voice Literary Supplement* (April 1988): 18-21. Wallace discusses recent criticism of Hurston's works, and looks carefully at writings by authors such as Mary Helen Washington, Barbara Christian, Henry Louis Gates, Jr. and Houston Baker.

1987

D129. Carr, Glynis. "Storytelling as Bildung in Zora Neale Hurston's *Their Eyes Were Watching God*." *CLA Journal* 31 (1987): 189-100. Provides a careful examination of Janie's voice and her mastery of language as she tells her story. Believes this mastery is crucial to defining who she is.

D130. Carroll, Suzanne. "Journey for Our Times: *Their Eyes Were Watching God*." *Currents: Issues in Education and Human Development*. 5, 2 (1987): 31-35 [ERIC Document ED 297 611]. Article is part of a special issue on "Integrating Materials About Women into the Curriculum." Says *Their Eyes Were Watching God* was chosen because its "characterizations, drama, humor, and imagery" mean it can be read on many levels.

D131. Davis, Jane. "*The Color Purple*: A Spiritual Descendant of Hurston's *Their Eyes Were Watching God*." *Griot* 6 (Summer 1987): 79-96. Notes major points of comparison between the two works--others making decisions for the main characters, using black dialect, and portraying women as possessions are just a few similarities.   Says it is clear that Walker is Hurston's spiritual descendant.

D132. Ferguson, Sally Ann. "Folkloric Men and Female Growth in *Their Eyes Were Watching God*." *Black American Literature Forum*. 21 Spring-Summer (1987): 185-197. Examines each of the men in Janie's life and how Janie grows as she moves from the first to the last. Also looks at Hurston's use of folklore to characterize the three men Janie married.

D133. Jones, Gayl. "Breaking Out of the Conventions of Dialect: Dunbar and Hurston." *Presence Africaine: Revue Culturelle du Mode Noir (Cultural Review of the Negro World)* 144 (1987): 32-46. Looks at minstrelsy and early literary dialects and uses Hurston and Dunbar to discuss the problems inherent in incorporating dialect and folklore in literature. "Gilded Six-Bits" puts reader inside community, not outside as dialect does in Dunbar.

D134. Kitch, Sally L. "Gender and Language: Dialect, Silence, and the Disruption of Discourse." *Women's Studies: An Interdisciplinary Journal* 14 (1987): 66-78. Believes Hurston uses *Their Eyes Were Watching God* to explore Lacon's psychosexual theory of female-inspired acquisition of language. Also discusses the novel's use of dialect, "phallic mothers," and the disruption and repression of discourse.

D135. Smith-Wright, Geraldine. "Revision as Collaboration: Zora Neale Hurston's *Their Eyes Were Watching God* as Source for Alice Walker's *The Color Purple*." *SAGE* 4, 2 (1987): 20-025. Sees "revision" as empathetic rather than competitive as theorized by Harold Bloom, and thinks black women writers need an "affirming audience" made up of their own peers. Says Walker spent a good deal of her professional career celebrating Hurston's gift to America, but that *The Color Purple* does not "correct" Hurston's novel. It does, however, correct years of silence and provide a forum for early "sister-writers" to be understood, to validate their efforts.

1986

D136. Byrd, James W. "Black Collectors of Black Folklore: An Update of Zora Neale Hurston and J. Mason Brewer." *Louisiana Folklore Miscellany* 6 (1986-87): 1-7. Looks at some approaches to collecting, notably that of Richard Dorson, and points out the differences between his technique and Hurston's and Brewer's. Critical of Dorson's collecting.

D137. Fannin, Alice. "A Sense of Wonder: The Pattern for Psychic Survival in *Their Eyes Were Watching God.*" *Zora Neale Hurston Forum* 1 (Fall 1986): 1-11. Discusses the trials Janie and Celie face on their journeys to achieving self-worth. Explores the love they both experience on the way and why both can finally survive alone.

D138. Jones, Kirkland C. "Folk Humor as Comic Relief in Hurston's *Jonah's Gourd Vine.*" *Zora Neale Hurston Forum* 1 (Fall 1986): 26-31. Discusses Hurston's use of humor in the novel and the use of Negro dialect and dialogue to embue the novel with wonderful humor. Feels the novel is successful due to the use of the Negro idiom and humor.

D139. Lupton, Mary Jane. "Black Women and Survival in *Comedy: American Style* and *Their Eyes Were Watching God.*" *Zora Neale Hurston Forum* 1 (Fall 1986): 38-44. Examines the notion of survival in the writings of Hurston and Fauset. Discusses the main reasons women survive.

D140. Newsom, Adele S. "The Fiery Chariot." *Zora Neale Hurston Forum*, 1, 1 (Fall 1986): 32-37. Writing in the first issue of this new journal, Newsom summarizes Hurston's plays which she feels are a "celebration of black folk art."

D141. Podrom, Cyrena N. "The Role of Myth in Hurston's *Their Eyes Were Watching God.*" *American Literature* 58 (May 1986) 181-202. Believes Hurston uses Egyptian and Babylonian myths as a means of "ordering, or giving a shape and a significance" to contemporary history. Feels a consideration of Hurston's novel in view of her use of myths yields an understanding of her views on race and spirituality.

D142. Reich, Alice. "Phoeby's Hungry Listening in Hurston's *Their Eyes Were Watching God.*" *Women's Studies: An Interdisciplinary Journal* 13 (1986): 163-169. Says the novel is the story of a woman's journey to find herself and her voice by refusing to accept limits as servant, wife or lover. Thinks the novel is "rich with imagery and black oral tradition," and feels Janie finds her voice as she relates her story to Phoeby.

D143. Wilentz, Gay. "White Patron and Black Artist: The Correspondence of Fannie Hurst and Zora Neale Hurston." *Library Chronicle of the University of Texas* 35 (1986): 20-43. Interesting investigation of the correspondence between the two writers.

1985

D144. Crabtree, Claire. "The Confluence of Folklore, Feminism and Black Self-Determination in Hurston's *Their Eyes Were Watching God*." *Southern Literary Journal* 71 (Spring 1985): 54-66. Looks at Hurston's intricate use of folklore and how she weaves it into the novel. Discusses Janie's journey toward self-determination.

D145. Johnson, Barbara. "Thresholds of Difference: Structure of Address in Zora Neale Hurston." *Critical Inquiry* 12 (Autumn 1985): 278-289. Looks at two Hurston essays--"How It Feels To Be Colored Me" and "What White Publishers Won't Print"--and *Mules and Men* to try to explain the difficulty of "double speak" that Hurston faced in addressing diverse audiences/readers.

D146. MacKetchan, Lucinda H. "Mother Wit: Humor in Afro-American Women's Autobiography." *Studies in American Humor* 4 (1985): 51-61. Examines three works for the "humor of mother wit" found in African American female autobiographical accounts. Believes humor has been "deviously employed since slavery by people denied access to all forms of power." Examines *Dust Tracks on a Road*.

D147. Marks, Donald R. "Sex, Violence, and Organic Consciousness in Zora Neale Hurston's *Their Eyes Were Watching God*." *Black American Literature Forum* 19 (Winter 1985): 152-157. Looks at Hurston's presentation of Janie's lovers and contends that Hurston chooses romance for Janie with Tea Cake instead of economic stability with Joe Starks.

D148. Matza, Diane. "Zora Neale Hurston's *Their Eyes Were Watching God* and Toni Morrison's *Sula*: A Comparison." *MELUS* 12 (Fall 1985): 43-54. Compares the two novels and how each deals with the dual problem of race and gender and how these two are handled by the individual within the community. Feels Hurston and Morrison allow themselves to portray their worlds as complex as they want them to be.

D149. Sandoff, Diane F. "Black Matrilineage: The Case of Alice Walker and Zora Neale Hurston." *Signs* 11 (Autumn 1985): 4-26. Examines the connection between Alice Walker and Hurston; feels that black women authors often "misread literary forebears."

D150. Schmidt, Rita T. "The Fiction of Zora Neale Hurston: An Assertion of Black Womanhood." *Ilha do Desterro: A Journal of Language and Literature* 14 (1985): 53-70. Cites the three decades of obscurity endured by Hurston as an example of what happens to many women writers. Provides some background information on the Harlem Renaissance before looking at what caused Hurston to be relegated to "subcategory status" and what caused her to be "revived." Article based on Schmidt's dissertation.

D151. Sheffey, Ruthe T. "Zora Neale Hurston's *Moses, Man of the Mountain*: A Fictionalized Manifesto on the Imperatives of Black Leadership." *CLA Journal* 29 December (1985): 206-220. Discusses Hurston's presentation of Moses, not as a Hebrew, but as an African leader, a powerful hero, and a genius. Believes that in this underrated novel, Hurston "reassembled this mystical leader--for the edification of an oppressed people--bone by bone."

1984

D152. Lewis, Vashti C. "The Declining Significance of the Mulatto Female as Major Character in the Novels of Zora Neale Hurston." *CLA Journal* 28 (1984): 127-149. Argues that unlike some earlier black female novelists, in Hurston readers find a new image of black females--not simply characters of mixed racial heritage, but strong female characters.

1983

D153. Kubitschek, Missy Dehn. "'Tuh de Horizon and Back': The Female Quest in *Their Eyes Were Watching God*." *Black American Literature Forum* 17 (Fall 1983): 109-115. Says the "quest motif structures the entire novel" and that Hurston successfully merges the quest pattern with call-and-response to form a group quest and a community renewal. Believes many critics ignore Janie's return to her community, and earlier critics did not allow her to be the heroine of her own story.

D154. Spillers, Hortense J.   "A Hateful Passion, a Lost Love." *Feminist Studies* 9 (Summer 1983): 293-323. Discusses Morrison's *Sula*, Margaret Walker's *Jubilee*, and Hurston's *Their Eyes Were Watching God*. Says Sula was born four decades before in the person of Janie in *Their Eyes Were Watching God*. Article "traces changes in female characterization" and looks at different agendas at work in each novel. Examines how each writer "translates sociomoral constructs into literary modes of discourse."

D155. Stetson, Erlene. "*Their Eyes Were Watching God*: A Woman's Story." *Regionalism and the Female Imagination* 4, 1 (1979): 30-36. Calls Janie Crawford an "anti-romantic symbol of the mulatto 'type'" and feels the novel's theme deals with black female survival.

D156. Willis, Miriam DeCosta. "Folklore and the Creative Artist: Lydia Cabrera and Zora Neale Hurston." *CLA Journal* 27 (September 1983): 81-90. Examines the similarities between the works of Cabrera and Hurston whom she calls two of the "most prolific writers of the twentieth century." They were similar in many ways: date of births, childhood experiences with black folks, collecting folklore, and each writer returned home to collect folklore. Despite these similarities, they had different views about life and art, and their difference in lifestyles is reflected in their works. Says Hurston was no poet, but she was a superb dramatist.

1982

D157. Howard, Lillie P. "Nanny and Janie - Will the Twain Ever Meet: A Look at Hurston's *Their Eyes Were Watching God*." *Journal of Black Studies* 12 (June 1982): 403-414. Discusses Nanny as the one with clear vision in the novel, as one who has Janie's best interest in mind--though Janie never understands Nanny's actions. Believes Nanny wants Janie to have what she never had.

D158. Hudson, Gossie Harold. "Zora Neale Hurston and the Alternative History." *MAWA Review* (Summer-Fall 1982): 60-64. Article discusses Hurston's contributions to the field of history by her "utilizations of folklore and oral tradition." Examines her as a collector of folklore and as an oral historian who used the speech of the "lowly" and left to Black historiography a rich tradition and legacy of storytelling.

D159. Lupton, Mary Jane. "Zora Neale Hurston and the Survival of the Female." *Southern Literary Journal* 15 (Fall 1982): 45-54. Discusses male-female conflicts and the sometimes violent struggle for female autonomy in *Their Eyes Were Watching God* and "Sweat." Traces Janie Starks from adolescence through her third marriage and examines her growth from "springtime" to "autumn."

D160. McCredie, Wendy J. "Authority and Authorization in *Their Eyes Were Watching God*." *Black American Literature Forum* 16 (Spring 1982): 25-28. Looks at three areas of Janie's search for herself and her voice-- "before, during and after" Tea Cake. Says Hurston "authorized" Janie with many voices which constantly unfold and that in the end she belongs to herself, so that "her voice articulates herself."

D161. Mikell, Gwendolyn. "When Horses Talk: Reflections on Zora Neale Hurston's Haitian Anthropology." *Phylon* 43 (September/Fall 1982): 218-230. A reprint of a paper presented at the Symposium on Zora Neale Hurston, this article examines Hurston's approach of being involved and participating in a culture in order to accurately depict it. Discusses Hurston's anthropological background, her experiences in Haiti, and concludes that Hurston's "travelogue" style was effective.

D162. Naylor, Carolyn A. "Cross-Gender Significance of the Journey Motif in Selected Afro-American Fiction." *Colby Library Quarterly* 18 March (1982) 26-38. Hurston's photo on the cover of this special on women and literature. Examines Morrison's *Song of Solomon*, Ellison's *Invisible Man*, Hurston's *Their Eyes Were Watching God* and a Richard Wright short story to support theory that there is a "'spiritual holistic' that characterizes the journey of women, but not that of men." Discusses the idea of *bildungsroman* as a vehicle of self-exploration and a symbol of healing and affirmation in *Their Eyes Were Watching God*, a novel in which the journey motif is established at the outset.

D163. Wilson, Margaret F. "Zora Neale Hurston: Author and Folklorist." *Negro History Bulletin* 45 (Oct.-December 1982): 109-110. This biographical sketch portrays the heritage of a "Negro Floridian" and was written for "young Americans" so that young blacks can see what they can achieve. Highlights Hurston's writings.

D164. Wolff, Maria Tai. "Listening and Living: Reading and Experience in *Their Eyes Were Watching God*." *Black American Literature Forum* 16 (Spring 1982): 29-33. Thinks Hurston's concern in novel is the impact Janie's story will have with her as the "teller" of the tale. Feels a reader's background would determine whether the story was effective and whether it had any significance.

1981

D165. Barksdale, Richard K. "Black Autobiography and the Comic Vision." *Black American Literature Forum* 15 (Spring 1981): 22-27. Discusses Hurston as one of three black authors who "provide the best examples of comic distancing in their autobiographical statements." Says *Dust Tracks on a Road* provides excellent examples of how "comic vision" works well in autobiographies.

D166. Lentz, Gunther H. "Southern Exposures: The Urban Experience and the Reconstruction of Black Folk Culture and Community in the Works of Richard Wright and Zora Neale Hurston." *New York Folklore Quarterly* 7 (1981): 3-39. Discusses the differences between Hurston's and Wright's use of folklore in their works and provides background information on "folk culture, ghetto culture, and black literature" from the Harlem Renaissance to the Great Depression. Says Hurston speaks in an "authentic voice," but her portrayal of the folk community is re-constructed and "ahistorical."

1980

D167. Howard, Lillie P. "Zora Neale Hurston: Just Being Herself." *Essence* 10 (November 1980): 100-101, 156. Article provides a good overview of Hurston's life and literary career and summarizes her major works. Discusses early negative criticism of her for not dealing with the race question, and her penchant for making "ill-conceived" remarks such as those she made about Jim Crow or school desegregation.

1979

D168. Borders, Florence Edwards. "Zora Neale Hurston: Hidden Woman." *Callaloo* 2, 2 (May 1979): 89-92. Discusses Hurston's inclusion in correspondence of others in the Amistad Collection at Dillard University and reprints one letter from Hurston to Countee Cullen dated March 5, 1943 in which Hurston said they both wrote from within "rather than catch the eye of those who were making the loudest noise."

D169. Dance, Daryl. "Following in Zora Neale Hurston's *Dust Tracks*: Autobiographical Notes by the Author of *'Shuckin' and Jivin'*." *Journal of the Folklore Institute* 16 (1979): 120-126. Dance discusses how the scarcity of studies on contemporary folklore led her to collecting black folklore. Comments on the problems of locating "informants" and how gender and "long-standing associations" are drawbacks while trying to interview informants. Recounts her successes, failures, and regrets as she collected, and discusses her indebtedness to Hurston and other folklorists.

D170. Washington, Mary Helen. "A Woman Half in Shadow." *Change* 11 (November 1979): 63-68. This is an excerpt from Washington's introduction to *I Love Myself When I am Laughing*.... She calls the harsh criticism of Hurston in the 1930s the "intellectual lynching of Zora Neale Hurston." Article provides biographical information and discusses several works.

1978

D171. Brown, Lloyd W. "Zora Neale Hurston and the Nature of Female Perception." *Obsidian* 4 (1978): 39-45. Examines Hurston's characters in *Their Eyes Were Watching God* and concludes that her female characters are not resigned to shattered dreams as the male characters seem to be.

D172. Cantarow, Ellen. "Sex, Race, and Criticism: Thoughts of a White Feminist on Kate Chopin and Zora Neale Hurston." *Radical Teacher* 9 (1978): 30-33. Looks at Janie in *Their Eyes Were Watching God* and compares her self-realization to Edna in *The Awakening* by Kate Chopin.

D173. Smith, Barbara. "Sexual Politics and the Fiction of Zora Neale Hurston." *Radical Teacher* 8 (May 1978): 26-30. Essay was delivered in 1975 at the Modern Language Association's Hurston seminar. Believes "sexual politics play a significant role" in Hurston's critical reception by men. Argues that only when "a heightened understanding of the way in which sexual politics affects Black women's lives emerges will the gifts of an artist like Hurston be fully understood and the ironies of her life fully mourned." Believes much of her fiction centers around marriage and family, and applauds Hurston's "complex psychological realities using seeming simple language."

1977

D174. Burke, Virginia M. "Zora Neale Hurston and Fannie Hurst as They Saw Each Other." *CLA Journal* 20 (June 1977): 435-447. Looks at the autobiographies of the two writers and compares what each disclosed about themselves and each other. Hurst's work reveals that Hurston was a minor player in Hurst's life, but Hurst was a major player in Hurston's life. Comments upon the enduring quality of Hurston's work compared to Hurst's relative obscurity today.

D175. Howard, Lillie P. "Marriage: Zora Neale Hurston's System of Values." *CLA Journal* 21 (December 1977): 256-268. Examines Hurston's views on marriage and problems in the marriage relationship--a theme that is seen in several of her short stories and three of her novels. Says Hurston, though a victim of several ill-fated unions, advocates marriage for her characters because she feels it was a valuable institution. Feels she presents marriage "frankly, replete with infidelity jealousy, violence, and hatred."

1976

D176. Hausman, Renee. "Their Eyes Were Watching God." *English Journal* 65 (January 1976): 61-62. Believes any investigation into Hurston's second novel must first examine the historical context of the novel. Feels the novel should stimulate many inquires: into the Harlem Renaissance era, slavery, folk culture, as well as African American history.

D177. Hemenway, Robert. "Folklore Field Notes From Zora Neale Hurston." *Black Scholar* 7 (April 1976): 39-46. Hemenway introduces Hurston's "Go Gator and Muddy the Water" and "Uncle Monday." Says her problem as a "social scientist was she was also an artist."

D178. Love, Theresa R. "Zora Neale Hurston's America." *Papers on Language and Literature* 12, 4 (Fall 1976): 422-437. Views Hurston's works through her use of folklore and dialect. Believes her study and stay in the Caribbean influenced her linkage of past and present.

D179. Rambeau, James. "The Fiction of Zora Neale Hurston." *Markham Review* 5 (1976): 6 1-64. Says Hurston's writings were influences more by her southern rural roots than anything else. Discusses her talent for "adaptation."

D180. Schwalenberg, Peter. "Time as Point of View in Zora Neale Hurston's *Their Eyes Were Watching God*." *Negro American Literature Forum* (10 (1976): 104-105, 107-108. Believes that Hurston used time to propel Janie from one dimension to another. Feels Hurston uses concrete and abstract time in the novel.

1975

D181. Giddings, Paula. "A Special Vision, A Common Goal." *Encore* 4, 12 (June 23-July 4, 1975): 44. Believes Janie in *Their Eyes Were Watching God* is a character who knows her mind and does not allow gender, race or narrow-minded neighbors to stand in her way.

D182. Harris, Trudier. "Zora Neale Hurston, Folklorist." Paper presented at the Modern Language Association Convention in San Francisco, December 1975. MLA conference focused national attention on Hurston, who at the time, was still a little-known member of the Harlem Renaissance whose books were mostly out of print.

D183. Walker, Alice. "In Search of Zora Neale Hurston." *Ms.* 3 (March 1975): 4-9. This is the Walker article purported to have launched numerous literary scholars--both black and white--on journeys to "discover" or rediscover Hurston. The article details Walker's pilgrimage to Hurston's home town of Eatonville, Florida to find and mark her grave with the phase "A Genius of the South." Walker recounts her meetings with some Eatonville "folk" who remember Hurston, including Dr. Benton, who declared that Hurston did not die of malnutrition. Relates her trek through the cemetery in search of Hurston's grave site.

D184. Walker, S. Jay. "Zora Neale Hurston's *Their Eyes Were Watching God*: Black Novel of Sexism." *Modern Fiction Studies* 20 (winter 1974-75): 519-527. Says an examination of the novel will show that Hurston was ahead of her time in writing about sexism and women's struggles for recognition. Believes she foreshadows the modern women's movement by several decades. Says women's lib came to Eatonville and everyone was better for it. Asserts that the novel is more about sexism than racism.

1974

D185. Jordan, June. "On Richard Wright and Zora Neale Hurston: Notes Toward a Balance of Love and Hatred." *Black World* 23, 10 (August 1974): 4-8. Argues that *Their Eyes Were Watching God* is a positive, defiant novel that affirms the power of black love. Jordan also explains why Hurston's works have been dismissed and belittled: "Zora Neale Hurston was a woman, and because we have been misled into devaluating the functions of Black affirmation, her work has been derogated as romantic/the natural purview of a woman."

D186. Neal, Larry. "A Profile: Zora Neale Hurston." *Southern Exposure* (Winter 1974): 160. A Carl Van Vechten photo from the Amistad Collection accompanies this article, a reprint that originally appeared in *Black Review*. Highlights Hurston's life and career, and states that she was a "precursor of the interest in folkways that shapes much of contemporary black fiction."

D187. Rayson, Ann. "The Novels of Zora Neale Hurston." *Studies in Black Literature* 5 (Winter 1974): 1-10. Asserts that Hurston's first novel, *Jonah's Gourd Vine*, establishes a pattern or formula or common plot her later novels follow. Article looks at each novel in view of this theory.

D188. Southerland, Ellease. "The Novelist-Anthropologist's Life/Works." *Black World* 20-30 (August 1974): 26. Summarizes each of Hurston's major works and provides background information on her life and career. Asserts that African culture survived in America due to oral folk traditions.

1973

D189. Rayson, Ann. "*Dust Tracts on a Road*: Zora Neale Hurston and the Form of Black Autobiography." *Negro American Literature Forum* 7 (Summer 1973): 39-45. Begins by announcing that Hurston is a "paradox among American black autobiographers." Feels that even though she is an "establishment" writer, Hurston is innovative in her independent style and her clever "manipulation of language, tone, and style."

1972

D190. Giles, James R. "The Significance of Time in Zora Neale Hurston's Their Eyes Were Watching God." *Negro American Literature Forum* 6 (Summer 1972): 52-53; 60. Article examines three competing concepts of time in the novel that Hurston uses to bring the basic conflicts in the novel into focus. These three are: a deterministic view--leading to death; a rationally controlled view--associated with work and making money; and a hedonistic view--personified by Tea Cake.

D191. Kilson, Marion. "The Transformation of Eatonville's Ethnographer." *Phylon* 33 (Spring 1972): 112-119. Examines Hurston's formal training as an ethnographer. Feels that Hurston changed during the early 1940s to become a "critical ethnographer."

D192. Washington, Mary Helen. "The Black Woman's Search for Identity." *Black World* 21 (August 1972): 68-75. Discusses how Janie leaves Nanny's world of "marriage for economic security" and seeks self-realization and freedom on her own terms.

1970

D193. Helmick, Evelyn T. "Zora Neale Hurston." *Carrell* 11 (June-December 1970): 1-19. Article provides biographical information and summaries of Hurston's major works. Says there are no stereotypes in Hurston's books and that she "rejected the kind of writing being done by other members of her race." Lauds Hurston's colorful and vibrant personality which spilled over into her work.

1960s

D194. Blake, Emma L. "Zora Neale Hurston: Author and Folklorist." *Negro History Bulletin* 29 (April 1966): 149-150+. A photograph accompanies this overview of Hurston's life and career. Summarizes each of her major works; *Jonah's Gourd Vine* mistakenly called "*Noah's Gourd Vine*."

D195. Hurst, Fannie. "Zora Neale Hurston: A Personality Sketch." *Yale University Library Gazette* 35 (1960): 17. Hurst recounts her first meeting with Hurston whom she describes as a "big-boned, good-boned young woman, handsome and light yellow." Article contains anecdotes of Hurston's laziness, humor, irresponsibility, and carelessness. Says she was the world's worse secretary so she switched her to chauffeur. Wrote that her books are "Negro Americana" but destined to endure.

D196. Lomax, Alan. "Zora Neale Hurston--A Life of Negro Folklore." *Sing Out* 10, 3 (October-November 1960): 12-13. Discusses his field work collecting folklore with Hurston.

D197. Pratt, Theodore. "Zora Neale Hurston." *Florida Historical Quarterly* 40 (July 1961): 37. Article states that Hurston was "absolutely and completely improvident." Regrets that she died in obscurity and without achieving recognition for her contributions to literature.

D198. Pratt, Theodore. "A Memoir--Zora Neale Hurston--Florida's First Distinguished Author." *Negro Digest* (February 1962): 52-56. Believes *Their Eyes Were Watching God, Mules and Men,* and *Jonah's Gourd Vine* to be in the "top rung of American writing." Provides biographical background on Hurston, recounts stories of their personal friendship and speaking at her funeral. Ends by noting that Hurston and her books are out of circulation, but the latter problem can be rectified.

1950s

D199. Brown, Sterling A. "A Negro Folk Expression." *Phylon* 21, 4 (1950): 318-327. Feels Hurston put too much credence in black folk speech and expression.

D200. Byrd, James W. "Zora Neale Hurston: A Negro Folklorist." *Tennessee Folklore Society Bulletin* 21, 2 (1955): 37-41. Says Hurston was unusual in her ability to use folk expressions, but in *Seraph on the Suwanee,* she mistakenly had whites using idioms only used by blacks.

1940s

D201. "Anisfield Awards to Hurston and Pierson." *Publisher's Weekly* 143 (February 27, 1943) 1023. Hurston received a $1,000 prize as winner of the John Anisfield Award in Racial Relations for best book of creative literature for 1942.

D202. Gloster, Hugh M. "Zora Neale Hurston: Novelist and Folklorist." *Phylon* 3 (April-June 1943): 153-156. Believes that Hurston's rural, southern heritage and her academic training as an anthropologist were the greatest influences on her creation of the "rich" language found in her writings.

D203. Hughes, Langston. "Harlem Literati in the Twenties." *Saturday Review of Literature* 22, 9 (June 22, 1940): 13-14. Calls Hurston "the perfect book of entertainment in herself." Provides some background on Hurston's life and work in Harlem.

1930s

D204. Asterlund, B. "Biographical Sketch." *Wilson Bulletin* 13, 8 (April 1939): 586. Gives a biographical sketch of Hurston and briefly discusses *Jonah's Gourd Vine, Their Eyes Were Watching God*, and *Tell My Horse*. Ends with Hurston's lament that her spirituals and work songs were not well received. Photo accompanies article.

D205. Preece, Harold. "The Negro Folk Cult." *Crisis* 43, 12 (December 1936): 364, 374. Says professional folklorists, especially whites, capitalize upon the "minstrelsy" of blacks and blasts Hurston for being short-sighted in "devoting her literary abilities to recording the legendary amours of terrapins." Calls her a "literary climber."

Reviews of Works
by Zora Neale Hurston

"Night came walking through Egypt swishing her black dress."

Moses, Man of the Mountain

Reviews of *Jonah's Gourd Vine*

E01. *Booklist* 30, 11 (July 1934): 351. Says the novel is a story about real "Negro country life in the far South" written by a Negro college woman.

EO2. New *York Herald Tribune Books* (May 6, 1934):7. Favorable review says Hurston understands her people and depicts them with objectivity and detachment. Feels language is poetic and Negro idiom is "delighted talk."

E03. Brawley, Benjamin. *The Negro Genius*. New York: Dodd, Mead & Company, 1937: 257-259. Unfavorable review claims the story is loosely organized and questions Hurston's choice of material. Feels Pearson's sermon may be the only redeeming feature in the book.

E04. Brickell, Herschel. *New Republic* 79 (July 1 1, 1934): 244. The favorable review says the novel is authentic but feels the use of dialect will prevent it from being very popular. Feels Hurston is talented and that his sermon is "magnificent." Author also reviewed novel in *North American Review* 238 (July 1934): 95.

E05. Burris, Andrew. *Crisis* 41, 6 (June 1934): 166-167. An unfavorable review which claims the characters are not realistic and the novel is a failure. Admits that "much about the book is fine and distinctive and enjoyable" but that Hurston needs more experience.

E06. Chamberlain, John. *New York Times* (May 3, 1934): 7. Says a "deep racial rhythm" runs through novel. Hurston ignores tradition, "steps out for herself" and shows her "remarkable ear for dialogue" with *Jonah's Gourd Vine.*

E07. Felton, Estell. *Opportunity* 612, 8 (August 1934): 252-253. A mixed review. Feels Hurston has an understanding of the "customs and traditions of her people," but her characterizations are weak and her "style at times falls out."

E08. Ford, Nick Aaron. *The Contemporary Negro Novel: A Study in Race Relations*. Boston: Meador Publishing, 1936. This unfavorable review says Hurston missed the unique opportunity to write a "masterpiece of the age," but failed from "lack of vision." Thinks Hurston's knowledge of her material unparalleled by any of "her race."

E09. Gayle, Addison, Jr. "The Outsider." *The Way of the New World.* Garden City, N.Y.: Doubleday, 1975: 143-144. Feels Hurston's representation of the black female stands out in this novel. Believes Hurston's female characters were more important than her males.

E10. Gruening, Martha. *New Republic* 79, 11 (July 1934): 244-245. Thinks *Jonah's Gourd Vine* is an excellent novel written by an "insider." Says, "Candor like Miss Hurston's is still sufficiently rare among Negro writers."

E11. *Nation* 138 (June): 683-684. A favorable review, despite "certain faults in construction." Feels Hurston has "enviable gifts of talent" and novel is refreshing because it does not "deal with the relations of Negroes and whites."

E12. Ovington, Mary White. *New York Age* 48, 35 (May 6, 1934): 6. Favorable review notes that the novel's diction and style are wonderful.

E13. Pickney, Josephine. "A Pungent, Poetic Novel About Negroes." *New York Herald Tribune Books* (May 6, 1934): 7. Says Hurston writes as a "Negro understanding her people," with objectivity and detachment. Discusses what she views as weaknesses in the novel--"some uncertainty" in the narrative and some unresolved conflicts. But feels story is set against a great background.

E14. Plomer, William. *Spectrum* 154 (January 4, 1935): 25. Favorable review says despite the complications of dialect, readers will be rewarded "by a genuine and in many ways admirable tale of Negro life." Appreciates the "touch of fantasy."

E15. *Times Literary Supplement* 18 (October 1934): 716-717. Favorable review thinks the story is well written and free of the violence often found in novels by Negroes. Says that the novel may seem like a "compilation of stories for after-dinner speakers" but it is scientific, including the materials on Hoodoo.

E16. Wallace, Margaret. "Real Negro People." *New York Times Book Review* (May 6, 1934): 6-7. This favorable review calls the novel "the most vital and original novel about the American Negro that has yet been written by a member of the Negro race." Praises the rich language and colorful idiom and says Hurston's talents as a storyteller saves the novel from mediocrity.

Reviews of *Mules and Men*

E17.   Boas, Franz. Introduction to *Mules and Men*. New York: Lippincott: 1935. Writes favorably of the Hurston's collection. Believes she was able to "penetrate through that affected demeanor by which the Negro excludes the White observer." Feels the work valuable to those interested in cultural history.

E18.   Brock, H. I. "The Full, True Flavor of Life in a Negro Community." *New York Times Book Review* 40 (November 10, 1935): 4. A favorable review of *Mules and Men*, Brock thinks Hurston's use of Negro dialect is successful and that the collection is an "amazing roundup of that color's very best stories." Believes Hurston provides a well-rounded view of Negro life in the book.

E19. Chubb, Thomas Caldecott. *The North American Review* 241, 1 (March 1936): 181-183. Believes *Mules and Men* a "well-filled source-book" for those interested in folklore, and that it will generally "delight" any audience, especially those interested in Negroes. Feels Hurston's portrayal of the Negro is a balanced one that shows their many sides.

E20. Daniels, Jonathan. "Black Magic and Dark Laughter." *Saturday Review of Literature* 12, 25 (October 19, 1935): 12. This favorable review thinks the work is a satisfying and "remarkable collection of Negro folk-tales." Believes some readers might be skeptical of Hurston's use of Hoodoo, but feels the book "rich enough to stand both skepticism and familiarity."

E21. Fallaize, E. N. *Manchester Guardian* (April 7, 1936): 7. Favorable review which notes, "Miss Hurston's native insight into Negro character gives her book a high value." Believes the average reader will find it "intensely amusing."

E22. Gannett, Lewis. *New York Herald Tribune Weekly Book Review* (October 11, 1935). Says he "can't remember better since Uncle Remus." Provides some excerpts from the collection which he calls a "rich experience."

E23. McNeill, B. C. *Journal of Negro History* 21, 2 (April 1936): 223-225. Favorable review calls *Mules and Men* "unique for a collection of folkways." Says it is written by an author who presents evidence of Voodooism.

E24. Moon, Henry Lee. "Big Old Lies." *New Republic* 85 (December 11, 1935): 142. This is a short review of *Mules and Men*. Believes the book provides a look at the lives of "simple" Negroes. Likes Hurston's observant presentation of the material without evaluating it.

E25. *Nature* 137 (April 25, 1936): 683. Favorable review believes collection provides an "illuminating view" of southern Negro society.

E26. Pickney. Darryl. "In Sorrow's Kitchen." *New York Review of Books* 25, 20 (December 21, 1978): 55-57. Believes the collection goes a long way in putting to rest some of the negative views about African Americans.

E27. Plomer, William. *Spectrum* 154 January 4, 1935): 25. Despite problems with dialect, feels the collection is an authentic representation of Negro life.

E28. Preece, Harold. "The Negro Folk Cult." *Crisis* 43, 12 (December 1936): 364. A negative review criticizes Hurston for the depiction of her own race. Calls her a "literary climber."

E29. Roberts, John. *Journal of American Folklore* 93, 370 (October-December 1980): 463-466. Reviews what he calls two "classics of Afro-American culture"--*Mules and Men* and *Their Eyes Were Watching God*. Feels Hurston's failure to explain how she collected and recorded her information leaves doubts about the authenticity of her transcriptions--a problem to professional folklorists. Believes *Their Eyes Were Watching God* is an "often overlooked classic" that is useful to anyone interested in folklore in literature.

E30. Stoney, Samuel Gaillard. *New York Herald Tribune Books* (October 13, 1935): 7. Praises Hurston for her lively and infectious style, and for looking objectively at her people.

E31. Turner, Darwin. "Zora Neale Hurston: Wandering Minstrel." *In a Minor Chord: Three Afro-American Writers and their Search for Identity*. Urbana: Southern Illinois University Press, 1971. Claims *Mules and Men* is the "more valuable of her two collections," but feels it is also evidence of Hurston's "talents as a reporter and her weaknesses as a scholar."

Reviews of *Their Eyes Were Watching God*

E32. *Booklist* 34, 4 (October 15, 1937): 71. Thinks the Negro dialect is easy to follow in the novel, and believes Hurston's story is a warm portrayal of Negro life.

E33. Brown, Sterling. "Luck Is a Fortune." *Nation* (October 16, 1937): 409-410. Brown writes a favorable review of the novel. Despite some "narrative gaps," lauds Hurston's use of folk speech and humor as original and successful. Feels bitterness is present in the novel, though sometimes oblique and sometimes forthright--which Hurston shows through "enforced folk manner."

E34. Ellison, Ralph. "Recent Negro Fiction." *New Masses* 5 (1941): 211.
Negative review faults Hurston for writing another "calculated burlesque"
show and setting her story in an all black town rather than in a realistic
setting where the South's brutalities might "intrude." Criticizes Hurston's
failure to deal with the race problem in her fiction.

E35. Ferguson, Otis. "You Can't Hear Their Voices." *New Republic* 92
(October 13, 1937): 276. A mixed review of a novel which Ferguson
thinks is dull and "superwordy." Feels the language and characterization
are too complicated for the setting of the novel and that Hurston's dialect
is "sloppy." Believes Hurston did not fully understand the rhythm of
dialect and consequently mishandled it in the novel. Despite its faults,
feels Hurston leaves the reader with a "good story where it never should
have been potentially."

E36. Forrest, Ethel. *Journal of Negro History* 23, 1 (January 1938): 106-
107. Favorable review says the novel is realistic and historical, a "gripping
story" that spins a realistic tale of the Negro in the South.

E37. Hibben, Sheila. *New York Herald Tribune Weekly Book Review*
(September 26, 1937): 2. Favorable review, feels the book is sensitive,
warm though black speech not as fully developed as in earlier works.
Believes the novel is mostly about life--"a swarming, passionate life."

E38. Hunton, W. A.   "The Adventures of the Brown Girl in Search for
Life." *Journal of Negro Education* 7,1 (January 1938): 71-72. Negative
review found little of redeeming value in the novel. Says the main concern
is a "study of the race-conscious introvert." Thinks Hurston has a "healthy
scorn" for those African Americans trying to pattern their lives after the
"bourgeois standards of whites."

E39. Locke, Alain. *Opportunity* (June 1, 1938). Mixed review calls the
novel "folklore fiction at its best" but objects to Hurston's "flashing on the
surface" instead of "diving down deep" to write about "motive fiction and
social document fiction." Believes her to be a gifted storyteller.

E40. Stevens, George. "Negroes by Themselves." *Saturday Review of
Literature* 16 (September 18, 1937): 3. Though story begins awkwardly,
believes, with exception of a few technical weak spots, the narrative in this
"simple and unpretentious" story is "exactly right." Believes there is an

undertone of "racial frustration" in the novel. Concludes that there is nothing else quite like it.

E41. *Time* 30, 12 (September 20, 1937): 71. One paragraph summary calls the novel the story of a "coffee-colored quadroon" who outlives her three men, goes back home, and makes her friends "eyes bug out" at her tales of life since she left home.

E42. Tompkins, Lucille. "In the Florida Glades." *New York Times Book Review* (September 26, 1937): 29. Favorable review calls *Their Eyes Were Watching God* a "beautiful," universal novel that is a "well nigh perfect story." Feels the dialect is easy to follow and the images are "irresistible."

E43. Wright, Richard. "Between Laughter and Tears." *New Masses* 25 (October 5, 1937): 22, 25. Critical, negative review of the novel. Thinks Hurston reinforces the stereotypical "minstrel" image of blacks. Criticizes Hurston's failure to deal with the race question. Says she can write but the novel has "no theme, no message, no thought."

Reviews of *Tell My Horse*

E44. Carmer, Carl. *New York Herald Tribute Books* (October 23, 19138): 96. Says Hurston came back from the Caribbean with a "harvest unbelievably rich." Believes there is no more beautiful story than the last one in the collection, "God and the Pintards."

E45. Courlander, Harold. "Witchcraft in the Caribbean Islands." *Saturday Review of Literature* 18, 25 (October 15, 1938): 6-7. Calls collection a "curious mixture of remembrances, travelogue, sensationalism, and anthropology." Concludes that Hurston was at her best with witchcraft; lauds her chapter on Zombies, and feels the photographs are "exceptionally good." Mixed review, believes Hurston succeeds in catching the "idiom of dialogue," but fails to fully digest her material.

E46. Locke, Alain. "The Negro: New or Newer." *Opportunity* 17 (February 1939): 38. Calls the book "anthropological gossip."

E47. "Lore of Haiti." *New York Times Book Review* (October 23, 1938): 12. Says collection written with sympathy and a level-headed balance in a "style which is vivid, sometimes lyrical, occasionally strikingly dramatic, yet simple and unstrained." Thinks the book is unusual and "richly packed with strange information."

E48. *New Republic* 97 (December 7, 1938): 155. Calls the book a "fine account of voodoo in Jamaica and Haiti." Says Hurston translates the "mumbojumbo" and ferrets out the reasonable without sacrificing the "drama and beauty" of the African ceremonies.

E49. *New Yorker* 14 (October 15, 1938): 95. Mixed review calls the collection a "witches brew" that is disorganized; however, feels it is an interesting account of Hurston's visit to the Caribbean.

E50. Thompson, Edgar T. *Rural Sociology* 4, 2 (1939): 261. Comparative review, believes Hurston's report on Voodoo in the Caribbean the best part of the collection.

E51. Woodson, Carter G. *Journal of Negro History* 24, 1 (January 1939): 116-118. Favorable review, Woodson feels the book is entertaining but is also an important discussion of the "conflict and fusion of cultures."

Reviews of *Moses, Man of the Mountain*

E52. *Booklist* 36, 7 (December 15, 1939): 150. Calls the novel a "fictionalized biography of Moses as a religious leader and a great voodoo man." Believes it to be a warm and human story told in Negro vernacular.

E53. Carmer, Carl. "Biblical Story in Negro Rhythm." *New York Herald Tribune Books* (November 26, 1939): 5. Favorable review, feels Hurston's prose "sparkles with characteristic Negro humor," praises her language and use of "Negro speech rhythms." Believes Hurston provides novels of her race that "few of her contemporaries are capable of writing."

E54. Ellison, Ralph. "Recent Negro Fiction." *New Masses* 40 (August 5, 1941): 22-26. Unfavorable review of *Moses, Man of the Mountain*, which he feels did "nothing for Negro fiction."

E55. Hutchinson, Percy. "Led His People Free." *New York Times Book Review* 44 (November 19, 1939): 21. A favorable review of *Moses, Man of the Mountain.* Thinks the narrative is powerful yet "warm with friendly personality and pulsating with homely and profound eloquence and religious fervor."

E56.   Jackson, Blyden.   "Some Negroes in the Land of Goshen." *Tennessee Folklore Society Bulletin* 19, 4 (December 1953): 1031-107. Believes Hurston wanted to show that "Negro folk experience" is as valuable as the experiences of any other people.

E57.   *New Yorker* 15, 39 (November 11, 1939): 75. Says story is Moses as a Voodoo man and told in Negro folk idiom. Believes it is the "real thing, warm, humorous, poetic."

E58.   Slomovitz, Philip. "The Negro Moses." *Christian Century* 56, 49 (December 6, 1939): 1504. Mixed review, believes Hurston created a "magnificent story" but that it is weak in its "treatment of the code of laws" handed down by Moses. Feels Hurston wrote a story that could only be written by a Negro.

E59.   Untermeyer, Louis. "Old Testament Voodoo." *Saturday Review of Literature* 21 (November 11, 1939): 11. Believes Hurston's "approach is as arresting as it is fresh." Feels main disappointment in book is Moses: the balance between his Egyptian breeding and his Hebraic adaption is not handled well and his growth is "weakly motivated." Even though not a "logically projected work," concludes that it is a novel from a gifted author.

Reviews of *Dust Tracks on a Road*

E60.   Bernstein, Dennis and Connie Blitt. *These Times* 6, 23 (May 8-14, 1985): 18-19. Briefly reviews several Hurston works. Appreciates the new release of her autobiography which contains more than 50 pages of new, "uncensored" material.

E61.   Bontemps, Arna. *New York Herald Tribute Books* (November 22, 1942): 3. Believes Hurston's autobiography "should not be read for its comments on the Negro as a whole." Says Hurston ignores the serious side of Negro life and has done "right well for herself" in the world she found.

E62.   Check, Joseph. *Harvard Educational Review* 55 (November 1985): 472. Favorably reviews the second edition of *Dust Tracks on a Road* and feels Hemenway's introduction provides good biographical materials on Hurston. Discusses the work in the context of its era.

E63.   Farrison, W. Edward. *Journal of Negro History* 28, 3 (July 1943): 352-355. Favorable review, feels Hurston presented material in an interesting manner--"whether fact or fancy." Notes that she lengthened the book by taking materials from several of her earlier works. Believes any problems in book are forgivable due to her wonderful narrative.

E64.   Gates, Henry Louis, Jr. "A Negro Way of Saying." *New York Times Book Review* (April 21, 1985): 1. Believes *Dust Tracks on a Road* is the story of Hurston's life, not a tale of "Negro problems." Feels she succeeds in using black oral traditions and speech, and that Hurston put her gender and profession before her race. Thinks Hurston was shaped by "double voice" of the "linguistic rituals of the dominant culture and those of the black vernacular tradition."

E65.   Hodges, J. O. *Choice* 23 (September 1985): 114. Reviews *Dust Tracks on a Road*. Believes that even with the addition of several chapters added by Hemenway, the new edition does not provide any proof for revisionists who want to put to rest the notion that Hurston was a "political accommodationist." Says the book reveals little about Hurston the individual and lacks the depth of serious autobiography, but the additional material in this edition does reveal a more "complex" Hurston.

E66.   Maja-Pearce, Adewale. *Times Literary Supplement* (May 2, 1986): 479. Reviews second edition of *Dust Tracks on a Road* and remarks that Hurston held fast to her vision.

E67.   *New Yorker* 18, 39 (November 14, 1942): 79. Calls Hurston a "Grade A folk writer" whose autobiography is "warm, witty, imaginative, and down to earth."

E68.   Preece, Harold. *Tomorrow* (February 1943). Negative review, calls autobiography the "tragedy of a gifted mind."

E69.   Rose, Ernestine. *Library Journal* 67 (November 1, 1942): 950. Mixed review says book written with "little finish" though told with "immense verve and gusto." Thinks libraries who want contemporary materials on Negroes will want this autobiography.

E70. Sherman, Beatrice. *New York Times Book Review* (November 29, 1942): 44. Favorable review calls Hurston a writer that any race would be proud to claim. Calls the book a "thumping story," one that is enjoyable for readers of any race.

E71. Strong, Phil. *Saturday Review of Literature* 25, (November 28, 1942): 6. Says the book is more "a summary than the autobiography it advertises itself as being." Says the "race-consciousness that spoils so much Negro literature is completely missing here." Concludes that it is a "fine, rich autobiography" and recommends it to readers of any race. The famous Schreiber drawing of Hurston accompanies the review.

D72. Weidman, B. S. *Commonweal* (October 4, 1985): 535-536. Reviews of *Dust Tracks on a Road*, second edition, and of *Moses, Man of the Mountain*, reprint of original edition. Reviews *Dust Tracks on a Road* and admonishes readers to examine Hurston's autobiography to learn the origins and context for her views. Believes the addition of three chapters provides details for a better understanding of what she believed and why.

Reviews of *Seraph on the Suwanee*

E73. *Christian Science Monitor* (December 23, 1948): 11. Favorably reviews *Seraph on the Suwanee* and feels book is "wholesome as a vegetable garden." Believes Hurston's setting the best thing about the novel.

E74. Hamilton, Edward. *America* 80, 13 (January 1, 1949): 354-355. Thinks the novel "shows promise," especially the first part where Hurston correctly represents native voice, but feels the ending is melodramatic and unsatisfactory.

E75. Hedden, Worth Tuttle. "Turpentine and Moonshine: Love Conquers Caste Between Florida Crackers and Aristocrats." *New York Herald Tribune Weekly* (October 10, 1948). A mixed review, Hedden thinks Hurston's characterization shows she knows Florida Negroes and whites, but does not fully develop them. Believes Hurston to be an "astonishing, bewildering talent" and the novel at its best when Hurston provides objective portrayals.

E76. Hughes, Carl Milton. *The Negro Novelist*. New York: Citadel Press, 1953: 172-178. Believes Hurston is a meticulous writer whose actions and episodes are related. Also believes she "paid homage to Sigmund Freud" in her development of Arvay Henson.

E77. Rogers, Michael. *Library Journal* 116,3 (February 15, 1991): 225. Says Hurston's story is a chronicle of poor Southern whites and her works are welcomed at anytime, especially for Black and Women's History months.

E78. Slaughter, Frank G. "Freud in Turpentine." *New York Times Book Review* 53 (October 31, 1948). A rather mixed review of *Seraph on the Suwanee*; feels Hurston used setting to great advantage but failed in her development of real characters. Discusses her use of Freudian psychology in developing the character Arvay Henson, although he feels some characters are "mechanical."

E79. Whitmore, Anne. *Library Journal* 73 (September 1, 1948): 1193. This favorable review states, "The colorful Florida 'cracker' language holds the mood throughout."

Reviews of "*I Love Myself When I Am Laughing...And Then Again When I Am Looking Mean and Impressive*": *A Zora Neale Hurston Reader* Edited by Alice Walker

E80. Blundell, J. B. *Library Journal* 104 (November 15, 1979): 2463. Appreciates Washington's introduction to the reader and Walker's efforts to produce an anthology that puts Hurston in her "proper place." Says the anthology "demonstrates the power and the humor of her unique voice."

E81. Boyd, Melba Joyce. *Black Scholar* 11, 8 (November-December 1980): 82-83. Calls the collection a "fine and necessary piece of literature." Lauds Alice Walker's arrangement of materials and her meticulous editing, which are strengths she found in this anthology.

E82. *Choice* 17 (June 1980): 538. Thinks the book is an important anthology which will be useful for scholarly and lay readers. Believes the fictional selections "represent Hurston's best characterizations and poetic imagery."

E83. *Ebony* 35 (January 1980): 24. A short blurb in the "Ebony Bookshelf" announces the books and claims it is the "first anthology of the writings of Zora Neale Hurston." Notes that much of what Walker includes has been out of print.

E84. Gornick, Vivian. "Catching Up With Hurston." *Village Voice* 24 (December 31, 1997): 34-35. Feels many of the essays in the collection are incomplete or are "heavy-handed in their irony;" acknowledges that Hurston's finest work is *Their Eyes Were Watching God*.

E85. Gregory, Carole E. "Hurston Revisited." *Freedomways* 20, 11 (1980): 305-307. Feels that Hurston was a genius at using black dialect and the oral storytelling traditions of her ancestors.

E86. Kennedy, Randall. *New York Times Book Review* (December 30, 1979): 8. Says the anthology is useful because of new trends in Afro-American and women's scholarship. Says Alice Walker "demands that her heroine's writing be considered on its own terms."

E87. Rushing, Andrea Benton. "Jumping at the Sun." *Callaloo*. 3,1-3 (1980): 228-230. Review calls work an "exciting volume of expertly-culled examples" of Hurston's work. Believes essays by Walker and Mary Helen Washington, as well as photographs, make this a "rich mine" for any reader.

E88. Skerrett, J. T. *MELUS* 7, 3 (1980): 90-91. Calls the collection a "godsend of pleasure and insight" for students and scholars. Thinks it increases the availability of Hurston's works and lauds Walker and Washington for their "useful introductions."

Reviews of *Novels and Stories* and *Folklore, Memoirs, and Other Writings* Edited by Cheryl A. Wall

E89.   Cornish, Sam.   "Hurston's Tales Illuminate Rural Black Culture."
Christian Science Monitor (May 31, 1985): 2 3-24.   Believes that as a
young educated Negro, Hurston had values which are considered
conservative.   Feels the stories deal with women caught between two
worlds.

E90.   Delbanco, Andrew.   "The Mark of Zora."   *New Republic* 213, 1 (July
3, 1995): 30-35.   Reviews of *Novels and Stories* by Zora Neale Hurston
edited by Cheryl A. Wall and *Folklore, Memoirs, and Other Writings* by
Zora Neale Hurston edited by Cheryl A. Wall.   Long review provides
biographical information on Hurston's life and career as well as summaries
of several of her primary works.   Says much of Hurston's work is
"preoccupied with the destructive force of love."   Believes one reason her
works will "abide" is the "universal disjunction between the limitless
human imagination and the constructions within which all human beings
live their lives."

E91.   Middleton, Joyce Irene.   "Where to Look for Zora."   *Women's
Review of Books* 13, 2 (November 1995): 28-29.   Thinks the release of this
two-volume work means Hurston's views on language, race, class and
gender are still relevant today.

E92.   Roberts, Michael.   "Classic Returns."   *Library Journal* 120 , 2
(February 1, 1995): 104.   Says Hurston's autobiography is presented for the
first time in an "unexpurgated form," and her "lesser-known
anthropological" works have been restored by editor Wall.

E93.   Sailer, Steve.   "The Secret Zora Neale Hurston."   *National Review*
47, 6 (April 3, 1995): 58-60.   Says Library of America honors Hurston by
selecting her works to reprint; however, feels that "selected" works would
have worked better than the two-volume work offered.   Says she is a
misunderstood and misread author, but thinks   the work "copiously
documents Miss Hurston's unfashionable world views."

E94.   Wilhelmus, T.   *Hudson Review* 48, 4 (Winter 1996): 672-678.
Thinks critics should examine Hurston's "'art' (or lack of it)" rather than
rejecting her for her racial and gender politics.   Believes her works are
"engaging in some fashion" but are artistically uneven.   Concludes that
however one feels about Hurston, the Library of American collection is
amply justified though should not be misread as an attempt to accredit

Hurston into the American literary canon. Wilhemus examines several of the pieces in the collection and provides critical commentary.

Reviews of Other Works Written by Hurston

E95. Ingoldsby, Grace. "Multiple Echo." *New Statesman* 14, 2936 (July 3, 1987): 29-30. A favorable review of "Spunk." Said to read Hurston is to learn how cautious many contemporary writers have become.

E96. Ingraham, Janet. Review of *Mule Bone, A Comedy of Negro Life*. Library Journal 116, 2 (February 1, 1991): 78. Thinks the accompanying correspondence, biography, and documentation of the Hurston-Hughes dispute which kept this work unproduced for sixty years is important for students and will "intrigue the general reader." Calls the play a "spirited black Southern folk story."

E97. Staples, Brent. *New York Times Book Review* (August 11, 1985): 14. Praises *Spunk* as a splendid collection that collocates stories often found in anthologies with not so well known ones. "Glossary of Harlem Slang" is included, and an excerpt from *Herod the Great* entitled "Herod on Trial" is appended.

F

Reviews of Works
about Zora Neale Hurston

*"Some folks needs thrones, and ruling-chairs and crowns tuh make they
influence felt. He don't. He's got uh throne in de seat of his pants."*

Their Eyes Were Watching God

**Hemenway, Robert. *Zora Neale Hurston: A Literary Biography*.
Urbana: University of Illinois Press, 1977.**

F01. Brittin, Ruth L. *Southern Humanities Review* 15 (Fall 1981): 369-
370. Objects to Robert Hemenway's "championing" of Hurston through his
biography. Feels Hurston does not need a "defender," only someone to
present her objectively. Believes, however, there is more to complement
than criticize in this impressive study of Hurston's life.

F02. *Choice* 15 (April 1978): 229. Says the books is "beautifully
documented" and should go a long way in reestablishing interest in
Hurston.

F03. Gates, Henry Louis, Jr. "Soul of a Black Woman." *New York Times
Book Review* (February 19, 1978):13. Calls book an "excellent biography"
and a "subtle blend of fact and close reading" that avoids sentiment and
oversimplification. Thinks Hemenway provides an honest portrayal of

Hurston, including the complexity of her politics, that should allow Hurston to be read again--"for all the right reasons."

F04.   Olney, James. *New Republic* (February 11, 1978):26. Believes Hemenway's careful research and scholarship will do much for Hurston's revival.   Lauds the "extensive, often acute summaries and analyses of all Hurston's extant work" and the meticulous, nearly complete research put into book.   Says his tale of Hurston is "by turns boisterous, sobering, cautionary, humorous, and pathetic."

F05. Pickney, Darryl. "In Sorrow's Kitchen." *New York Review of Books* 25, 20(December 21, 1978): 55-57. Favorable review of Hemenway's *Zora Neale Hurston: A Literary Biography*, a book he feels is needed to understand Hurston's development as a folklorist and writer of fiction.

Holloway, Karla. *The Character of the Word: The Texts of Zora Neale Hurston*. New York: Greenwood Press, 1987.

F06.   Deck, Alice. *Choice* 25 (September 1987): 124. Says Holloway's is a "fascinating study of the shifting language of the narrators" in each of Hurston's novels. Thinks she adequately supports all of her theories.

F07.   Haskins, Jim. *Florida Historical Quarterly* 67 (October 1988): 207-208.   Says the book is "elegantly written" and welcomes Holloway's complex linguistic analysis of Hurston's works--primarily her four novels.

F08.   McDowell, Deborah E. *Signs: Journal of Women in Culture and Society* 14 (Summer 1989): 948-452. A somewhat unfavorable review, says the blend of "biographical detail with textual analysis" is sometimes "lumpy." Some arguments are vague, and some approaches are "unevenly employed and not always clearly and sufficiently elaborated."

F09. Pondrom, Cyrena N. *American Literature* 60 (May 1988): 306. Mixed review believes that this text should be read for "useful insights into Hurston's texts...not for any sustained analysis or theoretical claims." Agrees that Holloway is justified in treating Hurston as a twentieth-century literary giant, and feels Holloway's study contributes to Hurston receiving a fuller understanding.

F10. Wall, Cheryl A. "Black Women Writers: Journeying Along Mother Lines." *Callaloo* 12, 2 (Spring 1989): 419-422. Comparative review examines Holloway's *The Character of the Word: The Texts of Zora Neale Hurston* and *Specifying: Black Women Writing the American Experience* by Susan Willis which discusses Hurston as the "mother" from whom contemporary African American female writers have descended. Says Willis' is a broad, bolder study, but some arguments in her chapter on Hurston are "problematic." Believes Holloway's linguistic training gives her tools with which to examine Hurston's complex language.

Bloom, Harold, ed. *Modern Critical Interpretations: Zora Neale Hurston's "Their Eyes Were Watching God."* New York: Chelsea House, 1987.

F11. Boesenberg, Eva. *Black American Literature Forum* 23, 4 (Winter 1989): 799-807. This review article examines two books in Bloom's Chelsea House series: *Modern Critical Views: Zora Neale Hurston* and *Modern Critical Interpretations: Zora Neale Hurston's Their Eyes Were Watching God.* The former includes essays by Hurston contemporaries such as Hurst, Hughes, Ford as well as recent sketches by Alice Walker and Mary Helen Washington.   Feels this "jigsaw puzzle" collection is unfinished because it omits any mention to Richard Wright. Claims the latter volume contains articles "notable for their sophisticated, substantial, and highly original scholarship."

Awkward, Michael. *New Essays on "Their Eyes Were Watching God."* Cambridge: Cambridge University Press, 1990.

F12. Madsen, Deborah L. *Journal of American Studies* 27, 3 (December 1993): 426-428. Review summarizes the essays included in Awkward's collection written by Hurston scholars, but provides no critical comment or recommendation.

F13. Kubitschek, Missy Dehn. "Re-Viewing *Their Eyes.*" *African American Review* 28, 2 (Summer 1994): 305-309. This lengthy, comparative review speaks favorably of Awkward's book, but objects to the recycled essays found in Harold Bloom's *Modern Critical Interpretations: Zora Neale Hurston's Their Eyes Were Watching God.* From Awkward's "exemplary introduction," to the diverse new essays included, Kubitschek feels *New Essays* offers something for both the "seasoned professional" and undergraduate readers. Comments upon several of the articles in the collection.

F14. Werner, Craig. *Choice* 29, 4 (December 1991): 594. Thinks this collection by established scholars of African American and women's literature is important to the reputation of Hurston. Notes Awkward's introductory essay and McKay's look at the "complex public position of black women writers."

Glassman, Steve and Kathryn Lee Seidel, eds. *Zora in Florida.* **Orlando: University of Central Florida Press, 1991.**

F15. Hunt, Charlotte D. *Florida Historical Quarterly* 70 (April 1992): 498-500. Says the essays in this book about Hurston's Florida roots will provide the reader with "insights that help explain some of the supposed contradictions" associated with her. Says the collection is "entertaining and substantive" and covers a good mix of topics.

F16. Hewett, Nancy A. *Journal of Southern History* 59, 1 (February 1993): 157-158. Thinks this book moves readers beyond the current fascination with *Their Eyes Were Watching God* to a look at some of Hurston's short stories, plays and nonfiction. Feels a "more forceful introduction" would have helped "guide readers through this somewhat eclectic collection."

F17. Isaacs, D. S. *Choice* 29, 3 (November 1991): 450. Thinks the collection is unique and readable with an "accessible style" which enables readers to get a good sense of the complexity in the simple stories found in Hurston's fiction and nonfiction.

Nathiri, N. Y. *Zora! Zora Neale Hurston: A Woman and Her* *Community.* **Orlando: Sentinel Communications, 1991.**

F18. Hirsch, Diana C. *School Library Journal* 37, 8 (August 1991): 211. Classes book as and "adult book for young readers," and says it is not a traditional biography but does contain a wealth of information including pictures. Thinks the Alice Walker essay and commentary from others "flesh out the now-celebrated writer's life."

F19. Johnson, George T. *Antioch Review* 49, 3 (Summer 1991): 465. A "lukewarm" review says the author wove her family's story of how they discovered Hurston into this book. Feels the volume is "attractive enough for popular consumption," but not for the serious Hurston scholar.

F20. Mitchell, Veronica. *Library Journal* 116 (March 15, 1991): 90. Favorable review believes author has brought together Hurston's friends and relatives for a better look at her life. Thinks the book is an "excellent companion" piece for Hurston's autobiography.

F21. Seaman, Diane. *Booklist* 87, 12 (February 15, 1991): 1173. Calls Nathiri's book a "fresh and informative volume" and a "gracious tribute" to Hurston, the wandering minstrel. John Hick's concise biography conveys Hurston's personality and creativity.

Brantley, Will. *Feminine Sense in Southern Memoir: Smith, Glasgow, Welty, Hellman, Porter, and Hurston.* Jackson: University of Mississippi Press, 1993.

F22. Robinson, Jo Ann O. *Journal of Southern History* 60, 3 (August 1994): 612-613. Feels the book would "benefit from more rigorous editing to streamline tedious rehearsals of scholarly debates." Thinks historians will benefit from the evaluation of the "evasions, omissions, and flat-out lies that occur in autobiography." One chapter is devoted to Hurston, and Robinson feels best thing about this book is the women speaking for themselves.

F23. Tischler, N. *Choice* 31, 2 (October 1993): 284-285. Calls the book an excellent and careful study which examines the threads that tie these southern women together. Feels Brantley has thoughtfully used "intertextual studies" and done much for a "reconsideration of the southern canon."

Lowe, John. *Jump at the Sun: Zora Neale Hurston's Cosmic Comedy.* Urbana: University of Illinois Press, 1994.

F24. Brantley, Will. *Contemporary Literature* 37, 1 (Spring 1996): 141-144. Reviews John Lowe's *Jump at the Sun*. Calls book the first "sustained examination...of Hurston's art--her humor, in all its complexity." Lauds Lowe for his inclusion of non-fiction pieces and for his "close and very detailed readings."

F25. Marrengane, Ntombi. *Black Scholar* 25, 2 (Spring 1995): 71. Brief paragraph review says book looks at Hurston's humor "as a vehicle for subversive observations on intolerable conditions."

F26. Nash, William R. "Illuminating Zora Neale Hurston's Laughter." *Southern Literary Journal* 28, 2 (Spring 1996): 124-127. Favorable review says the Lowe's book fills the gap dealing with Hurston's "creative use of comic elements in her novels and stories." Says the chapter "Laughin' Up a World: *Their Eyes Were Watching God* and the (Wo)Man of Words" is the "strongest section" of the book.

F27. Pondrom, Cyrena N. "The Americas - *Jump at the Sun: Zora Neale Hurston's Cosmic Comedy* by John Lowe." *Modern Fiction Studies* 42, 1 (Spring 1966): 149-152. Favorable review calls work a "welcome addition" to the body of literary criticism on Hurston. Feels Lowe's "wide reading and well-placed allusions" provide a new look at Hurston. Finds problematic, however, his "repeated efforts" to link some of his analysis to Hurston humor, but feels book deserves attention.

F28. Seidel, Kathryn. *Mississippi Quarterly* 49, 1 (Winter 1995): 160-161. Favorable review of Lowe's *Jump at the Sun*. Calls Lowe's work an "impressive study" and praises his insightful analyses of several of her works, especially *Their Eyes Were Watching God*. Thinks book is a "significant contribution to this second wave of Hurston scholarship."

Other Reviews

F29. Kidd, Stuart. *Journal of American Studies* 29 (December 1995): 465-466. Favorable review of Michael E. Staub's *Voices of Persuasion: Politics of Representation in 1930s America*--a work in which Hurston and James Agee are primary subjects.

F30. McCarthy, B. E. *Choice* 33, 9 (May 1996): 1481. Thinks *Every Tub Must Sit on Its Own Bottom: The Philosophy and Politics of Zora Neale*

Hurston, by Deborah Plant, "advances understanding of Hurston's intellectual identity." Feels book is widely researched and author writes with authority and intensity as she examines Hurston's philosophies, folklore and "sermon-based language." Also says by the end of Plant's study readers are reconciled to Hurston's conservative politics and its use within the "context of her contradictions."

F31.   Willis, Miriam DeCosta. *Sage* 4, 1 (Spring 1987): 76-77. Reviews the new periodical *The Zora Neale Hurston Forum*, the official publication of the Zora Neale Hurston Society housed at Morgan State University and headed by Ruthe T. Sheffey.

Reviews of Books about Hurston Written for Children

Miller, William. *Zora Neale Hurston and the Chinaberry Tree.* **Lee & Low, 1996.**

F32.   Emery, Francenia L.   *MultiCultural Review* 4 (March 1995): 79. Believes book is a wonderful story for children and is beautifully illustrated.

F33.   *Horn Book* 71 (January-February 1995): 69.   Thinks the "gentle, realistic watercolors perfectly match the story's various moods." Feels readers will welcome this book about a young girl who was taught she could do anything.

F34.   Lukehart, Wendy.   *School Library Journal* 40 (December 1994): 100.   Says Miller "not entirely successful in his treatment" of Hurston's challenging life.   Feels the narrative is too brief, and too much is left unsaid.

McKissack, Patricia. *Zora Neale Hurston*: **Writer and Storyteller. Springfield, NJ: Enslow Publishers, 1992.**

F35.   Keenan, Joan S.   *Childhood Education* 69, 1 (Fall 1992): 48. Review of children's book, *Zora Neale Hurston: Writer and Storyteller* by Patricia McKissack and *Jump at De Sun: The Story of Zora Neale Hurston* by A. P. Porter.   Says each book provides a "useful introduction to the unconventional life" of Hurston. McKissack's book is brief, and Porter's is more detailed with photographs, a bibliography and an index.

Porter, A.P. *Jump at De Sun: The Story of Zora Neale Hurston.* **Minneapolis: Caroirhoda Books, 1992.**

F36. Del Negro, Janice. *Booklist* 89 (December 15, 1992): 724. Says the book is easy to read and written in a "chatty, informal style" that is more chronology of Hurston's life than a narrative. Thinks more quotes from Hurston would have made it a better book.

F37. Laing, E. K. *Christian Science Monitor* (February 5, 1993): 11. Biography is an "honest and lovingly told appraisal of an often misunderstood woman." It is a wonderful introduction to Hurston's life and literary career.

F38. Sutton, Roger. *Bulletin of the Center for Children's Books* 46 (October 1992): 51. Says Porter uses a "down-home storytelling style" to tell his story of his "flamboyant subject." The book captures Hurston with all her complications and contradictions, and though she may be hard to pin down, believes Porter does a good job for the young reader.

F39. Welton, Ann. *School Library Journal* 39 (January 1993): 119. Favorable review believes the narrative is well-written and the black and white photographs appropriate. Says this is probably the most objective book about Hurston for young readers. Appreciates the "thorough" index and the bibliography.

Yannuzzi, Della A. *Zora Neale Hurston: A Storyteller's Life.* **Springfield, NJ: Enslow Publishers, 1996.**

F40. Bahrenburg, Dorothy. *Book Report* 15, 2 (September 1996): 46. Says book is a well written account of Hurston who "combined her knowledge of anthropology with her writing craft."

F41. *Publisher's Weekly* 238, 39 (August 30, 1991): 86. Calls work an "excellent introduction" to Hurston and her writings, and finds David Adams' illustrations "arresting."

F42. Rochman, Hazel. *Booklist* 88 (October 15, 1991): 435. Favorable review says Yates's account of Hurston's life is a "highly readable, sometimes lyrical account that conveys Hurston's remarkable spirit." Objects to lack of documentation and sources so children can follow up on the "smoothly integrated" quotes from Hurston herself. Appreciates the "dramatic linocut illustrations" done by David Adams, and feels the book will make you want to read more of the subject's works.

F43. Welton, Ann. *School Library Journal* 37 (October 1991): 132. Says Yates treatment of Hurston's life is "deceptively sunny" and that readers "will not empathize with Hurston's struggle." Believes some Hurston excerpts work well, but others do not, and the illustrations add little to the story.

Calvert, Roz. *Zora Neale Hurston, Storyteller of the South*. New York: Chelsea Juniors, 1993.

F44. Rochman, Hazel. *Booklist* 89 (May 1, 1993): 1585. Favorable review of this biography for middle school-aged children. Says Calvert tells Hurston's story well and celebrates her achievements as she frankly relates her struggles.

F45. Welton, Ann. *School Library Journal* 39 (June 1993): 114. This is a comparative review between Calvert's children's biography and that of A. P. Porter. Lukewarm describes her feeling toward Calvert's *Zora Neale Hurston, Storyteller of the South*, in which she feels the author tries to "gild a lily" that does not need it. Recommends Porter's *Jump at de Sun* as being more inclusive and livelier.

Lyons, Mary E. *Sorrow's Kitchen: The Life and Folklore of Zora Neale Hurston*. New York: Scribner's, 1990.

F46. Hill-Lubin, Mildred A. *Florida Historical Quarterly* 70 (January 1992): 391-392. Review of *Sorrow's Kitchen* by Mary E. Lyons. Says the "selections, organization, and storytelling" provide "an excellent overview of Hurston's incredible life." Appreciates her generous use of excerpts from Hurston's works, and feels Lyons is knowledgeable and up-to-date on Hurston scholarship. Notes that Lyons was awarded the Charlton W.

Tebau Book Award for "best book for young readers on a Florida personality" in 1991 by the Florida Historical Society for this book.

F47.   Sutton, Roger. *Bulletin of the Center for Children's Books* 44 (January 1991): 124. Mixed review believes that although the book is "occasionally disorganized," it does a "spirited job of conveying the subject's passions and accomplishments." Thinks Lyons selected well the excerpts from Hurston's works.

F48.   Tavegie, Sherry. *Reading Teacher* 45, 3 (November 1991): 220. Says Hurston wrote stories and articles that told of life during the "migration of thousands of Blacks from the American South to northern cities."

F49.   Watson, Elizabeth S. *Horn Book* 67 (March-April 1991): 216. Thinks author has written a "fascinating, enlightening, stimulating and satisfying" work which details the story of Hurston's life.   Says book liberally "sprinkled with photographs" and contains excerpts from Hurston's books.

F50.   Welton, Ann. *School Library Journal* 37 (January 1991): 119. Review of *Sorrow's Kitchen* by Mary E. Lyons. Favorable review, believes the inclusion of black and white photographs as well as excerpts from Hurston's writings add to this children's book.

Bibliographies and Guides to Works about Zora Neale Hurston

"He had a bow-down command in his face, and every step he took made the thing more tangible."

Their Eyes Were Watching God

G01.   Arata, Esther Spring. *Black American Playwrights, 1800 to the Present, A Bibliography*. Metuchen, NJ: Scarecrow Press, 1976. This works lists Hurston's plays as well as references where criticisms may be found.

G02.   Arata, Esther Spring, ed. *More Black American Playwrights: A Bibliography*. Metuchen, NJ: Scarecrow Press, 1978: 122. Lists *Mule Bone* with Langston Hughes and *Polk County* with Dorothy Waring as plays written by Hurston. Also lists "Sermon in the Valley" written in 1931. References to criticisms of Hurston and her individual works also listed.

G03.   Bruccoli, Matthew I. and Judith S. Baughman, eds. *Modern African American Writers*. New York: Facts on File, 1994: 32-38. Provides a listing of Hurston's books, then a selective list of bibliography, biography, and critical studies in books, essays, and articles about Hurston's writings.

G04.   Fairbanks, Carol.   *Black American Fiction: A Bibliography.*
Metuchen, NJ: Scarecrow Press, 1978. A bibliography of Hurston's work
and selected criticism is included.

G05.   Fairbanks, Carol.   *More Women in Literature: Criticism of the
Seventies.* Metuchen, NJ: Scarecrow Press, 1979: 178-179. Provides a
bibliography of critical materials written about Hurston during the 1970s.

G06.   French, William P., Michel J. Fabre, and Amritjit Singh, eds. *Afro-
American Poetry and Drama, 1760-1975: A Guide to Information Sources.*
Detroit: Gale Research, 1979: 320.   Lists Hurston's published and
unpublished plays; *Dust Tracks on a Road* under "biography and criticism."

G07.   Glikin,   Ronda.   *Black   American   Women   in   Literature: A
Bibliography, 1976-1987.* Jefferson, N C : McFarland & Company, 1989:
78-82. Entry lists Hurston's works by genre and provides a bibliography
of "textual criticism" of works by her.

G08.   Hatch, James V. and Omanii Abdullah, eds. *Black Playwrights,
1823-1977: An Annotated Bibliography of Plays.* New York: Bowker,
1977: 123. Lists *Mule Bone* as written by Hurston and Hughes in 1930,
Fast and Furious with Forbes Randolph in 1931 ("Moms" Mabley and Etta
Moten were cast members), and *Polk County* with Waring in 1944.

G09.   Hinding, Andrea and Ames Sheldon Bower, eds. *Women's History
Sources: A Guide to Archives and Manuscript Collections in the United
States.* New York: Bower, 1979: 157.   The entry provides the pages
where more information on collections where Hurston is included may be
found.

G10.   Holt, Elvin. "Zora Neale Hurston." In *Fifty Southern Writers After
1900: A Bio-Bibliographical Sourcebook.* Eds. Joseph M. Flora and Robert
Bain. Westport, CT: Greenwood Press, 1987:259-269. Holt provides
several pages of biographical information on Hurston's life and career,
discusses the major themes of her works, and gives a "survey of criticism"-
-including noted Hurston scholars Darwin Turner, Robert E. Hemenway,
Ruthe T. Sheffey, and Daryl C. Dance. The section, "Studies of Zora Neale
Hurston," includes journal articles and books about Hurston.

G11.   Jordan, Casper LeRoy, compl. *A Bibliographical Guide to African-
American Women Writers.* Westport, CT: Greenwood Press, 1993: 133-

140. Lists Hurston's articles, short stories, book-length works, and three pages of secondary sources which include journal articles and books written about Hurston.

G12. Lowe, John. "Zora Neale Hurston." *American Playwrights, 1880-1945: A Research and Production Sourcebook*. Ed. William W. Demastes. Westport, CT: Greenwood Press, 1995: 206-213. Provides background information on Hurston then discusses her theatrical reception and provides a summary and critical comments about each play. Says very little has been written on Hurston the dramatist and that her concentration on a "group culture" in her plays meant she sacrificed the strongly developed individual plots needed for the American stage.

G13. Margolis, Edward and David Bakish. *African-American Fiction, 1853-1976: A Guide to Information Sources*. Detroit: Gale, 1979: 62-63. Provides a list of critical studies of Hurston's works.

G14. Reilly, John M. In *Reference Guide to American Literature*. Ed. D. L. Kirkpatrick. Chicago: St. James, 1987. This entry cites her marriages, divorces, awards, various jobs then lists her publications. A short list of critical studies also included. Several other paragraphs briefly discuss *Mules and Men, Moses, Man of the Mountain*, and *Their Eyes Were Watching God*.

G15. Rush, Theressa Gunnels, Carol Fairbanks Myers, and Esther Spring Arata. *Black American Writers Past and Present: A Biographical and Bibliographical Dictionary*. Metuchen, NJ: Scarecrow Press, 1975: 405-409. Provides the standard biographical information, including mention of her folklore troupe and writing for Paramount Studios. A good sampling bibliographical references in journals and books is included. Interesting "Interjections" end the entry.

G16. Schwartz, Narda Lacey. *Articles on Women Writers: A Bibliography*. Santa Barbara, CA: ABC-CLIO, 1977: 123-125. Article on Hurston cites general works written about her and articles about individual Hurston titles.

G17. Southgate, Robert L. "*Their Eyes Were Watching God*." In *Black Plots & Black Characters: A Handbook for Afro-American Literature*. Syracuse: Gaylord Professional Publications, 1979: 163-165. Lists the important characters in the novel, brief critical comments, and a straightforward summary of the important action.

G18.   Spradling, Mary Mace, ed. *In Black and White: A Guide to Magazine Articles* 3rd ed. Detroit: Gale, 1985: 471. Notes that Hurston was "Mrs. Herbert A. Sheen" and a scholar, teacher and "raconteur." Provides an alphabetical list of works *about* Hurston, including Langston Hughes' *Big Sea*.

G19.   Spradling, Mary Mace, ed. *In Black and White: A Guide to Magazine Articles, Supplement.* 3rd ed. Detroit: Gale, 1985: 197. The entry cites same nine reference as earlier editions and states that Hurston was a "Full fledged member of the Harlem Renaissance." (p. 197).

G20.   Spradling, Mary Mace, ed. *In Black and White: Afro-Americans in Print: A Guide to Africans and Americans Who Have Made Contributions to the United States of America.* 2nd ed. Kalamazoo: Kalamazoo Public Library, 1976: 199. Lists nine references to works where information about Hurston is included and also includes several magazine and newspaper references

G21.   Werner, Craig. *Black American Women Novelists: An Annotated Bibliography.* Pasadena: Salem Press, 1989. 119-150. Werner provides a fairly comprehensive "selective" bibliography of the scholarship on Hurston. Entry divided into *biography*, *commentary*, and reviews and critical works of *selected titles*.

G22.   Whitlow, Roger. *Black American Literature: A Critical History.* Chicago: Nelson-Hall, 1973: 3-5, 103-106. A brief biography is given as well as critical comments about several of Hurston's works. Thinks *Their Eyes Were Watching God* contains the "finest dialect" of any American work.

G23.   Williams, Ora. *American Black Women in the Arts and Social Sciences: A Bibliographic Survey.* Metuchen, NJ: Scarecrow Press, 1978:158-160. Briefly lists books, articles, stories, and plays written by Hurston as well as other unpublished works--which include "Book of Harlem" and "The Emperor Effaces Himself in Harlem Language."

H

Biographical Information about Zora Neale Hurston

"The sunlight rose higher, climbed the rail and came on board."

Seraph on the Suwanee

The following sources provide biographical and bio/critical information on the life and works of Zora Neale Hurston. Some entries are brief, while others provide overviews of Hurston's life as well as fairly extensive critical assessments and evaluations of her published materials. Unless otherwise noted, all entries are entitled "Zora Neale Hurston."

H01. *Academic American Encyclopedia*. Danbury, CT: Grolier, 1996: 319. Brief paragraph says Hurston is "best known for her sympathetic portrayals of black life." Bibliography included.

H02. Andrews, William L. In *World Book Encyclopedia*. Chicago: World Book, 1996: 454. Entry provides a one sentence summary of Hurston's works and refers readers to Hemenway's *Literary Biography* and Lyons' *Sorrow's Kitchen*. Cites her date of birth as 1891.

H03. Ashby, R. and Deborah Gore Ohrn, eds. *Herstory: Women Who Changed the World*. New York: Viking, 1995: 220-222. Highlights

Hurston's life and says her early love of folktakes and storytelling stayed with her and charted the path to her career as a writer.

H04.   Barksdale, Richard and Keneth Kinnamon. *Black Writers of America: A Comprehensive Anthology*. New York: Macmillan, 1972: 611-613. Provides a biography of Hurston and notes that as a folklorist, her major contribution was *Mules and Men*. Lists book and journal references where more biographical information may be found.

H05.   Bastin, Wade and Richard N. Runes. *Dictionary of Black Culture*. New York: Philosophical Library, 1973: 221. A one-paragraph sketch states Hurston was the "first black writer since Charles Chesnutt to use folkloric materials significantly in fiction."

H06.   Bell, Bernard W. In *The Reader's Companion to American History*. Eds. Eric Foner and John A. Garraty. Boston: Houghton-Mifflin, 1991: 528-529. Bell calls Hurston "outspoken" and summaries each of her major works. He also provides critical comments on *Their Eyes Were Watching God* and notes that it is Hurston's "most critically acclaimed book" while *Dust Tracks on a Road* is her most "commercially successful" one.

H07.   *Benet's Reader's Encyclopedia*. New York: Harper & Row, 1987: 470. This one paragraph entry mentions four of Hurston's works and provides a one-phrase summary of each.

H08.   Bily, Cynthia A. In *Cyclopedia of World Authors*. Vol. II. Ed. Frank N. Magill. Pasadena: Salem Press, 1989: 745-746. The two paragraph entry briefly summarizes each of Hurston's major works and says she was a "controversial figure all her professional life." Notes her arrest on a morals charge. Bibliographical references included.

H09.   Blain, Virginia. *The Feminist Companion to Literature in English*. New Haven: Yale University Press, 1990: 554-555. Bio-bibliographical article traces Hurston's life, lists her major works as well as works about her life and other works. Also notes several articles she wrote.

H10. Block, Maxine, ed. *Current Biography*. Bronx: H.W. Wilson, 1941: 402-404. Schrieber's pencil portrait of Hurston accompanies this article which outlines her life and discusses her work. Block writes, "In 1942, although still a young woman, Miss Hurston can look back upon a rich and full life." Articles notes that Hurston is flamboyant, "wears exotic clothing and affects bizarre jewelry." References accompany the entry.

H11. Brignano, Russell C. *Black Americans in Autobiography: An Annotated Bibliography of Autobiographies and Autobiographical Books Written Since the Civil War*. Durham, NC: Duke University Press, 1984:10-11. Lists *Dust Tracks on a Road*, and notes that Hurston "exuberantly depicts her youth in Eatonville, Florida." Her education and career are presented. This revised and expanded edition says, *Tell him Horse* [*sic*] is a "highly personal account of an anthropology field trip to Jamaica and Haiti in the 1930s." The 1973 edition lists an entry for Hurston on page 28.

H12. Buck, Claire. *The Bloomsbury Guide to Women's Literature*. New York: Prentice Hall, 1992: 653. A smiling Hurston appears with this five paragraph entry, and her major works are summarized. Article says she died in 1959.

H13. Burke, William and Will D. Howe. *American Authors and Books, 1640 to the Present Day*. New York: Crown Publishers, 1972: 319. A brief paragraph indicates Hurston was a drama professor at "North Carolina College for Negroes."

H14. Clark, Judith Freeman. *Almanac of American Women in the Twentieth Century*. New York: Prentice Hall, 1987:67. Hurston included in chapter entitled "Working Against the Odds: 1931-1940." Brief biographical sketch provided.

H15. Cullen-DuPoint, Kathryn. *The Encyclopedia of Women's History in America*. New York: Facts on File, 1996: 100-101. This seven paragraph biographical sketch of Hurston's life and career notes that a "recently discovered birth certificate has resolved long-standing confusion as to Hurston's date of birth." Cites references for further information

H16. Dance, Daryl C. In *American Women Writers: Bibliographical Essays*. Eds. Maurice Duke, Jackson R. Bryer, and M. Thomas Inge. Westport, CT: Greenwood Press, 1983: 321-351. Hurston is the only "woman of color" included in this work which mainly deals with southern novelists. Her works are categorized by "full-length, short stories, essays and other writings, manuscripts and letters, and biography." Dance individually discusses each of Hurston's primary works, and a bibliography in included.

H17. Deck, Alice A. In *Notable Black American Women*. Vol 1. Ed. Jessie Carney Smith. Detroit: Gale Research, 1992: 543-548. Hurston's photograph appears on the cover of this book, and Deck's article is also accompanied by the same photograph. Hurston's life is summarized briefly and each of her major works is discussed and critiqued. A bibliography is appended, and collections where Hurston papers are housed is provided.

H18. Draper, James P., Ed. *Black Literature Criticism: Excerpts From Criticism of the Most Significant Works of Black Authors Over the Pat 200 Years*. Detroit: Gale Research, 1992: 1068-1089. A photograph accompanies the biography of Hurston, and her principal works are listed with dates of publication. Excerpts from previously printed critical essays written by noted Hurston scholars and critics are provided, including excerpts from the work of Robert Bone, Cheryl Wall, Michele Wallace, and Sherley Anne Williams. Also included are a photograph and a list of annotated readings.

H19. *Encyclopedia Britannica*. Chicago: Encyclopedia Britannica, 1994: 168. The standard encyclopedia entry is three paragraphs long and notes that Hurston collaborated with Langston Hughes on one play and that *Their Eyes Were Watching God* was "widely acclaimed and highly controversial."

H20. *Encyclopedia Americana*. Danbury, CT: Grolier, 1994: 615. The four paragraph entry cites her birth date as "1901(?)" and states that Hurston "captured the rich idiom of her native rural South."

H21. Estell, Kenneth, ed. *Reference Library of Black America*. Vol. 3. Detroit: Gale Research, 1994: 834-835. Photograph included with three-paragraph entry that notes Hurston "died in obscurity and poverty."

H22. Felder, Deborah G. *The 100 Most Influential Women of All Time: A Ranking Bast and Present*. New York: Carol Publishing Group, 1996:141-143. A photograph accompanies the Hurston entry, and 1901 is given as her date of birth. Says that today Hurston is "acknowledged as one of the most important black writers of the twentieth century."

H23. Foster, M. Marie Booth. *Southern Black Creative Writers, 1829-1953*. Westport, CT: Greenwood Press, 1988: 40. Brief entry lists Hurston's works with dates, her educational background, and honors.

H24. Gates, Henry Louis, Jr. and Nellie Y. McKay, eds. *The Norton Anthology of African American Literature*. New York: W.W. Norton, 1997. "Faith has't got no eyes" (part of John Pearson's sermon from Jonah's Gourd Vine). In another section, "Sweat" is printed along with three pages of biographical information.

H25. Glazier, Steven D. In *American Folklore: An Encyclopedia*. Ed. Jan Harold Brunvand. New York: Garland, 1996: 381-382. This new volume provides a photograph of Hurston and states her birth date as 1891. Of her autobiography, writes that she "masterfully represents herself within the context of African American folk traditions."

H26. Gombar, Christina. *Great Women Writers, 1900-1950*. New York: Facts on File, 1996. The book is part of the "American Profiles Series." Hurston discussed in article entitled "Zora Neale Hurston: Genius of the South."

H27. Hart, James D. *The Oxford Companion to American Literature*. 6th ed. New York: Oxford University Press, 1995:310. This updated entry provides more detail about *Their Eyes Were Watching God*, which it calls Hurston's masterpiece." Says the novel "celebrates the self-liberation of Janie."

H28. Hedgepeth, Chester. *Twentieth-Century African-American Writers and Artists*. Chicago: American Library Association, 1991: 150-151. A brief biographical sketch is given as well as brief critical commentary of three works. No comment is provided for *Their Eyes Were Watching God*. "Works By" and several "Works About" Hurston are appended.

H29. Herzberg, Max J. *The Reader's Encyclopedia of American Literature*. New York: Crowell, 1962: 504. This entry notes that Hurston's tales were "told naturally and skillfully, with accurate reproduction of Negro dialect and rhythm."

H30. Holloway, Carla F. C. In *Oxford Companion to Women's Writing in the United States*. Eds. Cathy N. Davis and Linda Wagner-Martin. New

York: Oxford University Press, 1995: 408-410. Notes Hurston wrote over
100 manuscripts--novels, plays, short stories, essays, articles, interviews,
and reviews. Says "...we know of these works largely because of the
popularity and acclaim that have come to her 1937 novel, *Their Eyes Were
Watching God.*" Bibliographical references are included with the
biography, summaries and critical commentary on each primary work.

H31. Holt, Elvin.   In *Fifty Southern Writers After 1900: A Bio-
Bibliographical Sourcebook.* Eds. Joseph M. Flora and Robert Bain. New
York: Greenwood Press, 1987:259-269. Holt provides several pages of
biographical information on Hurston's life and career, discusses the major
themes of her works, and gives a "survey of criticism"--including noted
Hurston scholars Darwin Turner, Robert E. Hemenway, Ruthe T. Sheffey,
and Daryl C. Dance. The section, "Studies of Zora Neale Hurston,"
includes journal articles and books about Hurston.

H32. Howard, Lillie P.   In *Dictionary of Literary Biography: Afro-
American Writers from the Harlem Renaissance to 1940.* Vol. 51. Ed.
Trudier Harris. Detroit: Bruccoli Clark Layman, 1987: 133-145. *DLB*'s
usual excellent bio-critical review of all genres of works by Hurston was
written by a Hurston scholar and includes a photograph, awards and honors,
bibliographical references, and Hurston's major works. Several periodical
publications also included. Howard provides critical comments and notes,
and states that interest in Hurston had "diminished long before her death."
She concludes, "Today, the Hurston renaissance is in full swing."

H33. Ireland, Norma Olin. *Index to Women of the World From Ancient to
Modern Times: A Supplement.* Metuchen, NJ: Scarecrow Press, 1988:347.
Index lists Hurston as an American anthropologist, folklorist, novelist and
teacher and refers readers to works by critics' last names and page numbers.

H34. Kali, Herman. *Women in Particular: An Index to American Women.*
Phoenix: Oryx Press, 1984: 3, 250. Hurston listed under two separate
headings--anthropology and literature. The duplicate entries note she was
an author, novelist, folklorist, cultural anthropologist, and cite additional
sources where more information may be obtained on Hurston.

H35.   Kellner, Bruce, ed.   *The Harlem Renaissance: A Historical
Dictionary for the Era.* Westport, CT: Greenwood Press, 1984: 1890-181.
Discusses Hurston's life and career; summarizes her primary works;

comments briefly on her relationship with Hughes, Thurman, Hurst, and Boas, and calls *Dust Tracks on a Road* a "not entirely reliable autobiography."

H36. Kunitz, Stanley, ed. *Twentieth Century Authors.* New York: H.W. Wilson, 1955: 472. A brief paragraph refers reader to the 1942 edition and lists works about Hurston.

H37. Kunitz, Stanley, ed. *Twentieth Century Authors.* First Supplement. New York: Wilson, 1955:472. Refers readers to the 1942 text for an autobiographical sketch and list of earlier works. Inaccurately cites *Seraph on the Suwanee* as *"Search on the Sewanee."* Lists several works "about" Hurston.

H38. Kunitz, Stanley, ed. *Twentieth Century Authors: A Biographical Dictionary of Modern Literature.* New York: H.W. Wilson, 1942: 695. Hurston wrote her own entry. She said she had "never been able to achieve race prejudice." "I just see people." Hurston also notes, "I made up my mind to write about my people as they are, and not to use the traditional lay figures." The article lists her favorite authors, principal works, and her materials "about" her.

H39. Locher, Frances Carol, ed. *Contemporary Authors. Vol 85-88.* Detroit: Gale Research, 1980: 268-269. The standard *CA* entry provides information on Hurston's personal life, career, and lists the titles and dates of her major works. Bibliographical and critical references included.

H40. Low, W. Augustus, ed. *Encyclopedia of Black America.* New York: McGraw-Hill, 1981: 457. Lists Hurston's birthday at 1907 and notes that she wrote radio scripts for a Cincinnati station and three articles in the *Encyclopedia Americana.*

H41. Magill, Frank N., ed. *Magill's Survey of American Literature.* North Bellmore, NY: Marshall Cavendish, 1991. A portrait is included with the biography of Hurston.

H42. Magill, Frank N., ed. *Encyclopedia of World Biography: 20th Century Supplement.* Vol. 14. Palatine, IL: Jack Heraty & Associates, 1987-1988: 203-204. Says the feminist movement of the 1970s focused attention on *Their Eyes Were Watching God* and that it is the "central text in the canon of literature about black women specifically and women writers generally." Photograph of an older, heavier Hurston included.

H43. Mapp, Edward. *Directory of Blacks in the Performing Arts.* Metuchen, NJ: Scarecrow Press, 1990: 249. Labels Hurston a playwright and lists her dramatic works and autobiography. Says she was a "technical advisor" at Paramount from 1941-42.

H44. Matuz, Roger, ed. *Contemporary Literary Criticism.* Vol. 61. Detroit: Gale Research, 1990: 235-276. The *CLC* entries on Hurston have grown from three pages in 1977 to more than 40 pages in 1990--testimony to the interest her life and works have generated over the last twenty years. This entry has excerpts from the works of Sterling Brown, Larry Neal, Michael Cooke, and Elizabeth Meese, to name a few.

H45. McKay, Nellie Y. In *Encyclopedia of African-American Culture and History.* Eds. Jack Salzman, David Lionel Smith, and Cornel West. New York: Macmillan Library Reference, 1996: 1332-1334. McKay's three page article provides biographical information, summaries of Hurston's major works, and critical comments. McKay also notes that Hurston received "mixed" reviews of her books during her own life time. She also states that Hurston's "rediscovery" has led to critical acclaim as the "essential forerunner of black women writers who came after her." A photograph accompanies the article, and a brief list of reference is included.

H46. *Merriam-Webster's Encyclopedia of Literature.* Springfield, MA: Merriam-Webster, 1995: 571. A two paragraph summary of Hurston's life is given. *Jonah's Gourd Vine, Their Eyes Were Watching God, Dust Tracks on a Road,* and *I Love Myself When I'm Laughing* are the only works listed in this source.

H47. Mendelson, Phillis Carmel and Dedria Bryfonski, eds. *Contemporary Literary Criticism.* Vol. 7. Detroit: Gale Research, 1977: 170-172. This is the standard *CLC* entry--providing biographical information and excerpts from works by Hurston scholars such as Robert Hemenway. A photograph is included.

H48. Oslen, Kirstin. *Chronology of Women's History.* Westport, CT: Greenwood Press, 1994: 751. Hurston mentioned in the following years: 1934 for *Jonah's Gourd Vine*; 1937 for *Their Eyes Were Watching God*;

1939 for *Moses, Man of the Mountain*; and 1954 for her criticism of the Supreme Court decision.

H49.   Ousby, Ian, ed. *The Cambridge Guide to Literature in English*. Cambridge: Cambridge University Press, 1993: 462-463. Gives Hurston's date of birth as 1903; provides a one sentence summary of major works, and notes that her "popularity and critical reputation have grown since her death."

H50.   Page, James A. *Selected Black American Authors: An Illustrated Bio-Bibliography*. Boston: G.K. Hall, 1977:132. Page lists Hurston's major works, and notes that she contributed short stories and articles to various magazines.   Also listed are honors, awards, memberships. References are cited.

H51.   Page, James A. and Jae Min Roh. *Selected Black American, African, and Caribbean Authors: A Bio-bibliography*. Littleton, CO: Libraries Unlimited, 1985:140. Lists only Hurston's major works and a one-paragraph summary of her life. A head-shot photograph included.

H52.   Parker, Peter. *Reader's Companion to Twentieth-Century Writers*. New York: Oxford University Press, 1996: 355. Six paragraph article says Hurston "was out of fashion for some decades before a revival of interest in the 1970s." States that she influenced Ralph Ellison and Toni Morrison.

H53.   Patterson, Tiffany R.   In *Black Women in America: An Historical Encyclopedia*. Ed. Darlene Clark Hine. Brooklyn: Carlson Pub., 1993: 598-603. This is a fairly comprehensive look at Hurston's life and work. Patterson calls *Dust Tracks on a Road* "a simulated story" of Hurston's life, and examines each of her major works. She also discusses Hurston's views on the 1954 Supreme Court decision to desegregate public schools. The bibliography includes selected works by Hurston and works about Hurston.

H54.   Perkins, Barbara and Philip Leininger, eds.   *Benet's Reader's Encyclopedia of American Literature*. New York: HarperCollins, 1991: 506. This brief entry summarizes Hurston's major works, and states, "Neglected as a writer for years before her death, Hurston is now widely read and celebrated by writers and critics."

H55.   Peterson, Bernard, Jr. *Early Black American Playwrights and Dramatic Writers: A Biographical Dictionary and Catalog of Plays, Films, and Broadcasting Scripts.* Westport, CT: Greenwood Press, 1990: 114-116. Gives Hurston's date of birth as 1890. After the biographical entry, a list of Hurston's "stage works" includes title, type of drama, length of work, date, and a summary of each. Works listed include *Spears, Color Struck, The First One, Fast and Furious, Sermon in the Valley, The Fiery Chariot, Mule Bone*, and *Polk County*.

H56. Pettis, Joyce. In *American Women Writers*. Vol. 2. Ed. Lina Mainiero. New York: Ungar Publishing, 1980: 363-366. Each of Hurston's book-length works are summarized and discussed. Notes that Hurston was the only writer of the Harlem Renaissance who had a "southern background." (p. 363) Says also that the inclusion of "folk elements gives a uniquely southern flavor to character and setting." References to other works are provided.

H57. Ploski, Harry A. ed. *Reference Library of Black America*. Vol. III. New York: Bellwether Publ., 1971: 21. Entry lists her major works and brief biographical information.

H58. Ploski, Harry A. and James Williams, eds. *Reference Library of Black America*. Vol. IV. New York: Afro-American Press, 1990: 1001. This brief entry gives Hurston's date of birth as 1903 and notes that she was a "figure in the Negro Renaissance."

H59. Reagon, Bernice Johnson. In *Dictionary of American Negro Biography*. Eds. Rayford W. Logan and Michael R. Winston. New York: Norton, 1982: 340-341. Reagon provides a brief but comprehensive picture of Hurston, discussing several of her short stories as well as her book-length works. She cites Darwin's Turner's *In a Minor Chord* and Arthur Davis's *From the Dark Tower* as sources of additional information says Hurston was "mystical, impulsive, restless, and driven."

H60. Reilly, John M. *Great Writers of the English Language*. New York: St. Martin's Press, 1979:615-616. Entry lists Hurston's fiction and non-fiction. Reilly notes, "The leading fact about Zora Neale Hurston is her identification with black folklore." He also provides brief summaries of four Hurston works.

H61. Reilly, John M. In *Reference Guide to American Literature*. Ed. D. L. Kirkpatrick. Chicago: St. James, 1987: 302-303. This entry cites her marriages, divorces, awards, various jobs then lists her publications. A short list of critical studies also included. Several other paragraphs briefly discuss *Mules and Men, Moses, Man of the Mountain*, and *Their Eyes Were Watching God.*

H62. Richmond, Joanne S. *Handbook of American Women's History.* Ed. Frances M. Kavenik. New York: Garland, 1990: 274-275. Richmond's three paragraph essay notes that Hurston was a "social and political nonconformist." Discusses Hurston generally as a writer and folklorist; does not mention any works by title.

H63. Roses, Lorraine Elena and Ruth Elizabeth Randolph. *The Harlem Renaissance and Beyond: Literary Biographies of 100 Black Women Writers, 1900-1945.* Boston: G. K. Hall, 1990: 181-192. A photograph of a young Hurston is included, and the editors cite Hurston's birth year as 1891. A selected bibliography lists Hurston's primary works by genre, and each is critically discussed. Notes that in her day, such critics as Sterling Brown, Alain Locke, and Richard Wright "missed the point" and criticized *Their Eyes Were Watching God* for "absence of social content and a lack of militancy." A list of secondary sources is provided.

H64. Rush, Theressa Gunnels, Carol Fairbanks Myers, and Esther Spring Arata, eds. *Black American Writers Past and Present: A Biographical and Bibliographical Dictionary.* Metuchen, NJ: Scarecrow Press, 1975: 405-409. Provides the standard biographical information, including mention of her folklore troupe and writing for Paramount Studios. A good sampling of bibliographical references in journals and books is included. Interesting "Interjections" at end the entry.

H65. Salzman, Jack, ed. *Cambridge Handbook of American Literature.* Cambridge: Cambridge University Press, 1986: 120-121. The one paragraph entry cites Hurston's birth year as 1903 and summaries her life and major works. Says her popularity has grown since her death.

H66. Seymour-Smith, Martin, ed. *Novels and Novelists.* New York: St. Martin's Press, 1980: 161. Brief entry states, "She retold, with great skill, the tales of the Negroes." Lists *Tell my Horse, Their Eyes Were Watching God*, and *A Zora Neale Hurston Reader.*

H67. Shafer, Yvonne. *American Women Playwrights, 1900-1950*. New York: Peter Lang, 1995: 403-408. States that Hurston was a "flamboyant personality who achieved great fame, suffered disgrace, was forgotten." Highlights her life and summarizes the plots of *The First One*, *Color Struck*, *Fast and Furious*, and *Mule Bone*. Says Hurston was never able to fully develop as a dramatist.

H68.   Sipal, Iva. In *Contemporary Black Biography: Profiles From the International Black Community*. Vol. 3.   Detroit: Gale Research, 1993: 91-94. Includes selected works written by Hurston, bibliographic sources and a photograph. Fairly comprehensive biography that traces Hurston's life and career and says she was dubbed "Queen of the Renaissance."

H69. Spradling, Mary Mace, ed. *In Black and White: Afro-Americans in Print: A Guide to Africans and Americans Who Have Made Contributions to the United States of America*. 2nd ed. Kalamazoo, Mich: Kalamazoo Public Library, 1976: 199. Lists references to works where information about Hurston is included and provides several magazine and newspaper references.

H70.   Spradling, Mary Mace, ed. *In Black and White: A Guide to Magazine Articles, Supplement*. 3rd ed. Detroit: Gale, 1985: 197. The entry cites same nine reference as earlier editions and states that Hurston was a "Full fledged member of Harlem Renaissance."

H71.   Spradling, Mary Mace, ed. *In Black and White: A Guide to Magazine Articles*, 3rd ed. Detroit: Gale, 1985: 471. Notes that Hurston was "Mrs. Herbert A. Sheen" and a scholar, teacher and "raconteur." Provides an alphabetical list of works about Hurston, including Langston Hughes' *Big Sea*.

H72. Stine, Jean C. and Daniel C. Marowski, eds. *Contemporary Literary Criticism*. Vol. 30. Detroit: Gale Research, 1984: 207-229. An excerpt from a Cheryl Wall's essay is one of several included in this updated entry on Hurston.

H73. *The New York Times Obituaries Index*. Vol. 1. New York: New York Times, 1980:496. Refers reader to the February 5, 1960, *New York Times* newspaper for its obituary of Hurston.

H74. Trager, James. *The Women's Chronology: A Year-by-Year Record from Prehistory to the Present.* New York: H. Holt, 1994. This chronology lists Hurston accomplishments by date. In 1928 Hurston "becomes first black graduate of Barnard" [p. 228]; *Mules and Men* published in 1935 [p. 243]; *Their Eyes Were Watching God* published in 1937 [p. 246]; *Moses, Man of the Mountain* published in 1939 [p. 250].

H75. Turner, Darwin T. *Southern Writers: A Biographical Dictionary.* Eds. Robert Bain, Joseph M. Flora, and Louis D. Rubin, Jr. Baton Rouge: Louisiana State University Press, 1979:239-240. Turner gives a three paragraph summary of Hurston's life, career and primary works.

H76. Unglow, Jennifer S., ed. *The Continuum Dictionary of Women's Biography.* New York: Continuum, 1989: 270. Says Hurston was "one of the first widely acclaimed black writers to assimilate folk tradition into modern literature." Only reference cited is Robert Hemenway's literary biography.

H77. Unglow, Jennifer S. *The International Dictionary of Women's Biography.* New York: Continuum/Macmillan, 1982:233. Brief paragraph entry condensed from *The Continuum Dictionary of Women's Biography* article. Notes her Guggenheim Fellowship to do research in Haiti and Jamaica.

H78. Valade, Roger M., III. *The Schomburg Center Guide to Black Literature: From the Eighteenth Century to the Present.* Detroit: Gale Research, 1996: 214-215. Notes that Hurston was born in 1891 and was a writer from the Harlem Renaissance who relied on folklore material for her works. A brief summary is provided of Hurston's primary works.

H79. Van Raaphorst, Donna. In *African American Women: A Biographical Dictionary.* Ed. Dorothy G. Salem. New York: Garland, 1993: 266-267. Notes that although Hurston's birth year is often given as 1901, "it now seems indubitable that the correct date was January 7, 1891." Says Hurston was a "controversial, independent, outspoken, eccentric, and racially proud woman." Points out the "Hurston revival" after Alice Walker's 1975 article in *Ms.* magazine.

H80. Walker, S. Jay. In *Dictionary of American Biography, Supplement Three: With an Index Guide to the Supplements.* Ed. John A. Garrary. New

York: Scribner, 1973: 313-315. Lists and summarizes Hurston's novels. Asserts that her "contribution to Afro-American literature was to incorporate into it an image of the rural black American leading an independent and dignified existence outside the framework of white neighbors and oppressors." Bibliographical references included.

H81.   Warfel, Harry R., ed. *American Novelists of Today*. New York: American Book Co., 1951: 223. Says *Jonah's Gourd Vine* is about a "yellow Negro preacher and his tiny brown wife." Entry summarizes each of Hurston's primary works.

H82.   Werner, Craig. In *Modern American Women Writers*. Eds. Elaine Showalter, Lea Baechler, and A. Walton Litz. New York: Scribner, 1990: 221-233. This long bio-critical article provides a comprehensive look at Hurston's life and works. Werner discusses the influences of blues, jazz, gospel, the black church, cultural anthropology, and folklore on Hurston's work and outlook on life. A selected bibliography includes Hurston's works--cited by genre, as well as secondary biographical and critical works related to Hurston.

H83. *Who's Who in America*. Chicago: Marquis Who's Who, Inc., 1942. The standard brief *Who's Who* entry lists Hurston's works and memberships in organizations.

H84.   Ziadman, Laura M. In *Dictionary of Literary Biography: American Short Story Writers 1910-1945*. Vol. 86. Ed. Bobby Ellen Kimbel. Detroit: Bruccoli Clark Layman, 1989: 159-171. University of South Carolina professor Ziadman write *DLB*'s article on Hurston for the period indicated in title. In addition to a photograph and bibliographical references, Hurston's primary works are listed by genre. A paragraph telling where major depositories of Hurston's manuscripts may be found is appended to the article. Like most scholars writing about Hurston, Hemenway's biography is noted as a "comprehensive appraisal" of her life and work. States that she "produced a substantial body of literature of intense human emotions."

I

Zora Neale Hurston's Works in Anthologies

"Jesus have always loved us from the foundation of the world
When God
Stood out on the apex of His power
Before the hammers of creation
Fell upon the anvils of Time and hammered out the ribs of the earth"

Jonah's Gourd Vine

"Characteristics of Negro Expression"

I01. Cunard, Nancy, ed. *Negro, An Anthology*. New York: Frederick Ungar, 1970.

I02. Wintz, Cary D. *The Politics and Aesthetics of "New Negro Literature."* New York: Garland, 1996. "Characteristics of Negro Expression" is photocopied directly from *Opportunity* magazine. A photograph of Hurston is included.

I03. Mitchell, Angelyn. *Within the Circle: An Anthology of African American Literary Criticism from the Harlem Renaissance to the Present*. Durham, NC: Duke University Press, 1994.

"Color Struck"

I04. Lewis, David Levering. *The Portable Harlem Renaissance Reader*. New York: Viking, 1994.

I05. Perkins, Kathy A., ed. *Black Female Playwrights: An Anthology of Plays Before 1950*. Bloomington: Indiana University Press, 1989.

I06. *Zora Neale Hurston, Eulalie Spence, Marita Bonner, and Others: The Prize Plays and Other One-Acts Published in Periodicals*. New York: G.K. Hall & Co., 1996.

"Drenched in Light"

I07. Kanwar, Asha, ed. T*he Unforgetting Heart: An Anthology of Short Stories by African American Women, 1859-1993*. San Francisco : Aunt Lute Books, 1993. "Isis" ("first published in December 1924 *Opportunity* magazine under the original title 'Drenched in Light.'")

I08. Lewis, David Levering. *The Portable Harlem Renaissance Reader*. New York: Viking, 1994.

I09. Mee, Susie. *Downhome: An Anthology of Southern Women Writers*. San Diego: Harcourt Brace, 1995.   Hurston's "Isis" included in section entitled "Growing Up."

Excerpts from *Dust Tracks on a Road*

I10. Blount, Roy. *Roy Blount's Book of Southern Humor*. New York: Norton, 1994. "I Get Born" an excerpt from *Dust Tracks on a Road*, is included in section one "My People, My People."

I11. Long, Richard A. and Eugenia W. Collier, eds. *Afro-American Writing: An Anthology of Prose and Poetry*. Vol. 2. New York: New York University Press, 1972. Includes "Wandering" from *Dust Tracks on a Road*.

"First One"

I12. Hamallian, Leo and James V. Hatch. *The Roots of African American Drama: An Anthology of Early Plays, 1858-1938*. Detroit: Wayne State University Press, 1991. Biographical information on Hurston and references included.

I13. Hatch, James V. and Ted Shine, eds. *Black Theatre USA: Plays by African-Americans from 1847 to Today*. (Revised and expanded edition) New York: The Free Press, 1996. "The First One" (1927) found in a section on "Legend and History." Has a brief bio-bibliography of Hurston.

I14. Perkins, Kathy A., ed. *Black Female Playwrights: An Anthology of Plays Before 1950*. Bloomington: Indiana University Press, 1989.

I15. *Zora Neale Hurston, Eulalie Spence, Marita Bonner, and Others: The Prize Plays and Other One-Acts Published in Periodicals*. New York: G.K. Hall & Co.

"Gilded Six Bits"

I16. Andrews, William L., ed. *Classic Fiction of the Harlem Renaissance*. New York: Oxford University Press, 1994.

I17. Barksdale, Richard and Keneth Kinnamon. *Black Writers of America: A Comprehensive Anthology*. New York: Macmillan, 1972.

I18. Clarke, John Henrik, ed. *American Negro Short Stories*. New York: Hill and Wang, 1966.

I19. Clarke, John Henrik, ed. *Black American Short Stories: A Century of the Best*. New York: Hill and Wang, 1993.

I20. Davis, Arthur P., J. Saunders Redding, and Joyce Ann Joyce, eds. *The New Cavalcade: African American Writing from 1750 to the Present*. Vol 1. Washington, DC: Howard University Press, 1991.

I21. Hamer, Judith A. and Martin J. Hamer, eds. *Centers of the Self: Short Stories by Black American Women from the Nineteenth Century to the Present*. New York: Hill and Wang, 1994.

I22. Hughes, Langston. *The Best Short Stories by Black Writers: The Classic Anthology from 1899 to 1967*. Boston: Little, Brown, 1967.

I23. Major, Clarence, ed. *Calling the Wind: Twentieth Century African-American Short Stories*. New York: HarperCollins, 1993.

I24. *Soul of a Woman*. London: X Press, 1996.

Excerpts from *Jonah's Gourd Vine*

I25.   Gates, Henry Louis, Jr. and Nellie Y. McKay, eds. *Norton's Anthology of African American Literature*. New York: Norton, 1996.

I26.   Washington, Mary Helen, ed. *Invented Lives: Narratives of Black Women, 1860-1960*. Garden City, New York: Doubleday, 1987. This is a companion volume to *Black-Eyed Susans/Midnight Birds* and has "His Over-the-Creek Girl" from *Jonah's Gourd Vine*

Excerpts from *Mules and Men*

I27.   Brown, Sterling, Arthur P. Davis, and Ulysses Lee, eds. *The Negro Caravan, Writings by American Negroes*. New York: Dryden Press, 1941. An excerpt from *Mules and Men* is included in the section on *folk literature*.

I28.   Davis, Arthur P. and Michael W. Peplow, eds. *The New Negro Renaissance, An Anthology*. New York: Holt, Rinehart and Winston, 1975.

I29.   Forkner, Ben and Patrick Samway, eds. *A Modern Southern Reader: Major Stories, Drama, Poetry, Essays, Interviews and Reminiscences From the Twentieth-Century South*. Atlanta: Peachtree Publishers, 1986.

I30.   Hoffman, Nancy and Florence Howe. *Women Working-An Anthology of Stories and Poems*. Old Westbury, NY: Feminist Press, 1979.

I31.   Lomax, John A. and Alan Lomax. *Folk Song, U.S.A., The 111 Best American Ballads*. New York: Duell, Sloan & Pearce, 1947 and 1967.

I32.   *The Norton Book of Women's Lives*. New York: W.W. Norton, 1993.

"Spunk"

I33. Roses, Lorraine Elena and Ruth Elizabeth Randolph. *Harlem's Glory: Black Women Writing, 1900-1950*. Cambridge: Harvard University Press, 1996.

I34. Wintz, Cary D. *The Emergence of the Harlem Renaissance*. New York: Garland, 1996. "Spunk" as printed in *Opportunity* magazine in June 1925. A copy of the original announcement in *Opportunity* awarding Hurston the second place prize for the short story "Spunk" is also included.

"Story in Harlem Slang"

I35. Roses, Lorraine Elena and Ruth Elizabeth Randolph. *Harlem's Glory: Black Women Writing, 1900-1950*. Cambridge: Harvard University Press, 1996. "Story in Harlem Slang: Jelly's Tale" is in part seven entitled "Harlem's Glory: A Woman's View."

I36. Lane, Eric, ed. *Telling Tales: New One-Act Plays*. New York: Penguin Books, 1993. Includes Hurston's "Story in Harlem Slang" which was adapted by George C. Wolfe.

"Sweat"

I37. Andrews, William L., ed. *Classic Fiction of the Harlem Renaissance*. New York: Oxford University Press, 1994.

I38. Gates, Henry Louis, Jr. and Nellie McKay, eds. *Norton Anthology of African American Literature*. New York: Norton, 1996.

I39. Gilbert, Sandra M. and Susan Gubar. *The Norton Anthology of Literature by Women: The Tradition in English*. New York: W.W. Norton, 1985 (and 1996). A three page biography is included with the short story.

I40. Mullane, Deirdre, ed. *Crossing the Danger Water: Three Hundred Years of African-American Writing*. New York: Doubleday/Anchor Books, 1993. A bio-bibliographical essay is included along with the story.

I41. Oates, Joyce Carol. *The Oxford Book of American Short Stories*. New York: Oxford University Press, 1992.

I42. Wagner-Martin, Linda and Cathy N. Davidson, eds. *The Oxford Book of Women's Writing in the United States*. New York: Oxford University Press, 1995.

I43.   Worley, Demetrice A., ed. *African American Literature: An Anthology of Nonfiction, Fiction, Poetry, and Drama.* Lincolnwood, IL: National Textbook Company, 1993.

Excerpts from *Their Eyes Were Watching God*

I44. Brown, Sterling, Arthur P. Davis, and Ulysses Lee, eds. *The Negro Caravan, Writings by American Negroes.* New York: Dryden Press, 1941. "Hurricane," from the novel *Their Eyes Were Watching God*, is included in the section on *novels*.

I45. Davis, Arthur P. and J. Saunders Redding, and Joyce Ann Joyce, eds. *The New Cavalcade: African American Writing from 1750 to the Present.* Vol 1. Washington, DC: Howard University Press, 1991. An excerpt from *Their Eyes Were Watching God* is included in this new edition of *Cavalcade.* The biographical entry has also been expanded to list "scholarly studies" on Hurston.

I46.   Thornton, Louise, and Jan Sturtevant, eds. *Touching Fire: Erotic Writings by Women.* New York: Carroll and Graf Publishers, 1990.

I47.   Washington, Mary Helen, ed. *Invented Lives: Narratives of Black Women, 1860-1960.* Garden City, NY: Doubleday, 1987. This is a companion volume to *Black-Eyed Susans/Midnight Birds* includes "Janie Crawford" from *Their Eyes Were Watching God.*

"Uncle Monday"

I48.   Cunard, Nancy, ed. *Negro, An Anthology.* New York: Frederick Ungar, 1970.

I49. *Black Scholar* April 1976: 41, 44.

Other Titles in Anthologies

I50. *Black Scholar* April 1976: 41, 44. "Go Gater"

I51. Cunard, Nancy, ed. *Negro, An Anthology.* New York: Frederick Ungar, 1970. "Conversions and Visions," "Shouting," "The Sermon,"

"Mother Catherine," and "Spirituals and Neo-Spirituals" found in this anthology.

I52. Davis, Arthur P. and Michael W. Peplow, eds. *The New Negro Renaissance, An Anthology*. New York: Holt, Rinehart and Winston, 1975. Contains excerpts from *The Eatonville Anthology*.

I53. Davis, Arthur P. and Saunders Redding, eds. *Cavalcade: Negro American Writing from 1760 to the Present*. Boston: Houghton-Mifflin, 1971. Hurston's "Folk Tales" included in chapter entitled "The New Negro Renaissance and Beyond: 1910-1954." A brief biography is also included.

I54. Gates, Henry Louis, Jr., ed. *Reading Black, Reading Feminist: A Critical Anthology*. New York: Meridian, 1990. Opens with Hurston's "Art and Such" an article Stetson Kennedy says was postmarked "Eatonville, Fla, January 13, 1938," when he received it. Its first printing is in this anthology.

I55. Gilbert, Sandra M. and Susan Gubar. *The Norton Anthology of Literature by Women: The Tradition in English*. New York: W.W. Norton, 1985 (and 1996). A three page biography is included with the article, "How It Feels to Be Colored Me."

I56. Harwood, Kirsten, ed. *Florida Stories: Tales From the Tropics*. San Francisco: Chronicle Book, 1993. "The Diving Bell" included.

I57. Knopf, March, ed. *The Sleeper Wakes: Harlem Renaissance Stories by Women*. New Brunswick, NJ: Rutgers University Press, 1993. "Bone of Contention" and   "John Redding Goes to Sea."

I58. Kouwenhoven, John Atlee and Janice Farrar Thaddeus, eds. *When Women Look at Men, An Anthology*. New York: Harper & Row, 1963. "The Frizzly Rooster" included.

I59. Lewis, David Levering. *The Portable Harlem Renaissance Reader*. New York: Viking, 1994. *Mule Bone* co-authored with Langston Hughes found in this reader.

I60. Miller, John, Ed. *Fish Tales: Stories From the Sea*. Harrisburg, PA: Stackpole Books, 1993. "Man and the Catfish."

I61. Mitchell, Angelyn. *Within the Circle: An Anthology of African American Literary Criticism from the Harlem Renaissance to the Present.* Durham, NC: Duke University Press, 1994. "What White Publishers Won't Print."

I62. Roses, Lorraine Elena and Ruth Elizabeth Randolph. *Harlem's Glory: Black Women Writing, 1900-1950.* Cambridge: Harvard University Press, 1996. "Black Death" is found in part eight entitled "In the Looking Glass."

J

Juvenile Literature about Zora Neale Hurston

"Years ago, she had told her girl self to wait for her in the looking glass. It had been a long time since she had remembered. Perhaps she'd better look."

Their Eyes Were Watching God

J01. Calvert, Roz. *Zora Neale Hurston, Storyteller of the South*. New York: Chelsea House Publishers, 1993. This biography is part of the "Junior Black Americans of Achievement Series" and is recommended for grades 3 - 6. Chronicles Hurston's life and career.

J02. *Female Writers*. New York: Chelsea House, 1994. Hurston included in this" Profiles of Great Black Americans Series" series. A short biographical sketch and bibliographical references are included.

J03. Goss, Linda and Clay Goss. *Jump Up and Say! A Collection of Black Storytelling*. (ERIC Document 395 329). Hurston is included as a storyteller. Document is not available from EDRS.

J04. Lyons, Mary E. *Sorrow's Kitchen: The Life and Folklore of Zora Neale Hurston*. New York: Collier Books, 1993. This biography is part of Collier's "Great Achievers Series," and describes the life and work of Hurston. Recommended for grades 7 and up.

J05.   Krull, Kathleen. *Lives of the Writers: Comedies, Tragedies (and What the Neighbors Thought*. San Diego: Harcourt Brace, 1994. This is a special edition for Scholastic Book Fairs which was illustrated by Kathryn Hewett. The section on Hurston is entitled, "She Jumped the Sun." Recommended for grades 3 - 7.

J06.   McKissack, Patricia. *Zora Neale Hurston, Writer and Storyteller*. Hillside, N.J.: Enslow Publishers, 1992. This biography depicts the life of one of the Harlem Renaissance's most prolific writers. Part of the "Great African American Series," this book is recommended for grades 1 - 4.

J07.   Miller, William. *Zora Hurston and the Chinaberry Tree*. New York: Lee & Low Books, 1994. Illustrated by Cornelius Van Wright, this juvenile biography traces Hurston's life. Recommended for grades 1 and up.

J08.   Neyland, Leedell W. *Twelve Black Floridians*. Tallahassee: Florida A & M University Foundation, 1970. Hurston is included as a "Florida daughter."

J09.   Porter, A. P. *Jump at de Sun: The Story of Zora Neale Hurston*. Minneapolis: The Lerner Group, 1992.   This illustrated children's biography is part of the Trailblazers Series and is recommended for grades 4 - 7.

J10.   Otfinoski, Steven. *Great Black Writers*. New York: Facts on File, 1994. Hurston is included as a folklorist and feminist, and the entry is illustrated with a photo of her dressed as a voodoo dancer beating a drum. Discusses her major works and notes that she spent her life nurturing her southern heritage and "recreating it with loving care."

J11. Rediger, Pat. *Great African Americans in Literature*. New York: Crabtree Pub., 1996. Hurston included as a twentieth-century African American writer. A book in the "Outstanding African American Series."

J12.   Rennert, Richard, ed. *Female Writers*. New York: Chelsea House, 1994. Hurston's seven page entry is illustrated with a photograph of her in a hat with a feather across the front. Calls her one of the most "distinctive voices in American literature."

J13. Weitzman, David L. *Human Culture*. New York: Scribner, 1994. Hurston is one of twenty-eight anthropologists and archaeologists with biographical entries. Recommended for grades 4 - 6.

J14. Witcover, Paul. *Zora Neale Hurston*. Los Angeles: Melrose Square Pub. Co., 1994. This illustrated book is one in the "Melrose Square Black American" series. The biography notes that Hurston was born in 1891. Her career as a collector of folklore is discussed; her work in Polk County, Florida, her study of "hoodoo," and her interview with ex-slaves are also included. The book is recommended for grades 5 and up.

J15. Yannuzzi, Della A. *Zora Neale Hurston: Southern Storyteller*. Springfield, N.J.: Enslow Publishers, 1996. Part of the "African-American Biographies Series," this biography is illustrated with photographs of Hurston from collections at Yale and Howard Universities and the Schomburg Center for Research in Black Culture. Opens with a chapter entitled "New York, Here I Come," and ends with "Solitude." A chronology and chapter notes are provided.

J16. Yates, Janelle. *Zora Neale Hurston: A Storyteller's Life*. Staten Island, N.J.: Ward Hill Press, 1991. Illustrated by David Adams, this biography is part of the "Unsung Americans Series." It begins with Hurston's family moving to Eatonville, traces her life and career, and provides a chronology and bibliography.

APPENDIX I

Media Related to
Zora Neale Hurston

Alice Walker on Zora Neale Hurston. San Francisco: American Poetry Archive, 1980. Walker discusses the life, work and contributions of Hurston in a one-hour videocassette housed at the Poetry Center of the Archive.

American Library Association. *Oprah Winfrey for American Libraries.* Chicago: American Library Association, 1987. Winfrey is holding a copy of Hurston's *Their Eyes Were Watching God* in the 22" x 34" color poster.

American Library Association. *Zora Neale Hurston - Ideas from Great Minds.* Chicago: American Library Association, 1991. Black and white poster of a young, smiling Hurston wearing a trademark hat and a coat with fur collar is 15" x 23" and has the statement: "Research is formalized curiosity. It is poking and prodding and prying with a purpose. It is seeking that he who wishes may know the cosmic secrets of the world and they that dwell within."

Dee, Ruby and Ossie Davis. *In Other Words....* Works of poetry and prose written by several African American writers, including Hurston, are performed by these two well-known African American actors. Available on video cassette.

Historic Black Personalities. Skokie, IL: Quartet Manufacturing, 1990. Hurston is one African-American featured on 14 oversized "study prints."

Hurston, Zora Neale. "Songs of Worship to Voodoo Gods." from *Tell My Horse*. Philadelphia: J.B. Lippincott Company, 1938: 279-301. On microfilm at the Library of Congress in Washington, DC.

In the Beginning. Nashville: METT. A 54 minute sound recording of short stories by African American authors. Hurston's "Man Makes, Woman Takes" from *Mules and Men* is featured.

Krull, Kathleen. *Lives of the Writers: Comedies, Tragedies (And What the Neighbors Thought)*. Northport, ME: Audio Bookshelf, 1996. This two-hour audio cassette provides biographical information about noted writers. "She Jumped at the Sun: Zora Neale Hurston" is the title of the piece included on Hurston.

Literary Greats. West Lafayette, IN: The Archives, 1995. Hurston one of the six American authors featured on this 30 minute videocassette.

McGhee-Anderson, Kathleen. *Jump at the Sun*. Los Angeles: LA Theatre Works, 1994. This is a recording of a live theater performance which chronicles Hurston's.

Speisman, Barbara. *Zora Neale Hurston*. Rohnert Park, CA: Sonoma State University, Department of English, 1995. In a videocassette, approximately one and one half hours long, Speisman examines Hurston's life and work. The video was recorded as part of the "New Voices From the South Series."

Taylor, Phyllis McEwan. *Zora Neale Hurston Revisited*. Miami Beach, FL: Colony Theater, 1994. This is a 36 minute videocassette of Taylor's one-woman performance portraying the life and stories of Hurston.

Voices of Diversity. Madison, WI: Knowledge Unlimited, 1995. Hurston included as one of eight to ten black and white posters that have a "photograph, biographical information, and a brief quotation from a work of each author included." (catalogers notes)

Waldron, Betty. "Charcoal Sketches." This is a one-woman show performed by a Florida actress and is a tribute to Hurston and Mary McLeod Bethune.

Women From History Postcards. Martinsville, IN: Helaine Victoria Press, 1975. Hurston is depicted on one of fourteen giant postcards that have biographies on the back.

World Institute of Black Communications. *1982 Communication Communications Excellence to Black Audiences (CEBA Awards)*. Washington, DC: Howard University, WHMM-TV, 1983. This is an hour-long U-matic videocassette of a program featuring Ruby Dee discussing Hurston's life between scenes of Dee's company performing "Zora is My Name!" at the CEBA Awards. (catalogers notes)

World Institute of Black Communications. *1982 Communication Communications Excellence to Black Audiences (CEBA Awards)*. Washintgon, DC: Howard University. Hurston is featured on one of twelve one-minute public service announcements for the upcoming 1982 CEBA Awards. PSAs aired in late 1981.

Zora is My Name! Beverly Hills, CA: Pacific Arts Video, 1989. One videodisc that is approximately 78 minutes long and based on the PBS production of the play "Zora is My Name!" starring Ruby Dee. Information for play taken from *Dust Tracts on a Road* and *Mules and Men*. This is a dramatization of Hurston's life.

Zora Neale Hurston Day. Sonoma, CA: Sonoma State University Department of English, (February 8, 1995). One videocassette of a program where Hurston's life, career, and works are discussed and some of her works are read.

APPENDIX II

World Wide Web Sites

Entering Zora Neale Hurston's name in any catalog or search engine used to access the World Wide Web yields hundreds of hits. Many are links to commercial sites selling books by and about Hurston. Others are connected to special library collections; some sites are compiled by faculty and graduate students at major universities, and many provide only passing reference to Hurston or her works. The sites here provide only a representative sampling of those available on Hurston. Please keep in mind that a site may be available one day and gone the next.

//yaleinfo.yale.edu:7700/00YaleLibraries/Beinecke/Manu/American/ Hurston/gop
> Zora Neale Hurston Collection at Beinecke Library, Yale University: List of materials by box and folder.

//marvel.loc.gov:70/00/research/reading.rooms/folklife/guides/ hurston
> List of recordings, manuscripts, and ephemera in the Archive of Folk Culture and other divisions of the Library of Congress.

//ntas.morgan.edu/events/events.htm
> Site for the Zora Neale Hurston Society housed at Morgan State University in Baltimore.

//karamelik.eastlib.ufl.edu/bookill/hurston/hurston.htm.
Site for "Rare Books & Manuscripts - Manuscript Group 6" for the correspondence, manuscripts, printed materials, biographical information, photographs, miscellaneous materials in the special collection of the University of Florida. Links to other collections such as Yale's Beinecke Library Collection.

//www.vcu.edu/hasweb/eng/hurston/index.html
Hurston/Wright Awards announcement for the $1,000 first place award for fiction and publication in *The New Virginia Review*, presented each spring and sponsored by Virginia Commonwealth University.

//nicg.fas.harvard.edu/~afam138/
Richard Wright and Zora Neale Hurston Seminar class offered at Harvard University. Includes course syllabus, readings, requirements, and a bibliography of works for Hurston and Wright.

//english.cla.umn.edu/lkd/vfg/Authors/Zora Neale Hurston
Hurston one of the women writers of color included. Biographical materials, excerpts from works, selected bibliographies, photographs, and links provided. Site authored by a graduate student at the University of Minnesota.

//kelvin.seas.virginia.edu/~/as5s/zora/background.htm
Links for Harlem Renaissance, Hurston books, folklore, a video clip, and other sites.

//pages.prodigy.com/zora/
Zora Neale Hurston site maintained by Kip Hinton at *Kip+@osu.edu* has excerpts from stories and other Hurston works, photographs, information, and links.

//www.princeton.edu/~jmercado/harlem/zora.html
"Zora Neale Hurston: Affirmation & Transcendence" is an essay written in 1996 by James A. Mercado.

//splavc.spjc.cc.fl.us/hooks/zora.html
"Conjured Into Being: Zora Neale Hurston's *Their EyesWere Watching God*" links to other Hurston sites.

//www.as.wvu/~ginsberg/sweat.htm
> "Sweat" site includes four pages of essays about the short story written by Rachel Miller, Wiliam Resh and Eric Moran.

//encarta.msn.com/schoolhouse/harlem/hurston.asp
> Biographical article from Microsoft's *Encarta Encyclopedia*.

//www.eb.com/poll/hurston.htm
> *Encyclopedia Britannica* online has a biographical entry for Hurston.

//gopher.uconn.edu/~GYD95001/
> Biography, photo of Hurston's grave stone, and works by Hurston.

//www.scf.usc.edu/~grenier/112.html
> Experimental Writing Links lists six sites for Hurston.

//www2.trincoll.edu/~emorgane/hurston.html
> American Modernist Writers site gives biography and links to bibliographies and other Hurston sites.

//www.womenconnect.com/wco/wh30861.htm
> Women's History Connection has a biography of Hurston.

//bizport.com/ua/artspeack/zora2.html
> N. Y. Nathiri, executive director of the Association for the Preservation of the Eatonville Community, wrote the biographical entry on Zora Neale Hurston for Artspeak.

cpl.lib.uic.edu/001hwlc/litlists/harlemren.html
> This site on the Harlem Renaissance compiled by librarians at Chicago's Harold Washington Public Library. Selected Zora Neale Hurston works listed.

//ww.hsc.usc.edu/~gallagher/hurston/hurston.html
> Biography of Hurston, list of her works that are "readily available," and links.

//www.geocities.com/Tokyo/12224/lhurston

"Genuis of the South" includes biography, selected bibliography, selected works, "Zora on the Web," and links to other African-American pages.

//www-dept.usm.edu/~soq/hurstoncall2.html.

Southern Quarterly at the University of Southern Mississippi is planning a special Zora Neale Hurston issue for spring 1998 edited by Anna Lillios, and the call for proposals is listed at this site.

APPENDIX III

Special Collections of Hurston Manuscripts, Correspondence, Photographs, and Memorabilia

Amistad Research Center. Tulane University. Cullen Collection. Includes correspondence with Hurston.

American Philosophical Society. Philadelphia, Pennsylvania. Hurston correspondence with Franz Boas.

Boston University. Mugar Memorial Library. Hurston correspondence with Dorothy West as well as photographs of Hurston found here.

Fisk University. Black Oral History Collection. Charles S. Johnson Papers. Special Collections has papers and correspondence related to Hurston.

Fisk University Library. Rosenwald Foundation Papers. Special Collections has some Hurston papers and correspondence.

Hebrew Union College. American Jewish Archives. Cincinnati, Ohio. Hurston correspondence.

Howard University Library. Alain Locke Collection and the Langston Hughes Papers at Founders Library.   Moorland-Spingarn Research Center has Hurston papers and correspondence.

Library of Congress. Manuscript Division has Hurston manuscripts. Ten carbon copies of play manuscripts were found in spring 1997.

Library of Congress. American Folklife Center. Archive of Folk Culture has recordings and ephemera related to Hurston.

New York Public Library. Schomburg Center for Research in Black Culture. Hurston Collection has Hurston manuscripts and correspondence.

Papers of Tracy L'Engle Angas include nine pieces of correspondence between Angas and Hurston.

University of Florida. Gainsville. P. K. Young Library. Rare Books and Manuscripts Department. Hurston Collection has Hurston correspondence, manuscripts, financial records, leaflets, newspaper clippings, and other papers from 1926-1960. Hurston correspondence also found in the Marjorie Kinnan Rawlings papers housed there. Some papers from the "Negro Unit" of the WPA are also stored at the University of Florida.

University of North Carolina. Chapel Hill. Carolina Southern Historical Collection has papers and correspondence from 1938-1939 relating to the Florida office of the Federal Writers' Project and a folder of "miscellaneous materials" relating to Hurston. These are mostly photocopies of original papers retained by Stetson Kennedy.

University of South Florida Library. Florida Historical Society Papers house material on the Florida Negro and Florida slaves. Hurston directed workers in the Negro Writers' section of the Federal Writers' Project as they interviewed ex-slaves. Materials on Hurston also included in a manuscript section on "The Florida Negro."

University of Texas at Austin. Fannie Hurst Collection. Harry Ransom Humanities Research Center has correspondence between Hurst and Hurston.

Yale University. James Weldon Johnson Collection. Beinecke Library. Rare Books and Manuscripts as well as the Carl Van Vechten Papers have papers related to Hurston.

Chronological Listing of Works Written by Zora Neale Hurston

Jonah's Gourd Vine. Philadelphia: J. B. Lippincott, 1934.
    Reprinted, with an introduction by Larry Neal, Philadelphia:
      J. B. Lippincott, 1971.
    Reprinted, New York: HarperCollins, 1990.

Mules and Men. Philadelphia: J. B. Lippincott, 1935.
    Reprinted, London: Kegan Paul & Co, 1936.
    Reprinted, New York: Negro Universities Press, 1969.
    Reprinted, with an introduction by Darwin Turner, New York:
      Harper and Row, 1970.
    Reprinted, Chicago: University of Illinois Press, 1978.
    Reprinted, New York: HarperCollins, 1990.
    Reprinted, San Bernardino: Borgo Press, 1990.

Their Eyes Were Watching God. Philadelphia: J. B. Lippincott, 1937.
    Reprinted, London: J. M. Dent & Sons, 1937
    Reprinted, Greenwich, CT: Fawcett Publications, 1965.
    Reprinted, New York: Negro Universities Press, 1969.
    Reprinted, Westport, CT: Greenwood Publishing Group, 1970.
    Reprinted, Urbana: University of Illinois Press, 1978.
    Reprinted, with a foreword by Mary Helen Washington. New
      York: HarperCollins, 1990.
    Reprinted, San Bernardino: Borgo Press, 1990.

Reprinted, with an introduction by Sherley Anne Williams.
Urbana: University of Illinois Press, 1991.
Reprinted, Reading, MA: Addison-Wesley, 1995.

Tell My Horse. Philadelphia: J. B. Lippincott, 1938.
Reprinted, with an introduction by Bob Callahan, as *Voodoo
Gods: An Inquiry into Native Myths and Magic in Jamaica
and Haiti*. Berkeley: Turtle Island Foundation, 1981.
Reprinted, with a new foreword by Ishmael Reed. New York:
Harper Perennial, 1990.

Moses, Man of the Mountain. Philadelphia: J. B. Lippincott, 1939.
Reprinted, London: J.M. Dent & Sons, 1941.
Reprinted, Chatham, NJ: Chatham Bookseller, 1974.
Reprinted, with an introduction by Blyden Jackson, as *The Man
of the Mountain*. Chicago: University of Illinois Press, 1984.
Reprined, San Bernardino: Borgo Press, 1991.

Dust Tracks on a Road. Philadelphia: J. B. Lippincott, 1942.
Reprinted, London: Hutchinson & Co., 1944.
Reprinted, with an introduction by Darwin Turner. New York:
Arno Press, 1969.
Reprinted, with an introduction by Larry Neal. New York: J. B.
Lippincott, 1971.
Reprinted, (with additional, original chapters) edited with an
introduction by Robert Hemenway. Urbana: University of
Illinois Press, 1984.
Reprinted, New York: HarperPerennial, 1996.
Reprinted, San Bernardino: Borgo Press, 1996.

Seraph on the Suwanee. New York: Charles Scribner's Sons, 1948.
Reprinted, Ann Arbor: University Microfilms, 1971.
Reprinted, New York: AMS Press, 1974.
Reprinted, San Bernardino: Borgo Press, 1991.
Reprinted, New York: HarperCollins, 1991.

**"I Love Myself When I am Laughing...and Then Again When I am
Looking Mean and Impressive": A Zora Neale Hurston Reader**.
Edited by Alice Walker, with an introduction by Mary Helen
Washington. Old Westbury, NY: Feminist Press, 1979.

Sanctified Church. Foreword by Toni Cade Bambara. Berkeley: Turtle Island Foundation, 1981.

Spunk: The Selected Stories of Zora Neale Hurston. Berkeley: Turtle Island Foundation, 1985.

Gilded Six-Bits. Minneapolis: Redpath Press, 1986.

Mule Bone, a Comedy of Negro Life. (with Langston Hughes) Edited by George Houston Bass and Henry Louis Gates, Jr. New York: HarperCollins, 1991.

Spunk, Three Tales. New York: Dramatists Play Service, 1992.

Folklore, Memoirs, and Other Writings. Ed. Cheryl A. Wall. New York: Library of America, 1995. (Includes *Mules and Men, Tell My Horse, Dust Tracks on a Road*, and selected articles)

Novels and Stories. Ed. Cheryl A. Wall. New York: Library of America, 1995. Stories selected by Cheryl A. Wall; *Jonah's Gourd Vine* has new foreword by Rita Dove; *Mules and Men* has the original Franz Boas preface, illustrations by Miguel Covarrubias, and a foreword by Arnold Rampersand; *Their Eyes Were Watching God* has a foreword by Mary Helen Washington. *Seraph on the Suwanee* and *Moses, Man of the Mountain* also included.

The Complete Stories of Zora Neale Hurston. Introduction by Henry Louis Gates, Jr. and Seiglinde Lemke, afterword by Henry Louis Gates, Jr. New York: HarperCollins, 1995.

Bottle Up & Go: The Illustrated Zora Neale Hurston Reader. Ed. Bob Callahan. New York: Marlowe & Company, 1995.

Sweat. Edited by Cheryl A. Wall. New Brunswick NJ: Rutgers University Press, 1996.

1920s

"John Redding Goes to Sea." *Stylus* 1 (May 1921): 11-22. Reprinted in *Opportunity* 4 (January 1926): 16-21.

"O Night." *Stylus* 1 (May 1921): 42.

Poem. *Howard University Record* 16 (February 1922): 236.

"Drenched in Light." *Opportunity* 2 (December 1924): 371-74.

"Spunk." *Opportunity* 3 (June 1925): 171-73. Reprinted in *The New Negro*, edited by Alain Locke. New York: Albert and Charles Boni, 1925.

"Magnolia Flower." *Spokesman* (July 1925): 26-29.

"The Hue and Cry about Howard University." *Messenger*, 7 (September 1925): 315-19, 338.

"Muttsy." *Opportunity* 4 (August 1926):; 246-5.

"Possum or Pig?" *Forum* 76 (September 1926): 465.

"The Eatonville Anthology." *Messenger* 8 (September-November 1926): 261-62+.

Color Struck: A Play. *Fire!* 1 (November 1926): 7-15.

"Sweat." *Fire!* 1 (November 1926): 40-45.

The First One: A Play. In *Ebony and Topaz*. Ed. Charles S. Johnson. New York: National Urban League, 1927.

"Cudjo's Own Story of the Last African Slaver." *Journal of Negro History* 12 (October 1927): 648-63.

"Communication." *Journal of Negro History* 12 (October 1927): 664-67.

"How It Feels to Be Colored Me." *World Tomorrow* 11 (May 1928): 215-16.

<u>1930s</u>

"Dance Songs and Tales from the Bahamas." *Journal of American Folklore* 43 (July-September 1930): 294-312.

"Hoodoo in America." *Journal of American Folklore* 44 (October-December 1931): 317-418.

"The Gilded Six-Bits." *Story* 3 (August 1933): 60-70.

In *Negro: An Anthology*. Ed. Nancy Cunard. London: Wishart, 1934:
       "Characteristics of Negro Expression"
       "Conversions and Visions"
       "Mother Catharine"
       "The Sermon"
       "Shouting"
       "Spirituals and Neo-Spirituals"
       "Uncle Monday"

"The Fire and the Cloud." *Challenge* 1 (September 1934): 10-14.

"Race Cannot Become Great Until It Recognizes Its Talent."*Washington Tribune* (December 29, 1934).

"Full of Mud, Sweat and Blood." (Review of *God Shakes Creation* by David Cohn). *New York Herald Tribune Books* (November 3, 1935): 8.

"Fannie Hurst." *Saturday Review* (October 9, 1937): 15-16.

"Star-Wrassling Sons-of-the-Universe." (Review of *The Hurricane's Children* by Carl Carmer). *New York Herald Tribune Books* (December 26, 1937): 4.

"Rural Schools for Negroes." (Review of *The Jeanes Teacher in the United States* by Lance G. E. Jones). *New York Herald Tribune Books* (February 20, 1938): 24.

"Stories of Conflict." (Review of *Uncle Tom's Children* by Richard Wright). *Saturday Review* (April 2, 1938): 32.

"Now Take Noses." In *Cordially Yours*. Philadelphia: J. B. Lippincott, 1939: 25-27.

1940s

"Cock Robin, Beale Street." *Southern Literary Messenger* 3 (July 1941): 321-323.

"Story in Harlem Slang." *American Mercury* 55 (July 1942): 84-96.

"Lawrence of the River." *Saturday Evening Post* (September 5, 1942): 18, 55-57. Condensed in *Negro Digest* 1 (March 1943): 47-49.

"The 'Pet Negro' System." *American Mercury* 56 (May, 1943): 593-600. Condensed in *Negro Digest* 1 (June, 1943): 37-40.

"High John de Conquer." *American Mercury* 57 (October 1943): 450-458.

"Negroes Without Self-Pity." *American Mercury* 57 (November 194): 601-603.

"The Last Slave Ship." *American Mercury* 58 (March 1944): 351-58. Condensed in *Negro Digest* 2 (May 1944): 11-16.

"My Most Humiliating Jim Crow Experience." *Negro Digest* 2 (June 1944): 25-26.

"The Rise of the Begging Joints." *American Mercury* 60 (March 1945): 288-294. Condensed in *Negro Digest* 3 (May 1945).

"Crazy for This Democracy." *Negro Digest* 4 (December 1945): 45-48.

"Bible, Played by Ear in Africa." (Review of *How God Fix Jonah* by Lorenz Graham). *New York Herald Tribune Weekly Book Review* (November 24, 1946): p. 5.

"Jazz Regarded as Social Achievement." (Review of *Shining Trumpets* by Rudi Blesh). *New York Herald Tribune Weekly Book Review* (December 22, 1946): 8.

"Thirty Days Among Maroons." (Review of *Journey to Accompong* by Katharine Dunham). *New York Herald Tribune Weekly Book Review* (January 12, 1947): 8.

"The Transplanted Negro." (Review of *Trinidad Village* by Melville Herskovits and Frances Herskovits). *New York Herald Tribune Weekly Book Review* (March 9, 1947): 20.

Caribbean Melodies for Chorus of Mixed Voices and Soloists. Arr., William Grant Still. Philadelphia: Oliver Ditson, 1947.

Review of *Voodoo in New Orleans* by Robert Tallant. *Journal of American Folklore* 60 (October-December 1947): 436-438.

"At the Sound of the Conch Shell." (Review of *New Day* by Victor Stafford Reid). *New York Herald Tribune Weekly Book Review* (March 20, 1949): 4.

1950s

"Conscience of the Court." *Saturday Evening Post* (March 18, 1950): 22-23, 112-122.

"I Saw Negro Votes Peddled." *American Legion Magazine* 49 (November 1950): 12-13, 54-57, 59-60.

"Some Fabulous Caribbean Riches Revealed." (Review of *The Pencil of God* by Pierre Marcelin and Philippe Thoby Marcelin). *New York Herald Tribune Weekly Book Review* (February 4, 1951): 5.

"What White Publishers Won't Print." *Negro Digest* 8 (April 1950): 85-89.

"Mourner's Bench, Communist Line: Why the Negro Won't Buy Communism." *American Legion Magazine* 50 (June 1951): 14-15, 55-60.

"A Negro Voter Sizes Up Taft." *Saturday Evening Post* (December 8, 1951): 29, 150.

"Zora's Revealing Story of Ruby's First Day in Court." *Pittsburgh Courier* (October 11, 1952).

"Victim of Fate." *Pittsburgh Courier* (October 11, 1952).

"Ruby Sane." *Pittsburgh Courier* (October 18, 1952).

"Ruby McCollum Fights for Life." *Pittsburgh Courier* (November 22, 1952).

"Bare Plot Against Ruby." *Pittsburgh Courier* (November 29, 1952).

"Trial Highlights." *Pittsburgh Courier* (November 29, 1952).

"McCollum-Adams Trial Highlights." *Pittsburgh Courier* (December 27, 1952).

"Ruby Bares Her Love." *Pittsburgh Courier* (January 3, 1953).

"Doctor's Threats, Tussle over Gun Led to Slaying." *Pittsburgh Courier* (January 10, 1953).

"Ruby's Troubles Mount." *Pittsburgh Courier* (January 17, 1953).

"The Life Story of Mrs. Ruby J. McCollum." *Pittsburgh Courier* (February 28, 1953, and during March, April and May 1953).

"The Trial of Ruby McCollum." In *Ruby McCollum: Woman in the Suwannee Jail*. William Bradford Huie. New York: E. P. Dutton, 1956: 89-101.

"This Juvenile Delinquency." *Fort Pierce Chronicle* (December 12, 1958).

"The Tripson Story." *Fort Pierce Chronicle* (February 6, 1959).

"The Farm Laborer at Home." *Fort Pierce Chronicle* (February 27, 1959).

"Hoodoo and Black Magic." *Fort Pierce Chronicle* (July 11, 1958-Aug. 7, 1959).

RECOVERED WORKS

"Art and Such." (January, 1938). Printed for the first time in *Reading Black, Reading Feminist: A Critical Anthology*. Ed. Henry Louis Gates, Jr. New York: Meridian Book, 1990: 27. Stetson Kennedy writes that he had the article in his possession since he received it postmarked "Eatonville, Fla., January 13, 1938."

"Under the Bridge." *American Visions* 11 (December/January 1997): 14-19. Short story found in a Zeta Phi Beta Sorority notebook by collector Wyatt Houston Day in 1996.

FORTHCOMING WORKS

Complete Essays. New York: HarperCollins Publishers. (due in two volumes in 1997 and 1999)

Collected Essays. New: HarperCollins Publishers. (projected date 1998)

Complete Plays. New York: HarperCollins, nd.

Hurston Reader. New York: HarperCollins, nd.

References

The following sources were consulted in researching the list of works written by Zora Neale Hurston.

Books in Print and *World Catalog* [Online]. Available: FirstSearch Online Databases. March, 1997.

Books in Print. New York: R. R. Bowker, 1996-1997.

Hemenway, Robert. *Zora Neale Hurston, A Literary Biography*. Urbana: University of Illinois Press, 1977.

International Index to Periodicals. New York: H. W. Wilson, 1924-1962.

Readers' Guide to Periodical Literature. New York: H. W. Wilson, 1924-1963.

Author Index

Entries prefixed with an "A" are found in the chapter "Books about Zora Neale Hurston;" those items prefixed with "B" refer to Dissertations and Theses; items marked "C" are found in "Essays and Book Chapters;" "D" indicates Periodical Literature; "E" refers to "Reviews of Works Written by Zora Neale Hurston;" "F" points to "Reviews of Works about Zora Neale Hurston," "G" indicates Bibliographies and Guides; "H" is for Biographical entries, and "J" is for Juvenile Literature. Numerical references guide readers to pages in the appendices.

Subject Index

Entries prefixed with an "A" are found in the chapter "Books about Zora Neale Hurston;" those items prefixed with "B" refer to Dissertations and Theses; items marked "C" are found in "Essays and Book Chapters;" "D" indicates Periodical Literature; "E" refers to "Reviews of Works by Zora Neale Hurston;" "F" points to "Reviews of Works about Zora Neale Hurston;" "G" indicates Bibliographies and Guides; "H" is for Biographical entries, and "J" is for Juvenile Literature. Numerical references guide readers to pages in the appendices.

About the Compiler

ROSE PARKMAN DAVIS is Assistant Professor and Coordinator of Library Instruction at Dacus Library, Winthrop University. Her research has appeared in *Mississippi Libraries*, and she is also a published poet.

ISBN 0-313-30387-8

HARDCOVER BAR CODE